A CASE FOR IRONY

The Tanner Lectures on Human Values

A Case for Irony

Jonathan Lear

With Commentary by
Cora Diamond
Christine M. Korsgaard
Richard Moran
Robert A. Paul

HARVARD UNIVERSITY PRESS
Cambridge, Massachusetts, and London, England 2011

Library of Congress Cataloging-in-Publication Data
Lear, Jonathan.
A case for irony / Jonathan Lear ; with commentary by Cora Diamond . . . [et al.].
p. cm.—(The Tanner lectures on human values)
Includes bibliographical references (p.   ) and index.
ISBN 978-0-674-06145-3 (alk. paper)
1. Irony. I. Title.
BH301.I7L43 2011
128—dc22   2011014608

FOR GABRIEL, SOPHIA, AND SAM

Contents

CONTENTS

Preface

I have come to think over years of reading Kierkegaard and Plato that irony is fundamental to the human condition, but poorly understood. The misunderstanding is pervasive in contemporary culture; it has also affected intellectual life, including our contemporary philosophical understanding of irony. It is not, I think, an accident that this should be so. We both do and do not want to live with routine understandings of ourselves; but insofar as we do, we are motivated to live with routine understandings of irony. In this book I try to break through those routines, to make clear what irony is and why it matters. But I need to say a word about what I mean by this. Obviously, people may call all sorts of related phenomena "irony," and if the use sticks, you can eventually read about it in the *Oxford English Dictionary*. The *OED* aspires to give an authoritative account of the historical uses of the word; and if one thinks that that is all there is to irony, it can seem as though there is nothing more to find out. The idea that one still needs to grasp what irony *really is* can look like mystifying hokum. And yet, what if the *OED* gives us the history of our *routines* with the word, but there is also a phenomenon that underlies and disrupts these routines? What if this little disrupter is crucial to the human condition? In my opinion, irony is revealed neither by a majority vote of those who use the term nor by a glimpse of a transcendent idea, but by a grasp of what should matter when it comes to living a distinctively human life.

This, I believe, was the route Kierkegaard took—and he has everywhere been my teacher. Socrates was his teacher. But what Kierkegaard learned from Socrates is itself a source of confusion. Kierkegaard was a passionate Christian, a religious thinker. Whatever one's own commitments (or lack of commitment), one cannot understand Kierkegaard unless one makes an effort to understand Christianity. (I hasten to say: I am not a Christian.) He is thus often passed over in secular philosophy departments. The dominant attitude among athiests is: why bother? On occasion when one wants to know Kierkegaard's views on Socratic irony, one tends to consult (dare I say dip into?) his book *The Concept of Irony: With Continual Reference to Socrates*. But that book was literally a student thesis: Kierkegaard wrote it for his *Magister* degree. The mature Kierkegaard came to think of it as the misguided view of a very young man.

In general, the philosophical reception of "the problem of Socratic irony" has been unironic about its own activity. The debate has focused on whether or not Socrates is dissembling, wearing a mask, saying the opposite of what he means.[1] How has this come to be the debate? Well, at various points in the Platonic dialogues some of Socrates' more challenging interlocutors— Alcibiades, Thrasymachus, and Callicles—accuse Socrates of deploying his typical *eirōneia*. That Greek term, from which the English word descends, does mean putting on a mask, dissimulation. Although there can be complex levels of masking—and thus room for nuance—it nevertheless seems that ultimately there are only two positions: either to agree with the charge leveled against Socrates, or to disagree by interpreting the texts in such a way that Socrates is no deceiver.

Kierkegaard, as I understand him, broke through this either/or. He had his eye on the fact that Thrasymachus, Callicles, and Alcibiades are unreliable narrators. Each in his own way is a brilliant but flawed character. So one should expect them to be focusing *on something* when they make their charge, but to have a distorted view of what that something is. In his irony about irony, Kierkegaard treats Thrasymachus, Callicles, and Alcibiades as though they were involved in a naming ceremony. He lets their use of *eirōneia* fix rigidly on the activity of Socrates (whatever it is) that elicits this criticism from his interlocutors. He does not expect them to understand what that activity is. And then Kierkegaard asks, what was Socrates actually doing? The answer to that question is, for the mature Kierkegaard, what Socratic irony is.

Well, not quite. For Kierkegaard, what it is to learn from Socrates is not to write an academic treatise explaining the marks and features of Socratic irony; it is to *be ironic* in the service of helping oneself and one's readers to move in the direction of virtue. Thus instead of a later academic work in which he revises his earlier views on irony, we have the creation of pseudonymous authors who go on to write (or edit) their own ironic and humorous texts. The aim of these texts is not to *explain* irony, but to *instill* it. In this book, I would like to make clear why that matters.

These are the Tanner Lectures on Human Values that I gave at Harvard University, along with responses by commentators and my responses to their comments. I think that the back-and-forth of this conversational style—with the inevitable disagreements, misunderstandings, revisions, and elaborations—is a better literary form for illuminating irony than a straightforward narrative.

One of the joys in doing philosophy is the conversation one gets to have. When a conversation comes alive, I have a sense that this is what a musician must feel when the right musicians have come along.[2] I have been in conversation for years with Gabriel Lear and Candace Vogler on the topic of these lectures. There is no thought expressed here that has not been influenced by them. I have also had enduring and sustaining conversations with Irad Kimhi and Sebastian Rödl. James Conant and I taught a series of seminars on Kierkegaard together in 2001–2002, and it is in those stimulating conversations that I began to think about irony. Agnes Callard, John Coetzee, David Finkelstein, Anton Ford, Michael Forster, Jonathan Galassi, Ross Harrison, Jim Hopkins, Michael Kremer, Jennifer Lockhart, Christopher Peacocke, David Possen, Timothy Smiley, Jonny Thakkar, and Katharine Withy have been wonderful conversation partners along the way.

It is difficult to describe the extraordinary graciousness with which Harvard University welcomed me. President Drew Faust's thoughtful introduction upended my sense of what presidents do on such occasions. And from then on, every conversation with faculty and students was a treat. But the biggest honor was from my commentators: for me, Cora Diamond, Christine Korsgaard, and Richard Moran set contemporary standards of how to do philosophy; the same is true for Robert Paul with respect to psychoanalysis.

As the reader will see, we often do not agree, but I could not have had a better time. My responses to their comments gave me an opportunity to elaborate my position.

I am indebted to the Tanner Foundation and to the Tanner Committee at Harvard for giving me the occasion to present these thoughts on irony as a human value. I am also indebted to the Center for Advanced Studies of Norway, where I was able to continue my research on Socratic irony; to the King's College Cambridge Research Centre, for inviting me to present work in progress; and to the Franke Institute for the Humanities at the University of Chicago, where I worked on these lectures as a senior research fellow. I would also like to express profound gratitude to the Andrew W. Mellon Foundation for awarding me their Distinguished Achievement Award. This has given me the time to turn these lectures and responses into a book. I would like to thank the students and colleagues at the University of Chicago with whom I have read Kierkegaard and Platonic texts over many years. I have spoken on irony at Berkeley, the Catholic University of America, Columbia, Emory, Michigan State, New York University, Notre Dame, Purdue, Rutgers, Swarthmore, UCLA, the University of Arkansas, the University of Helsinki, the University of New Mexico, the University of South Carolina, Wellesley College, Williams College, and Yale; as well as at the American Psychological Association, the Boston Psychoanalytic Society, the Chicago Psychoanalytic Society, the Toronto Psychoanalytic Society, and the Western New England Institute for Psychoanalysis. I am grateful for the many questions that continued to resonate as I wrote this book.

No one is satisfied to acquire things believed to be good; they seek *good things*. Here everyone is contemptuous of mere belief . . . Every soul pursues that and does everything for its sake—having a hunch that the good is something, but *perplexed* and unable to grasp adequately what it is.

—Socrates in Plato, *Republic* VI.505d–e (my translation)

Irony is an existence-determination, so nothing is more ridiculous than to suppose it to be a figure of speech, or an author's counting himself lucky when once in a while managing to express himself ironically.

—Johannes Climacus (a pseudonymous author of Søren Kierkegaard)

I

The Lectures

I

To Become Human Does Not Come That Easily

"To become human does not come that easily." So wrote
Søren Kierkegaard in his journal on December 3, 1854, and by now the claim
would seem to be either familiar or ridiculous.[1] Ridiculous in the sense that
for those of us who are human, becoming human was not up to us and was
thus unavoidable; for those creatures who are not human, becoming human
is out of the question. There is, of course, a distinguished philosophical tradition that conceives of humanity as a task. This is the familiar sense in which
being human involves not just being a member of the species but living up to
an ideal. Being human is thus linked to a conception of human excellence;
and thus becoming human requires getting good at being human. We see this
thought reflected in such ordinary expressions as "that was a humane thing
to do": in doing the humane thing, a person might be performing an act that
almost all members of the biological species would evade.[2] Kierkegaard's entry could then be understood as meaning that becoming human requires that
one become humane, and that is a difficult task. Of course, if one wants to
treat this as more than an uplifting metaphor, one needs an argument. And
philosophers from Plato to the present have taken up the challenge, arguing
that self-constitution is indeed an achievement.[3] Rather than contribute to

that discussion directly, I would like to take an oblique turn. For I suspect that this claim has become too familiar. Kierkegaard is getting at something unfamiliar: it has less to do with the arduousness of a task than with the difficulty of getting the hang of it. It is not that easy to get the hang of being human—and becoming human requires that we do so. In this lecture, I would like to render this familiar claim—that becoming human does not come that easily—unfamiliar.

§1. Excavating Kierkegaardian Irony

Christine Korsgaard, the contemporary philosopher who argues most thoroughly for the task-oriented nature of self-constitution, claims that our difficulty arises out of two fundamental features of our condition: the structure of human self-consciousness and the fact that we constitute ourselves via a practical identity. Given any item that enters self-conscious awareness—a temptation, desire, thought, "incentive"—we have the capacity to step back from it in reflective consciousness and ask whether it gives us reason to act (or to believe).[4] And for self-constitution to be a genuine possibility, Korsgaard argues, we must ask this question from the perspective of our practical identity: "a description under which you value yourself, a description under which you find your life to be worth living and your actions to be worth undertaking."[5] My practical identity commits me to norms that I must adhere to in the face of temptations and other incentives that might lead me astray.

> Our ordinary ways of talking about obligation reflect this connection to identity. A century ago a European could admonish another to civilized behavior by telling him to act like a Christian. It is still true in many quarters that courage is urged on males by the injunction "be a man!" Duties more obviously connected with social roles are of course enforced in this way. "A psychiatrist doesn't violate the confidence of her patients." No "ought" is needed here because the normativity is built right into the role.[6]

If we accept that becoming human requires that we inhabit a practical identity well, and that doing so requires both that we reflectively endorse (or criticize) the various incentives presented to consciousness and actually live by our judgment, then we can see how becoming human might be an arduous task. It can be tough work fending off those temptations that would undo our claim to be the person we are; it is, on occasion, tough work to live up to the demands that, given our practical identity, are required; and it can be tough work to hold the apparently competing demands of life together. Fidelity to oneself is not for the fainthearted. Thus we do have here an interpretation of what it might mean for becoming human to be not that easy.

However, this does not seem to be the difficulty Kierkegaard is talking about. In that journal entry he writes:

> In what did Socrates' irony really lie? In expressions and turns of speech, etc.? No, such trivialities, even his virtuosity in talking ironically, such things do not make a Socrates. No, his whole existence is and was irony; whereas the entire contemporary population of farm hands and business men and so on, all those thousands, were perfectly sure of being human and knowing what it means to be a human being, Socrates was beneath them (ironically) and occupied himself with the problem—what does it mean to be a human being? He thereby expressed that actually the *Trieben* [drives] of those thousands was a hallucination, tomfoolery, a ruckus, a hubbub, busyness . . . Socrates doubted that one is a human being by birth; to become human or to learn what it means to be human does not come that easily.[7]

The suggestion here is *not* that if only we would reflect on what our practical identity already commits us to then we would be taking on the difficult task of becoming human. The contrast Kierkegaard is drawing is not between unreflective and reflective life. Rather, it is between "the entire contemporary population" and Socrates—and to understand the depth of Kierkegaard's point, it is crucial not to caricature the population. There is plenty of reflection in the contemporary population's goings-on. Ordinary life is constituted by people assuming practical identities and then, in reflection, asking what is required of them. And Plato dramatizes the reflectiveness of ordinary life when, at the beginning of the *Republic*, Socrates goes to the home of Cephalus, a wealthy businessman who enjoys conversation. Cephalus makes it clear that not only does he have a practical identity as a businessman, but that he has been careful in life to stick to its norms. His grandfather had been wealthy, through inheritance and business acumen, but his father had lost the fortune. Cephalus has spent his life rebuilding the family fortune. (I.330a–b). And when Socrates asks him, in reflective conversation, "What do you think is the greatest good you've received from being very wealthy?," Cephalus has a remarkable answer, clearly an outcome of reflective self-questioning (I.330d–331b). Cephalus is a man with a practical identity, a person who has had to stick to its norms in the face of challenges, and someone who has thought about what it all means. And yet, as he leaves the conversation to make a religious sacrifice, it is clear that this is part of the "hubbub, busyness" that Socrates' life exposes.

The contrast Kierkegaard is drawing is between Socrates, whose "whole existence is and was irony," and everyone else. We caricature everyone else if we think of them all as unreflectively going through automatic routines. Obviously, we do not yet know what Socrates' irony consists in. But Kierkegaard is explicit that it is not—as the contemporary world would have it—about witty turns of speech, or even about saying the opposite of what one means. Irony is a form of existence. The contrast Kierkegaard draws is with everyone else who is *"perfectly sure* of being human and knowing what it means to be a human being." So irony would seem to be a form of not being perfectly sure—an insecurity about being human that is at once constitutive of becoming human and so remarkable that, in all of Athens, only Socrates embodied it. The important point for now is that the perfectly-sure / not-perfectly-sure divide does not coincide with the division between unreflective and reflective life. At least some of those who are perfectly sure are quite capable of reflecting on the demands of their practical identity. Indeed, that very reflection may manifest their confidence. So the mere fact of reflection on the basis of one's practical identity is not sufficient to take one out of the "hubbub, busyness" that Kierkegaard describes.

It would seem then that the route out of this busyness is not a trivial matter. Kierkegaard names it irony, and he ascribes it to himself as well as to Socrates:

> My entire existence is really the deepest irony.
>   To travel to South America, to descend into subterranean caves
> to excavate the remains of extinct animal types and antediluvian

TO BECOME HUMAN DOES NOT COME THAT EASILY

fossils—in this there is nothing ironic, for the animals extant there now do not pretend to be the same animals.

But to excavate in the middle of "Christendom" the types of being a Christian, which in relation to present Christians are somewhat like the bones of extinct animals to animals living now—this is the most intense irony—the irony of assuming Christianity exists at the same time that there are one thousand preachers robed in velvet and silk and millions of Christians who beget Christians, and so on.[8]

Irony does seem to arise here from some feature of practical identity—in this case, from being a Christian. One can easily read this passage as a complaint about historical transmission—that long ago there were Christians, something got lost, and now there are only impostors—but one thereby misses the irony. One can make that complaint in the flat-footed way I just did. Rather, the occasion for irony arises from trying to figure out the types of being a Christian by excavating *"in the middle of Christendom."* Kierkegaard used "Christendom" to refer to socially established institutions of Christianity, the ways in which understandings of Christianity are embedded in social rituals, customs, and practices.[9] The picture here is of me trying to reflect on the types of being a Christian by consulting available church histories, the received accounts of the division of the church into sects, available accounts in sermons, books, editorials, and articles about Christian life. Again, it is easy enough to caricature my activity—choosing which church to join as though I were inspecting different species in the Galápagos—but the power of irony emerges when one portrays me as a more serious figure. So, I am engaged in what I take to be the practical task of living up to the demands of a practical identity—being a Christian—but I am doing so by working my way through Christendom. Note that this activity is essentially reflective—I am stepping back from ordinary life and asking what a properly Christian life consists in— and it may be undertaken in a genuine mood of sincerity and with intellectual sophistication. The problem is that, however thoughtful and sincere the questioning is, the reflection itself is a manifestation of the assumption that Christianity exists. It is a form of being "perfectly sure." This shows itself in my reliance on Christendom to give me the materials for my reflection. But what if Christianity does not exist? What if nothing in the world—including this activity of reflection—answers to the call of Christian life? Then my reflection on my practical identity via an excavation of Christendom would be mere hubbub, busyness.

The Christendom of Kierkegaard's Europe no longer exists; and I expect this audience to be largely secular, and those that do live a religious life will do so in different ways. Thus, *we* can step back from that Christendom and treat it as an object for reflective consideration of the standard type. But if we *were* inhabitants of that Christendom, reflection would be possible, reflection on our practical identity as Christians would be possible, reflection on Christianity would be possible—but all of this would be further acts within Christendom. Christendom aims to be (and when it is vibrant it for the most part is) *closed under reflection:* for its inhabitants, reflection is possible, even encouraged, but is not itself sufficient to get one outside it.[10] Elsewhere Kierkegaard called Christendom a "dreadful illusion," and I take it he is talking not only about its degree of falsity, but about its all-encompassing nature.[11] The illusion of Christendom is that it is the world of Christianity—that when it comes to Christianity, there is no outside—and its success as illusion thus depends on its ability to metabolize and contain reflection on Christian life. One can thus easily see that when a culture is in the grip of a vibrant illusion, philosophical discourse about our ability to step back in reflection can function as ideology, reinforcing our confinement in the name of liberating us from it.

And I see no reason for assuming that for any illusion there will always be discrepancies, disagreements, contradictions within it such that reflecting on them will be sufficient to get us out of them. When Christendom was vibrant there were plenty of discrepancies, disagreements, and contradictions—and reflecting on them was the stuff of Christendom. I suspect that the thought that reflective consciousness ought in principle to be able to recognize an illusion from the inside derives not only from the well-known narratives of Hegel and Marx, but from the plausible thought that if we are to give content to the idea of something's being an illusion, we need to give content to the idea of our coming to recognize it as illusion. However, one can accept that thought and nevertheless be skeptical that reflection is the mode of recognition. On occasion we fall in love, then we fall out of love, and then we give ourselves reasons for why our love failed. On occasion we fall into illusion, and over time illusions may lose their grip, and then we can see contradictions, discrepancies, and disagreements as reasons for giving it up. What grounds our confidence that our reflective reasons are the cause of giving up the illusion, rather than it being the illusion's fading that facilitated the reflection?

However that may be, it is precisely the moment when reflective consciousness unwittingly participates in the illusion that is the occasion for "the most intense irony"—at least, in Kierkegaard's opinion. The instance that concerned him was the one he took to be of greatest practical importance to himself and his neighbors: trying to figure out how to be a Christian. Notice that the occasion for irony arises not merely for the vain and the hypocritical, the shallow and the silly; even if I am smart and sincerely want to think about how to be a Christian, if I do so by excavating Christendom—that is, engaging in reflection within Christendom—this activity, too, is an occasion for irony. And this at least suggests that when a person is misleading himself about the point of his own reflective engagement, irony may be of help. Thus it behooves us to understand what Kierkegaard took irony to be.[12]

§2. The Experience of Irony

To get clear on what irony is I want to distinguish *the experience of irony* from the development of a *capacity for irony;* and to distinguish those from what Kierkegaard calls *ironic existence.* In a nutshell, the experience of irony is a peculiar experience that is essentially first-personal: not simply in the sense that all experience is the experience of some I, but that in having an experience of irony I experience myself as confronted by that very experience. Developing the capacity for irony is developing the capacity to occasion an experience of irony (in oneself or in another). We tend to think casually of "the ironist" as someone who is able to make certain forms of witty remarks, perhaps saying the opposite of what he means, of remaining detached by undercutting any manifestation of seriousness. This, I shall argue, is a derivative form; and the deeper form of ironist is one who has the capacity to occasion an experience of irony. Ironic existence is whatever it is that is involved in turning this capacity for irony into a human excellence: the capacity for deploying irony in the right way at the right time in the living of a distinctively human life. It is ironic existence that is the not-that-easy of becoming human. In this section, I want to focus on the experience of irony.[13]

To bring the idea to light, Kierkegaard makes a constitutive contrast using an archeological metaphor; but we don't need to go on an imagined trip or even carry out an imagined dig. If, say, a duck is waddling across the courtyard, it does not matter whether there are bones of its ancient ancestors buried in the ground. The reason is that the duck, in its waddle, is not thereby pretending to be the same as its ancestors. Here is the pivot-point of irony: it becomes possible when one encounters animals who pretend.

Let us not get stuck trying to insist upon a categorial difference between humans and the rest of animal life. We are only beginning to grasp the sophisticated cognitive capacities of dolphins and chimpanzees. And we still have so much to learn about the forms of communication within other species. I would not be surprised to learn that some forms of animal communication deserve to be called pretense. But Kierkegaard makes his point, not to delineate the absolute limit of non-human animal life, but to bring to light a crucial characteristic of human life.

When Kierkegaard says that other animals don't pretend, he is not making a point about make-believe. Rather, he is using "pretend" in the older sense of *put oneself forward* or *make a claim*.[14] Think of the pretender to a throne: she is someone putting herself forward as the legitimate heir. Now in the most elemental sense, pretense goes to the heart of human agency. Even in our simplest acts, pretense is there, at least as a potentiality. You see me bent over and ask, "What are you doing?" and I say, "Tying my shoes." Right there in that simple answer I am making a claim about what I am up to, in this case one in which I have nonobservational first-person authority.[15] Human self-consciousness is constituted by our capacity to pretend in this literal and nonpejorative sense: in general we can say what we are doing; and in doing *that* we are making a claim about what we are up to. Of course, the capacity for pretense opens out in myriad ways: in occupying social roles, maintaining a sense of identity, declaring our beliefs, and so on. And so, practical identity as Korsgaard understands it is a species of pretense in Kierkegaard's sense. It is a regular feature of pretense that, as we put ourselves forward in one way or another, we tend to do so in terms of established social understandings and practices.[16] Our practical identities tend to be formulated as variations of available social roles.

Social roles provide historically determinate, culturally local accounts of various ways in which one might be good at being a human being. So, for instance, given that humans are essentially social animals, who spend a comparatively long time developing, who are born largely in ignorance of the world into which they are born, it is at least plausible that the category of *teacher* should provide one route of human well-being. A teacher, broadly construed, would be someone who can help his neighbors learn. This is at least a plausible candidate for one way of being good at being human, and thus one way of becoming human. A social role would be a socially available way of putting oneself forward as a teacher. So, for instance, one way of being a teacher would be to be a *professor*. In the United States and Europe at the beginning of the twenty-first century there is a fairly well-established range of teaching styles—in seminar, tutorial, and lecture course—and a fairly well-established range of evaluative techniques, such as grades. There is even a range of dress you can expect a professor to wear, a way of being in front of a lectern and delivering a paper. And there are socially acceptable ways of demurring from the role: special ways of not wearing the right clothes, not giving a standard talk. That, too, can be part of the social pretense. But in this variety of socially recognized ways, I put myself forward *as* a professor. In this way a whole range of activity—including dress, mannerisms, a sense of pride and shame—can all count as pretense in that they are all ways of putting oneself forward *as* a professor. Since even our simplest acts are regularly embedded in our sense of who we are, the possibility of irony is pervasive. Note that putting oneself forward does not on any given occasion require that I say anything: I may put myself forward as professor in the way I hunch my shoulders, order a glass of wine, in my choice of shoes, socks, and glasses. Conversely, when I do put myself forward verbally it need not be in any explicit statement to that effect. It's right there in such ordinary statements as "I've switched to a Mac."

The possibility of irony arises when a gap opens between pretense as it is made available in a social practice and an aspiration or ideal which, on the one hand, is embedded in the pretense—indeed, which expresses what the pretense is all about—but which, on the other hand, seems to transcend the life and the social practice in which that pretense is made. The pretense seems at once to capture and miss the aspiration. That is, in putting myself forward as a teacher—or, whatever the relevant practical identity—I simultaneously instantiate a determinate way of embodying the identity and fall dramatically short of the very ideals that I have, until now, assumed to constitute the identity. Note that thus far we have captured only a condition that makes the experience of irony possible. The cases that primarily concerned Kierkegaard were not of individual hypocrisy, but ones in which the individual was an able representative of a social practice that itself fell short. As we have seen before, to grasp the power of Kierkegaard's critique it is crucial not to caricature Christendom. Obviously, there were vain priests within Christendom who cut a ridiculous figure; and the spiritless bourgeois who went to church on Sunday in order to be seen. And Kierkegaard did lampoon them. But Christendom also included self-conscious and disputed histories of the church, conflicts about what it is to be Christian, disputes about practices, rituals, ceremonies as well as about how to interpret them. Christendom contained the Reformation and division into sects. And thus there are people within Christendom asking tough questions about what it is to be Christian. So Christendom itself contains a discomfort, disagreement, and reflection on its own practice. It is thus a mistake—and it diminishes Kierkegaard's point—to think of Christendom as unreflective or unself-critical. Christendom is the social pretense of Christianity, the *myriad* ways in which the social world and its inhabitants put themselves forward as Christian. The problem would not be so difficult and irony would not be so important if reflection and criticism were not already part of the social practice, in this case Christendom. What we need to understand is how Kierkegaardian irony is not captured by any of these myriad forms or calls to self-consciousness.

Kierkegaard's fundamental ironic question is:

(1) In all of Christendom, is there a Christian?

Or, to put it more bluntly,

(2) Among all Christians, is there a Christian?

It is a striking fact about us that we can immediately hear that there is a question being asked, rather than a meaningless repetition. The form of the question is a tautology; yet we do not hear it as a tautology: and it is, I think, a revealing fact about us that this should be so. The question asks of a purported totality whether *any* of its members live up to the aspirations that purportedly characterize the totality. In this case, the question asks whether amongst all who understand themselves as Christian there is anyone who is living up to the requirements of Christian life.

If, by contrast, we were to ask,

(*) Among all the ducks, is there a duck?

it is not clear what, if anything, is being asked. Unlike human life, duck life does not involve pretense: ducks do not make claims for themselves, they do not put themselves forward *as* anything at all. Of course, *we* may make claims for the ducks: a master chef standing in front of a pond and planning this evening's *canard à l'orange* may utter just such a sentence, but it would not be based on any claims the ducks were making. Thus there is no room for a gap opening between their pretense and aspiration.[17] And that is why, though we can provide an unusual context in which the sentence does make sense, upon a first hearing it strikes us as strange. Duckly life does not have a place in it for practical reflection, and thus there is no place for irony to take hold. Notice that ducks are social animals and, in their sociality, they do adhere to norms. On occasion a duck will fail in the social requirements of duckly life. Still, none of this opens up ducks to the possibility of irony, because none of this involves making a claim about what they are up to. By contrast, it is characteristic of human life—either explicitly or in our behavior—that we do make claims about who we are and the shape of our lives. This quintessentially human activity of putting oneself forward as a certain kind of person can, in certain circumstances, set us up for the fall: this can occur when the pretense simultaneously expresses and falls short of its own aspiration. Irony, for Kierkegaard, is the activity of bringing this falling short to light *in a way that is meant to grab us.*

It is this way of being grabbed (when we are) that is so tricky to capture, yet is crucial to the experience of irony. The ironic question on its own is neither necessary nor sufficient to generate an experience of irony—and, as we shall see, it is important that this should be so. If, for example, Christendom were fairly obviously a rundown institution, then one might use a sentence like

(1) In all of Christendom, is there a Christian?

in an absolutely straightforward reflection in which one steps back from the practices and questions them in the familiar way. One might even call this reflection "ironic"—but, philosophically speaking, one would be using the term in a derivative sense. That is, one would be missing the philosophically significant sense of irony that (I think) Kierkegaard is trying to capture and provoke. And, by calling that turn of phrase irony, one might thereby hide from oneself that anything is missing.

So, how might a question like (1) be an occasion for an experience of irony? Let us develop Kierkegaard's example. A hallmark of Christian life is loving one's neighbor as oneself. The difficult part, the reason irony is needed, is that Christendom ostensibly already contains this teaching—*as well as* an understanding of what it is to fall short. Indeed, there are *within Christendom* many opportunities to reflect on what it means to love one's neighbor, reflect on how well or poorly one is living up to the ideal, and so on. This is a crucial part of the problem: reflection is a process that can be used in the service of keeping one firmly ensconced within Christendom. Christendom even contains its own (restricted) version of irony. I spend Sunday morning listening to a sermon about ways we fail to live up to that ideal. I leave the church and pass a beggar on the street; he irritates me; then I remember the priest's sermon. I turn around and give the beggar a dollar. He says, "You must be listening to your priest." What is he saying? We'll never know. But I may understand him in a number of different ways. I may, first, take him simply to be remarking that it is a memory of the priest's words that pricked my conscience. Or I may take him to be speaking ironically in the familiar sense of exuding sarcasm about the paltry nature of my donation. He's telling me in his "ironic" way—saying the opposite of what he means in a way that I can recognize—that I should have given him a twenty. So far, we haven't left Christendom: my sense of falling short of the ideal, my sense of his "irony," all fall within received social understandings. But suppose now that it occurs to me that I *have* learned from my priest *and that is my problem!*

Here, the manner of this occurring is all-important: I am shaken. It is not merely that I have a sincere propositional thought with this content; it is that the having of this thought is the occasion for disruption and disorientation. It is as though Christianity has *come back* to show me that *everything* I have hitherto taken a Christian life to be is ersatz, a shadow. Even when I am pricked by conscience and experience myself falling short—that *entire package* I learned in Christendom bears at best a comical relation to what it would actually be to follow Jesus' teaching. Notice, I use the same terms as I used before, but I am disoriented with respect to them; they seem strange yet compelling. I may not yet know in any detail what the requirements of loving one's neighbor are; I may have only the barest inkling of the transformations

I would have to undergo to be someone capable of such love; but at the same time I vividly recognize that the range of possibilities that Christendom has put forward as the field of loving one's neighbor is wildly inadequate to the task. In that sense, irony breaks open a false world of possibilities by confronting one with a practical necessity. The form of this confrontation is disruption: disruption of my practical identity as a Christian, disruption of my practical knowledge of how to live as a Christian.

So when I get to an ironic question like

(3) Among all those who love their neighbors, does anyone love his neighbor?

for it to function as a genuine occasion for irony it must shed its ordinary garb of a tame Sunday sermon; it must lose its familiar sense of an appeal to a standard act of reflection. Indeed, when the question reaches its target, it shows our standard activities of reflection to be ways of avoiding what (we now realize) the ideal calls us to. It is as though an abyss opens between our previous understanding and our dawning sense of an ideal to which we take ourselves already to be committed. This is the strangeness of irony: we seem to be called to an ideal that transcends our ordinary understanding, but to which we now experience ourselves as already committed.

The experience of irony thus seems to be a peculiar species of uncanniness—in the sense that something that has been familiar returns to me as strange and unfamiliar.[18] And in its return it disrupts my world. For part of what it is to inhabit a world is to be able to locate familiar things in familiar places. Encountering strange things per se need not be world-disrupting, but coming to experience what has been familiar as utterly unfamiliar is a sign that one no longer knows one's way about. And the experience of uncanniness is enhanced dramatically when what is returning to me as unfamiliar is what, until now, I have taken to be my practical identity.

This is what makes irony compelling. It is the mirror image of an oracle. An oracle begins with an outside source telling a person who he is in terms he at first finds alien and enigmatic. Then there is an unsettling process of familiarization: the person comes to understand what the oracle means as he comes to recognize that he is its embodiment. And, of course, the recognition of the meaning of the oracle represents more than an increase in propositional knowledge—for example, that I am the one who murdered his father and married his mother. It is the occasion for a more or less massive disruption of my sense of who I am; and a disorientation in a world that, until now, had been familiar. With this robust form of irony, the movement is in the opposite direction: a person gives a familiar designation to himself. He takes on a practical identity. As the irony unfolds, not only does the designation become weirdly unfamiliar; one suddenly experiences oneself as called to one-knows-not-what, though one would use the same language as before: to love one's neighbor as oneself.

Oracles regularly depend for their power on the structure and ambiguity of their wording, so it is worth noting that the basic form of the ironic question has the structure of uncanniness. The first occurrence of the term in the sentence

Among all Christians . . .

gives us the pretense, the familiar. But the second occurrence which gives the aspiration:

. . . is there a Christian?

is also the repetition and return of Christianity, this time as strange, enigmatic, unfamiliar. Of course, the ironic question on its own does not guarantee ironic uptake—the experience of irony. But when the experience does occur, it has the structure of uncanniness.

§3. Teaching

I have been using Kierkegaard's example of Christendom, but the possibility for irony does not depend on the religious nature of the example. So let me give a secular example. We have already seen that the experience of irony has basically two moments: first, there is the bringing out of a gap between pretense and pretense-transcending aspiration. Second, there is an experience of ironic uptake that, I have suggested, is a peculiar species of uncanniness. And it is time to bring into relief a crucial feature of irony that has been in the background: namely, that in the paradigm case, it is radically first-personal, present tense. Of course, conversation with another—say, with Socrates—might be an occasion for an ironic experience, just as reading Descartes' *Meditations* might be an occasion to go through the cogito. But just as no one else can go through the cogito for me, similarly with irony: in the paradigm case, for each I, irony is something *that disrupts me now.* The fact that ironic experience is paradigmatically first person, present tense may at first seem strange because the basic form of the ironic question does not explicitly have the first-person pronoun in it. However, for the question to hit its target—for it to occasion ironic uptake—for some particular I, there must be a peculiar first-personal disruption.

So, I am sitting at home in the evening grading papers, and I begin to wonder what this has to do with actually teaching my students. For a while, this is a normal reflection in which I step back and wonder about the value of my activity. I still have a sense of what the ideal is; I am just reflecting on how well the activity of grading contributes to it. I decide to talk this over with my colleagues at a department meeting: perhaps we can figure out a better way to evaluate students, one more in line with our core function of teaching. This sort of reflection is part and parcel of inhabiting a practical identity. Thus far I am at the level of reflection that might lead me to engage in educational reform. But then things get out of hand. I am *struck* by teaching in a way that disrupts my normal self-understanding of what it is to teach (which includes normal reflection on teaching). This is not a continuation of my practical reasoning; it is a disruption of it. It is more like vertigo than a process of stepping back to reflect. When it comes to previous, received understandings of teaching—even those that have been reflectively questioned and adjusted in the normal ways—*all bets are off.* No doubt, I can still use general phrases like "helping my students to develop"; but such phrases have become enigmatic, open-ended, oracular. They have become signifiers whose content I no longer grasp in any but the most open-ended way. I no longer know who my "students" are, let alone what it would be to "help them develop." Are my students the individuals coming into my classroom at the appointed time . . . or are they to be located elsewhere? Are they in the younger generation . . . or are they my age or older? Might they come along in a different generation altogether . . . maybe in the next century? And if my classroom is where my students are, where is my classroom? What am I to make of the room I actually do walk into now? Where should I be to encounter my students? What would it be to *encounter* them? And if I were to encounter them, what would it be to help them, rather than harm them? What is development? Already I have enough questions to last a lifetime, and I do not even know where to begin.

This is a different order of concern from something that might at first look a lot like it. In a different mode, a normal mode, I consider myself a serious teacher. It might take me a lifetime of practice before I really get good at it. I am dedicated to this practical identity. I treat teaching as a master-craft, an arduous but noble calling; and even after all these years, I still think of myself as an apprentice, en route. On occasion I do wonder about those around me who assume that teaching is easy, or even those who find it difficult, but assume they know what it is: what *are* they up to? Nevertheless, in this reflective and questioning mode, I still have a fairly determinate sense of the path I am on. Of course, the path essentially involves reflective questioning of what I am doing; and as a result of the questioning I may alter my direction one way or another. Yet, I know what to do today and tomorrow; and I trust that if I keep practicing and developing my skills I will get better at it. Maybe I'll even get good at it. In this mode, I act as though I have practical knowledge of how to go about acquiring the skill, even if, in my view, true mastery lies off in the future.

By contrast, in the ironic moment, my *practical knowledge* is disrupted: I can no longer say in any detail what the requirements of teaching consist in; nor do I have any have any idea what to do next. I am also living through a breakdown in *practical intelligibility:* I can no longer make sense of myself (to myself, and thus can no longer put myself forward to others) in terms of my practical identity. That I have lost a sense of *what it means* to be a teacher is revealed by the fact that I can now no longer make sense of what I have been up to. That is, I can certainly see that in the past I was adhering to established norms of teaching—or standing back and questioning them in recognized ways. In *that* sense, my past continues to be intelligible to me. But I now have this question: What does *any of that* have to do with *teaching?* And if I cannot answer that question, my previous activities now look like hubbub, busyness, confusion. I have lost a sense of how my understanding of my past gives me any basis for what to do next. That is why, in the ironic moment, I am called to a halt. Nothing any longer makes sense to me as the next step I might take *as a teacher.* Until this moment of ironic disruption, I had taken various activities to be unproblematic manifestations of my practical identity. Even in this moment, I might have no difficulty understanding what my practical identity requires, just so long as practical identity is equated with social pretense, or some reflected-upon variant. My problem is that I no longer understand what practical identity so construed has to do with my practical identity (properly understood).

Ironic disruption is thus a species of uncanniness: it is an *unheimlich* maneuver. The life and identity that I have hitherto taken as familiar have suddenly become unfamiliar. However, there is this difference: in an ordinary experience of the uncanny, there is mere disruption: the familiar is suddenly and disruptively experienced as unfamiliar. What is peculiar to irony is that it manifests passion for a certain direction. It is because I care about teaching that I have come to a halt as a teacher. Coming to a halt in a moment of ironic uncanniness is how I manifest—in that moment—that teaching matters to me. I have a strong desire to be moving in a certain direction—that is, in the direction of becoming and being a teacher—but I lack orientation. Thus the experience of irony is an experience of *would-be-directed* uncanniness. That is, an experience of standard-issue uncanniness may give us goose bumps or churn our stomachs; the experience of ironic uncanniness, by contrast, is more like losing the ground beneath one's feet: one longs to go in a certain direction, but one no longer knows where one is standing, if one is standing, or which direction is the right direction. In this paradigm example, ironic uncanniness is a manifestation of utter seriousness and commitment (in this case, to teaching), not its opposite.[19] As Johannes Climacus, one of Kierkegaard's pseudonymous authors, puts it, "From the fact that irony is present, it does not follow that earnestness is excluded. That is something only assistant professors assume."[20]

It is often assumed that irony is a form of detachment. From the perspective of those who are embedded in the social pretense—who just don't get what is going on with me—it may well *appear* that irony is a form of detachment, a lack of commitment or seriousness. For, after all, it is a peculiar form of detachment *from the social pretense*. And, as we shall see, it may be the occasion for a peculiar form of re-attachment. But if, in one's blinkered view, social pretense is all there is, then it is easy to view irony as it regularly is viewed. "Lear hasn't handed in his grades—typical; and now he's jabbering on about not knowing how to grade. *Of course* he knows how to grade; he's just being ironic. It would be better if we had a colleague who was committed to teaching." To the socially embedded, it is precisely this manifestation of commitment that will appear as lack of commitment—perhaps as dissembling or as sarcasm. (That is, of course, precisely how Socrates seemed to some of his interlocutors.)

If we get away from misleading appearance, and try to capture what is really going on with me, the language that suggests itself is that of Platonic Eros: I am *struck* by teaching—by an intimation of its goodness, its fundamental significance—and am filled with longing to grasp what it is and incorporate it into my life. I can no longer simply live with the available social understandings of teaching; if I am to return to them it must be in a different way. Thus the initial intuition is that there must to be something more to teaching than what is available in social pretense. Irony is thus an outbreak (or initiation) of pretense-transcending aspiring. The experience of ironic uncanniness is the form that pretense-transcending aspiring takes. Because there is embodied in this experience an itch for direction—an experience of uncanny, enigmatic longing—it is appropriate to conceive the experience of irony as an experience of *erotic uncanniness.*

Plato gave this experience a mythical and metaphysical interpretation. A person is struck by beauty here on earth and is driven out of his mind because he is reminded of the true beauty of the transcendent forms. This is the "greatest of goods," Socrates tells us: "god-sent madness is a finer thing than man-made sanity" (*Phaedrus* 244a–d, 245b–c, 249d–e).[21] Platonic metaphysics has been out of fashion, and thus there is a tendency to treat Plato's account of this experience as though it were at best an intriguing moment in the history of philosophy. Plato emphasizes the importance of the disruptive, disorienting experience as that from which philosophical activity emerges.[22] I think he is right that such moments of disruption are philosophically significant: thus if we are not willing (or not ready) to accept his metaphysical account, it is incumbent upon us to find another. Though Socrates is describing an intense moment of god-sent madness—and thus his language is dramatic—the structure of the experience fits the ironic uncanniness I have been trying to isolate. Those who are struck in this way *"do not know what has happened to them for lack of clear perception"* (250a–b). They are troubled by "the strangeness [atopia] of their condition" (251e), but they also show "contempt for all the accepted standards of propriety and good taste"—that is, for the norms of social pretense. Yet all along "they follow the scent from within themselves to the discovery of the nature of their own god" (252e–253a). If we demythologize this point and put it in the context of the example I have been developing, it looks like this. I have already taken on the practical identity of a teacher. I have internalized its values: its principles are to some extent within me. This is the "scent from within": precisely by following the values of my practical identity, reflecting on its norms and on how well or badly I live up to them . . . I am led to a breakdown in these normal goings-on. There is something uncanny about, of all things, teaching. It *seems* as though there is something about teaching that transcends (what now seems like) the dross of social practice. There is something about my practical identity that breaks my practical identity apart: it seems larger than, disruptive of, itself. This is the experience of irony.

Call this an existential crisis if you will, but this is not how the expression is normally used. In—forgive the expression—a normal existential crisis, life comes to seem empty, and I throw it all overboard in order to do something dramatically different. Perhaps I move to the Arctic to take up the life of a hunter-gatherer.[23] By contrast, in the ironic experience, it is my *fidelity* to teaching that has brought my teacherly activities into question. For a similar reason, irony also differs from the experience of absurdity that Thomas Nagel describes.[24] It is not an experience of the meaninglessness of life so much as of its value: it is because my life as a teacher matters to me that I am disrupted. Nagel argues that the experience of absurdity arises from an inherent feature of the standard form of reflective self-consciousness: that we are able to step back from daily life and view it "with that detached amazement which comes from watching an ant struggle up a heap of sand."[25] On this view, reflective consciousness itself has no commitments; it is just a detached observer of commitment. I suspect there is idealization in this picture of reflection: that in seeing ourselves in the humble position of an ant we thereby give ourselves a God's-eye perspective. In any case, ironic experience, by contrast, is a peculiar form of *committed* reflection.

I have been describing a dramatic moment to bring the large-scale structure of irony into view, but I believe there are petite moments of ironic uncanniness that are over almost as soon as they begin. These moments happen to us, we get over them quickly and move on, remembering at best a shadow of their occurrence. This is of more than psychological significance. It is not peculiar to me that such an ironic moment could occur—and there is more to be learned from this moment than that at any moment any one of us could go nuts. There is a question of the philosophical significance of the possibility of such a moment. The weakest claim one might make is that this moment shows that practical identity has a certain instability built into it. It seems internal to the concept of *teacher*, for example, that, on the one hand, it must be realized and realizable in social practices that establish and maintain its norms (including revisions based on reflective criticism), but, on the other hand, there is also the possibility of disrupting one's sense of the validity of that practice in the name of the very norms the practice was meant to establish. But, as I shall argue, a stronger claim is warranted: namely, developing a capacity for ironic disruption may be a manifestation of seriousness about one's practical identity. It is not merely a disruption of one's practical identity; it is a form of loyalty to it. So, my ironic experience with teaching manifests an inchoate intimation that there is something valuable about teaching—something excellent as a way of being human—that isn't quite caught in contemporary social pretense or in normal forms of questioning that pretense. This is not social critique. No doubt, a social critic with good rhetorical skills might deploy irony to shake his listeners up in the name of the cause she wishes to advance. But it is a mistake to think that if we just got our social practice—say, of teaching—into good shape, there would no longer be room for ironic disruption of practical identity. It is constitutive of our life with the concepts with which we understand ourselves that they are subject to ironic disruption.

§4. Plato's Socrates on Practical Identity

Kierkegaard took inspiration from Plato's Socrates; and we can certainly see this form of ironic questioning of practical identity in the dialogues. In the *Gorgias,* for example, Socrates asks whether

(4) Among all politicians (in Athens), is there a single politician? (513e–521e)

His answer is that no one in the entire cohort of those who put themselves forward as politicians qualifies, nor do those whom we standardly take to have been great politicians, like Pericles; for none of them have genuinely been concerned with making the citizens better. "I am one of the few Athenians—not to say the only one—who understands the real political craft and practice politics—the only one among people now" (521d).

Similarly with rhetoric, Socrates asks:

(5) Among all rhetoricians, is there a single rhetorician? (502d–504a)

His answer again is that no one who puts himself forward, or anyone so reputed from earlier times, has been engaged in anything more than shameful flattery and gratification (503a–d). The true rhetorician looks to the structure and form of the soul, and crafts his speech so as to lead souls toward virtue and away from vice (504d–e, 503e–504a) Plato's implication is that if there is a single rhetorician in all of Athens, it is Socrates. And again:

(6) Among all doctors, is there a doctor? (*Charmides* 156e–157b, 170e–171c, *Gorgias* 521a; *Republic* III.405a–408e, 409e–410e; VIII.563e–564c; X.599b–c)

Plato's answer: There is Socrates, for he is the one genuinely concerned with promoting health. Those who put themselves forward as doctors are in effect gratifiers and drug-dealers: helping those who are addicted to an unhealthy life extend their sick lives.

(7) Among all shepherds, is there a shepherd?

Plato: there is Socrates, because only he understands that a true shepherd looks to the good of his flock, not to those who feed off of them (*Republic* I.345b–e).[26]

(8) Among all the wise, is there a wise person?

There is Socrates, for he alone knows that he does not know (*Apology* 23a–b). And so on. These questions all have the same form—and in each case the possibility for irony arises by showing that the pretense falls short of its own aspiration. That is, a social pretense already contains a pretense-laden understanding of its aspiration, but irony facilitates a process by which the aspiration seems to break free of these bounds. In each case a purported totality is interrogated as to whether *any* of its members actually fits the bill. So, irony interrogates a totality not for its alleged inclusiveness, but for whether it has anything at all to do with the totality it purports to be. It is a movement that exposes a pretense in the nonpejorative sense to be pretense in the pejorative sense.

But we misunderstand the ironic movement if we think of Socrates as simply providing a revised set of criteria—for example, as arguing that a true doctor doesn't prescribe diet pills, but rather puts his patients on an exercise regimen. If this were all that was going on then the standard model of reflective endorsement would be adequate both for established practice and for the proposed Socratic revision. And this would be what was going on if Socrates had been an Aristotelian. That is, we begin with a practical identity such as *doctor*, and Socrates quickly links it to human excellence. Why doctoring matters is that it is the capacity for and activity of promoting health in humans. Now if Socrates were an Aristotelian, the next step would be simply to determine the marks and features of human health. Socrates, by contrast, repeatedly and insistently declares his ignorance of what human excellence consists in. I do not think we can understand the movement of Socratic irony until we understand Socrates' profession of ignorance—and I shall turn to this topic later. But, for the moment, notice that Socrates' ironic questioning seems to maintain a weird balancing act: simultaneously (i) calling into question a practical identity (as socially understood), (ii) living that identity; (iii) declaring ignorance of what it consists in. If becoming human requires holding all of that together, no wonder Kierkegaard thinks it is not that easy to get the hang of it.

Note that this account of Socratic irony provides an overarching unity to Socrates' method that would otherwise go unnoticed. The Socratic method is usually identified as refutation, the elenchus, which is then characterized formally as an attempt to elicit a contradiction—p and not-p—from an interlocutor. When the figure of Socrates in the dialogues abandons the elenchus, he is portrayed as having given up on his own method. There is then the famous charge that he has just become a mouthpiece for Plato.[27] But if one thinks of Socratic irony in terms of this broader form of activity—exposing the gap between pretense and aspiration—then the elenchus can be seen as one species of this method. Often the interlocutor is someone who puts himself forward, as knowing, say, what justice or piety is. On occasion, the interlocutor is puzzled as well, but he ends up speaking on behalf of a social pretense. The interlocutor is then shown either to fall short of aspirations that he himself espouses, or to speak for a social pretense that he can no longer make sense of. By concentrating on the formal feature of contradiction, commentators have ignored an essential nonformal feature: that it brings out the gap between pretense and aspiration. Thus when Socrates shifts from the elenchus to other ways of bringing out this gap, he need not be seen as giving up on Socratic method, nor as having become a mouthpiece for Plato; rather, he is taking up myriad forms of one method, Socratic irony.[28]

§5. Ironic Pretense-Transcending Activity

The point, then, is not about leaving the social world behind, but about a peculiar way of living in relation to it. When irony hits its mark, the person who is its target has an uncanny experience that the demands of an ideal, value, or identity to which he takes himself to be already committed dramatically transcend the received social understandings. The experience is uncanny in the sense that what had been a familiar demand suddenly feels unfamiliar, calling one to an unfamiliar way of life; and yet the unfamiliarity also has a weird sense of familiarity; as though we can recognize that this is our commitment. The important point right now is that the transcendence at issue is of available social pretenses, and this is a possibility that can be realized in human life. We are not talking about transcendence of the human realm altogether. For Kierkegaard, whatever the difficulties, it was possible to become (and be) a Christian; for Socrates, whatever the difficulties, it was possible to become (and be) a doctor (properly understood). For each of them, these were ways of becoming human.

These genuine human possibilities of pretense-transcending activity tend to escape our notice. In part this is because the social pretense puts itself forward as an adequate understanding of what, say, medicine consists in. But it is also true that the social sciences tend to overlook this possibility of pretense-transcending aspiring. This is because, in general, the social sciences want to collect data that are measurable, repeatable, and statistically analyzable. Irony escapes such measurement. If we look at the ironic questions, we can see they establish two columns:

Christian	Christian
Politician	Politician
Rhetorician	Rhetorician
Doctor	Doctor
Shepherd	Shepherd
Sage	Sage
. . . .	. . . .
. . . .	. . . . . .

The left-hand column is formed from the first occurrence of the relevant term, which expresses the social pretense; in the right-hand column, there is the second occurrence of the same term, which invokes the aspiration. Roughly speaking, the left-hand column gives us the domain of the social sciences. It gives us the domain that is accessible when it comes to collecting data that are measurable. The perennial challenge for social scientists is to figure out ways to operationalize a question: and that task will inevitably tend one's research in the direction of the left-hand column. So, for example, if one wanted to understand religion in America, one might try to establish reliable statistics for what percentage of the population attends church each week, what percentage self-describes as religious, and so on. These are all data that come from the left-hand column. Though a life exemplifying any of the categories in the right-hand column is neither ineffable nor supernatural, it does not lend itself to straightforward data collection or measurement. There is no statistically reliable way to answer the ironic question, "Among the millions who pray on Sunday, does anyone pray?"

§6. Two Students

So what, then, is the transcendence of the right-hand column? It is difficult to say, not because it is supernatural or an ineffable mystery, but, first, because everything one wants to say admits of interpretation that is appropriate to the left-hand column. Second, what one needs to grasp is the evanescence of the right-hand column. It has all the substantiality of the Cheshire cat's smile. It is as though one already has to have some capacity for irony to grasp what it is about. Let us use an example that is close to home, the category of student. The left-hand column is easy enough to establish: a *student* is someone who is enrolled in a recognized school. Now we might be tempted to think that if we add on a few conditions we can move on over to the right. But, as we shall see, the right-hand column is not the sort of thing that can be captured simply by trying to add necessary and sufficient conditions. *Everything is going to depend on how those conditions are themselves understood.*[29] That is, one needs an ironic ear to hear the conditions in the right sort of way. So, imagine trying to add conditions to the practical identity of student: a student in this deeper sense would be someone who takes on the life-task of becoming a person who is open to the lessons that the world, nature, others have to teach her. In so doing, she recognizes that the task is as never-ending as it is vora-cious. She may in fact direct her studies to this or that established area of re-search, but her identity as student is not exhausted by that commitment. Thus being/becoming a student in this sense is what contemporary philoso-phers call an infinite end.[30] Obviously, satisfying these conditions takes one well beyond the run-of-the-mill student; but there are ways of doing it that remain within received understandings. Ditto if one tries to nail it down by adding that one needs to take individual responsibility for what all this con-sists in. These statements need not take one out of the realm of social pre-tense. Indeed, this is the language of social pretense when it comes to describing a serious and dedicated student. And yet they also seem to me to be the right sort of statements to make.

One might think one could nail it down by adding more radical condi-tions. For example: the ideal of openness must include an openness to the possibility that all previously received understandings of what openness con-sists in themselves fall short of what openness really demands. And taking responsibility must consist in a willingness to orient oneself according to this revised understanding, regardless of what the social pretense recognizes or demands. But even these claims are open to left-handed interpretations. Thus one cannot capture the right-hand column simply by listing more conditions, no matter how right-thinking they may sound.

To see more clearly what this difficulty is, it is helpful to consider a pro-vocative example offered by Christine Korsgaard:

> you are visiting some other department, not your own, and fall
> into conversation with a graduate student. You discover that he is
> taking a course in some highly advanced form of calculus, and
> you ask him why. With great earnestness, he begins to lay out an
> elaborate set of reasons. "Philosophers since the time of Plato,"
> he says, "have taken mathematics to be a model for knowledge:
> elegant, certain, perfect, beautiful and utterly a priori. But you
> can't really understand either the power of the model or its limits
> if you have an outsider's view of mathematics. You must really
> get in there and do mathematics if you are to fully appreciate all
> this . . ." And just when you are about to be really impressed by
> the young man's commitment and seriousness, another student

comes along smiling and says "and anyway, calculus is required in our department."[31]

The first student, Korsgaard says, "seems like a phony. Since he had *that* motive for taking the course, all the rest seems a little irrelevant." As she puts it: "Although the student might appreciate the reasons why it is a good idea that the course should be required, it would be a little odd to say that that is his motive, since he has a decisive reason for taking the course whether he understands those reasons or not."[32]

Korsgaard admits that if the course had not been required and the first student took it for the reasons he gave, then "in one sense" he would be more autonomous than the student who merely takes it because it is required.

> He would be guided by his own mind, not that of another. But if he is required to take it, the reasons he gives should not be his motive. This may seem odd, since in a sense they are better reasons. But even if he understands them, they are excluded by his practical identity. Because his practical identity in this case is being a student. And this has two implications. First, to the extent that you identify yourself as a student, you *do* act autonomously in taking a course that is required. And second, it is an essential part of the idea of being a student that you place the right to make some of the decisions about what you will study in the hands of your teachers. And that means that when one of those decisions is in question, you are not free to act on your own private reasons any more, no matter how good those reasons are in themselves.[33]

Korsgaard is aware that the example may at first "seem odd," but she thinks that it lends insight into the relation of practical identity and autonomy. And it does—*if* one is considering practical identity as a left-hand phenomenon. Korsgaard says, "to the extent that you identify yourself as a student, you *do* act autonomously in taking a course that is required." One thus inhabits a practical identity by committing to the norms of the established social practice. In effect, Korsgaard has established one left-hand meaning for "autonomous."

But the important point right now is to see that even the student as social critic does not thereby make it to the right-hand lane of life. Let us develop Korsgaard's vignette. If we think of the first student, the one who is giving all his reasons for taking the required course, there are three salient possibilities of who he might be. He might be the phony Korsgaard takes him to be. Or he might be a more serious figure trying to think through what the requirements of a graduate education in philosophy ought to be. Let us imagine that last year, in his role as committed student, he led a successful campaign to have the department abolish the foreign-language requirement, and argued that first-order logic should count as a "foreign language." This person has a practical identity of student that is richer either than that of the phony or of the second student who simply says, "it's required." On occasion it requires him to invite his teachers to rethink what the educational requirements should be. He thus might be an interesting and challenging figure. But as yet we have no evidence of any irony that would move him over to the right-hand column. The fact that necessary and sufficient conditions are themselves not sufficient to move a person from left- to right-hand column may at first seem odd. After all, this student is spending his time challenging a social pretense, an established practical identity. But this form of challenge is itself a social pretense: it is a socially available way of putting oneself forward as a student. That is why it is important not to caricature the left-hand column of social pretense.

Allow me now to play fast and loose with space, time, and historical fact. Imagine that Korsgaard's conversation occurred in the philosophy department at the Pontifical University centuries ago and that her first interlocutor was the young Martin Luther. Apparently, just before their meeting, young man Luther had been haranguing the faculty on the entire curriculum of Christian education. The only course that survived his withering scrutiny was the course on calculus. (Never mind that calculus had not yet been invented.) Now imagine this outcome: as a result of his harangues there is a social transformation throughout Europe that results in the establishment of churches, the reorganization of nation-states and society. If Luther were just an extreme version of the previous example—a student protestor on steroids—then this would be a magnificent outcome. But if Luther were an ironist this would be a disaster. For what we have here, for all its social momentousness, is the establishment of the version of Christendom that Kierkegaard ironized. On this imagined example, we have not yet left the realm of social pretense; we have only envisaged its transformation. And though Christendom *mark one* and Christendom *mark two* differ on doctrinal issues, modes of ritual, and forms of hierarchy, they partake of a shared social pretense: they each put themselves forward as adequate to embody and express ideals that, when ironized, break their bounds. That is, they put themselves forward as though irony were not amongst their possibilities.[34] Ironically, if Luther had been an ironist, the only Lutheran in all of Christendom would have been Kierkegaard, who devoted his life to imploding the pretense of Lutheran Christendom.

§7. Ironic Existence

I have thus far been trying to capture the experience of irony. I would like to conclude with a preliminary account of ironic existence. Ironic existence is a form of life in which one develops a capacity for irony—that is, a capacity for occasioning an experience of irony (in oneself or another)—into a human excellence. That is, one has the ability to deploy irony in the right sort of way at the right time in the living of one's life. This gives us the basis for asking the ironic question:

(9) Among all ironists, is there an ironist?

One aim of this lecture has been to argue that there are at least two, Socrates and Kierkegaard. But what does this ironic existence consist in? Let us start by marking out what it is not. First, ironic existence does not entail that one act in one particular way rather than another with respect to established social practices. One may abandon the established social forms, finding them thin, hollowed out, hypocritical; but, conversely, to take Kierkegaard's example, one may return to the church one had been attending and participate in established rituals. Ironic existence need not show up in any particular behavioral manifestation—though how one inhabits the social pretense will nevertheless be transformed. Second, ironic existence does not imply that one is occasioning ironic experiences all the time. Ironic existence is rather the ability to live well all the time with the *possibility* of ironic experience. This requires practical wisdom about when it is appropriate to deploy irony. More important, it requires practical understanding that irony is a possibility in life. We need to capture a more robust sense of what this means. Third, ironic existence does not require alienation from established social practice. It is true that irony involves opening a gap between pretense and pretense-transcending aspiration—and in this sense, irony takes off from established social understandings—but acknowledging this gap is compatible with passionate engagement in social life.

To understand ironic existence, consider the modal structure of practical identity. To have a practical identity is in part to have a capacity for facing life's possibilities. As a teacher, to continue with the example, I have the capacity to face what comes my way *as a teacher would*. In particular, I can rule out as impossible, acts that would be incompatible with being a teacher. Thus I have internalized an implicit sense of life's possibilities, and have developed a capacity for responding to them in appropriate ways. This is what it is to inhabit a world from the perspective of a practical identity. In normal circumstances, this capacity for dealing with life's possibilities is an inheritance from, an internalization of, available social practices. I learn how to be a teacher from people I take to be teachers, and, in the first instance, I take society's word for who the teachers are. Obviously, as I develop, I may subject various norms to reflective criticism: that is part of my normal development as a teacher. Ironic experience is, as we have seen, a peculiar disruption of this inherited way of facing life's possibilities. This is not one more possibility one can simply add to the established repertoire. It is a disruption of the repertoire—and, in the disruption, it brings to light that the established repertoire is just that.

In ironic existence, I would have the capacity both to live out my practical identity as a teacher—which includes calling it into question in standard forms of reflective criticism—*and* to call all of that questioning into question; not via another reflective question, but rather via an ironic disruption of the whole process. In this twofold movement I would both be manifesting my best understanding of what it is about teaching that makes it a human excellence *and* be giving myself a reminder that this best understanding itself contains the possibility of ironic disruption. No wonder that getting the hang of it does not come that easily. Done well, this would be a manifestation of a practical understanding of one aspect of the finiteness of human life: that the concepts with which we understand ourselves and live our lives have a certain vulnerability built into them. Ironic existence thus has a claim to be a human excellence because it is a form of truthfulness. It is also a form of self-knowledge: a practical acknowledgment of the kind of knowing that is available to creatures like us.

If we take seriously the thought that ironic existence is a form of human excellence—peculiar to be sure—then there are certain lessons we can learn from Plato and Aristotle. First, we should not expect to be able to specify ahead of time in any detail what the appropriate ironic thing to do is in any particular circumstances. We learn how to live with irony appropriately by learning from those who already are living an ironic existence. Our most notable exemplar is Socrates. Second, we can think of ironic existence as lying in a mean between excess and defect: the defect would be the familiar "ironic" wit who forever remains detached from committed life; the excess would be the perpetual disrupter of social norms, lacking good judgment about appropriateness.

To grasp the peculiar ironic mean, it is helpful to return to Socrates. What is so astonishing about Socrates' life, and one that tends to escape the notice of commentators, is how effortlessly he blends positive and negative aspects of ironic existence. People tend to associate Socrates with the so-called method of refutation, the elenchus. Of course, the elenchus is structured so that a sincere interlocutor, in the midst of his pretense, is brought to a halt. But in terms of the shape of Socrates' life, what is most striking about the elenchus is not any formal or informal feature of the argument considered in isolation, but rather how Socrates deployed it: *in enthusiastic endless repetition.* He takes it as his divine task to cross-examine everyone he meets who has a pretense to knowledge of virtue—and thus he is not simply undermining interlocutors, he is honoring the god. He takes up a god-given task, and thereby tends to, reminds us of, the boundary between knowledge that is accessible to humans and the transcendent-divine.[35] His interlocutors are not simply defending their own beliefs: they are trying to put into words and defend a common social understanding of a virtue. Thus in questioning them he is questioning an aspect of social pretense. When they come up short, they manifest that this attempt to ground a social practice has fallen apart. And Socrates never relents. He is engaged in the endless task of undoing any particular claim to know. And if there is life after death, Socrates plans to go on endlessly cross-examining everyone he meets in Hades.

The young Kierkegaard could see only the negative side of this activity, and that is why he said that irony is "infinite negativity."[36] The late (and marvelous) Gregory Vlastos poured scorn over this expression: "fished out of

Hegel," as he put it, it renders Kierkegaard's interpretation "hopelessly per-plexed by this dazzling mystification." For Vlastos, "what irony means is simply expressing what we mean by saying something contrary to it."[37] Of course, that is what irony would look like if we had to make sense of it solely in terms of the left-hand column of meanings. Vlastos missed what Kierke-gaard was getting at, as has the Anglo-American tradition that followed him.[38] Funnily enough, though, the mature Kierkegaard himself came to pour scorn on the young author of the expression "infinite negativity." In a later work, *Concluding Unscientific Postscript,* the pseudonymous author Johannes Clima-cus criticizes "Magister Kierkegaard" for bringing out "only the one side" of irony.[39] "As can be inferred from his dissertation," Climacus tells us, "Magister Kierkegaard" has "scarcely understood" Socrates' "teasing manner."[40] I take the mature Kierkegaard to be making fun of himself as a young man: *The Concept of Irony,* his *Magister's* thesis, was written too much under the influ-ence of Hegel, and thus focused one-sidedly on the negativity of irony. What we need to understand is how ironic activity can be as affirming as it is negat-ing. Certainly, we need a better understanding of how it could be that, though he spends his life undermining each particular pretense to virtue, Socrates never falls into nihilism, questioning the reality of human virtue. Indeed, he takes his activity to be one of protecting virtue from the false masks that would be put upon it. Nor does his elenchic questioning necessarily pull him out of the related social practices.

So, consider Alcibiades' wonderful depiction of Socrates on the battlefield. What does Socrates do during the campaign for Potidaea? Well, for one thing, he stands still:

> One day, at dawn, he started thinking about some problem or other; he just stood outside trying to figure it out. He couldn't resolve it, but he wouldn't give up. He simply stood there, glued to the same spot. By midday, many soldiers had seen him and, quite mystified, they told everyone that Socrates had been stand-ing there all day, thinking about something. He was still there when evening came, and after dinner some Ionians moved their bedding outside, where it was cooler and more comfortable (all this took place in the summer), but mainly in order to watch if

Socrates was going to stay out there all night. And so he did; he stood on the very same spot until dawn! He only left next morning, when the sun came out, and he made his prayers to the new day. (*Symposium* 220c–d)[41]

Does Alcibiades suppose that Socrates cannot think and walk at the same time? In portraying Socrates as thinking about "some problem or other"—perhaps the proof of an especially difficult geometrical theorem!—Alcibiades shows that he just doesn't get it. Socrates is standing still not because he is too busy thinking, but because he *cannot walk,* not knowing what his next step should be. I take this to be a moment of erotic uncanniness: *longing* to move in the right direction, but not knowing what that direction is. He is uprooted only by the conventional religious demands of a new day. Yet when the actual battle comes, Socrates behaves with extraordinary bravery—*by the standard lights* of accepted social behavior. As Alcibiades says, "during that very battle, Socrates single-handedly saved my life! He absolutely did! He just refused to leave me behind when I was wounded, and he rescued not only me but my armor as well. For my part, Socrates, I told them right then that the decoration really belonged to you" (220d–e). It is as though the moment of standing still invigorates him, at the right moment, to perform *extraordinary acts of conventional bravery.* And rather than their being two disparate moments in a disunified life, Alcibiades has an intimation that they form some kind of unity. In describing how Socrates bravely helped Laches in the retreat from Delium, Alcibiades says:

> in the midst of battle he was making his way *exactly as he does around town,* "with swaggering gait and roving eye." He was observing everything quite calmly, looking out for friendly troops and keeping an eye on the enemy. Even from a great distance it was obvious that this was a very brave man, who would put up a terrific fight if anyone approached him. That is what saved both of them. (221b; my emphasis)

And yet, Alcibiades also says that Socrates' bravery cannot be compared to that of Achilles or anyone else (221c–d). Why ever not, if all we are talking about is battlefield bravery? The answer must be that Socratic ignorance (in this case, about courage), far from being a distinct moment in Socrates' life (in the study, as it were), and far from sapping confidence in the ordinary demands of bravery, can, in certain circumstances, invigorate the enactment of the ordinary requirements. The irony must be *right there,* in the obviously brave acts, otherwise Socrates' bravery would be comparable with Achilles'. This is what makes Socrates, in Alcibiades' words, "unique": "he is like no one else in the past and no one in the present—this is by far the most amazing thing about him." He is able to act bravely (according to the lights of social pretense), all the while holding firm to his ignorance. This isn't just negativity; it is a peculiar way of *obviously* contributing to polis life. Socrates isn't merely a gadfly: he's a gadfly who, on appropriate occasions, is willing to fight to the death in conventional battle.[42]

Similarly with Socrates' classic examination of courage in the *Laches*. To be sure, by the end of the dialogue Socrates admits that he and his fellow inquirers have failed to discover what courage is (199e). However, he is able to enter the conversation to begin with only because his interlocutors trust him as a worthy interlocutor—and they trust him because he is well known for having lived courageously, according to the received norms of courage. Lysimachus says to Socrates that he keeps up his father's good reputation, and that he was the best of men. And Laches elaborates: "I have seen him elsewhere keeping up not only his father's reputation but that of his country. He marched with me in the retreat from Delium and I can tell you that if the rest had been willing to behave in the same manner, our city would be safe and would not then have suffered a disaster of that kind" (181a–b).[43] So Socratic ignorance is compatible with behaving with outstanding courage *as socially understood*. It is not a way of withdrawing from battle on behalf of the polis, but a way of participating in it. Even the inquiry into the nature of courage is not an abstract "philosophical" inquiry (as that term is often used), but a response to an impassioned, urgent plea for help. Lysimachus and Melisius— two of the interlocutors—are the undistinguished sons of great men who are now worried about transmitting virtue to *their* sons (178c–d). No culture is stronger than its ability to pass on its values to the next generation, so this is a conversation born of social anxiety. Anxious representatives of the social practice are turning to Socrates for help, and Socratic examination is his response. It does not leave them empty-handed. Rather, they are convinced that they need to find a proper teacher *for themselves*. "I like what you say,

Socrates," Lysimachus says, "and the fact that I am the oldest makes me most eager to go to school along with the boys." Socrates agrees to meet again tomorrow so they can *all* begin to search for the best possible teacher (201a–c). Do I have any takers for the bet that should they find that teacher, not only will he not know what courage is, but he will not know what teaching is either? The point of Socratic irony is not simply to destroy pretenses, but to inject a certain form of not-knowing into polis life. This is his way of teaching virtue. And it shows the difficulty of becoming human: not just the arduousness of maintaining a practical identity in the face of temptation, but the difficulty of getting the hang of a certain kind of playful, disrupting existence that is as affirming as it is negating. It is constitutive of human excellence to understand—that is, to grasp practically—the limits of human understanding of such excellence. Socratic ignorance is thus an embrace of human openendedness.

The height of his irony comes when, convicted of corrupting the youth and introducing new gods, Socrates proposes his own punishment. As absolutely conventional as he was in courageously defending the polis from external attack, he is absolutely unconventional in defending the polis from its own internal disease. It is one and the same virtue that is a manifestation of both. And he faces death in both cases with the same equanimity. If the appropriate punishment is what he deserves, "Nothing is more suitable, gentlemen, than for such a man to be fed in the Prytaneum much more suitable for him than for any one of you who has won a victory at Olympia with a pair or a team of horses. The Olympian victor makes you think yourself happy; I make you be happy" (*Apology* 36d–e).[44] The irony is utter earnestness: this *is* what he deserves. And it is an occasion for disruption: to vote for this proposal the Athenians would have had to disrupt the world of social expectations. In the extreme moment of facing death, Socrates does not deviate an iota from ironic existence. If the Athenians had accepted Socrates' proposal, I am confident he would not have missed a beat, continuing his conversations while enjoying dinner at public expense. That Socrates got the hang of it is attested by Vlastos's astute observation: "In the whole of the Platonic corpus, in the whole of our corpus of Greek prose or verse, no happier life than his may be found."[45]

§8. Getting the Hang of It

In the diary entry with which I began, Kierkegaard says: "becoming human or learning what it means to be human is not that easy." If one takes this claim with ontological seriousness, it turns out that these disjuncts are equivalent. Human being would be understood in terms of human excellence. So being human would be a matter of becoming human—the practical task of achieving human excellence and this would be learning what it means to be human. But the practical knowledge that is human excellence contains a moment of ignorance internal to it. Part of what it is to be, say, courageous is to recognize that one's practical understanding of courage is susceptible to ironic disruption. Part of what it is to be courageous is courageously to face the fact that living courageously will inevitably entangle one in practices and pretenses and possible acts all of which are susceptible to the question, what does *any of that* have to do *with courage?* Ironic existence is the ability to live well with that insight.

Kierkegaard says that "no genuinely human life is possible without irony."[46] On the interpretation I have been developing this would mean: It is constitutive of human excellence that one develop a capacity for appropriately disrupting one's understanding of what such excellence consists in. Human flourishing would then partially consist in cultivating an experience of oneself as uncanny, out of joint. This is what it would mean to get the hang of it, the erotic uncanniness of human existence.

Appendix 1: Comment on Richard Rorty's Interpretation of Irony

Richard Rorty, who is well known for having articulated a contemporary philosophical conception of irony, defines an ironist as someone who, first, "has radical and continuing doubts about the final vocabulary she uses, because she has been impressed by other vocabularies or books she has encountered." (A final vocabulary is that which one uses to formulate basic projects, important hopes, doubts, praise, and blame.) Second, she has "realized that the arguments phrased in her current vocabulary can neither underwrite nor dissolve these doubts"; and, third, "insofar as she philosophizes about her situation, she does not think that her vocabulary is closer to reality than others, that it is in touch with a power not herself."[47] This seems to me a thin conception of irony and its possibilities; and it is worth noting how different it is from Kierke-gaard's conception. For Kierkegaard, irony is a way of achieving a deeper un-derstanding of—and ultimately a more earnest commitment to—what comes to emerge as one's final vocabulary.

Note that Rorty's ironist need never leave the left-hand lane of life. To continue with an example we have been using, imagine an inhabitant of Christendom who starts to have doubts about the institutionalized practices. Something about it she experiences as routine, hollowed out. She then *looks sideways* over at other final vocabularies. So, she reads books about Judaism and Islam, reads about Confucianism and Buddhism, even tries out some New Age spirituality. Perhaps she visits temples, mosques, and other shrines. The temptation to caricature her is enormous; but let us refrain from doing so. The point is that in investigating these other final vocabularies, there is no pressure thereby generated to question the various social pretenses other than in terms of other pretenses. From Kierkegaard's perspective, Rorty's ironist is not an ironist at all, but someone confined to the left-hand meanings of social pretense, misleading himself about his freedom via the plethora of meanings at his disposal and his lack of commitment to any of them. Differ-ent final vocabularies are treated as though they were objects of disinterested choice: one could choose them on the basis of being struck by doubt with one's own final vocabulary.[48] In a Kierkegaardian vein, this looks like a weari-ness that does not recognize itself as such.[49]

But the point here is not to criticize Rorty. In fact, Rorty's irony is what irony would look like if there were no right-hand resonances in life. Then there would be only the disenchantment with a given social pretense (and its final vocabulary) while the only alternatives on offer were other social pre-tenses (and their final vocabularies). That is why there is reason to think that there are not simply two different uses of the word "irony," but that contem-porary use is a diminished version of what Kierkegaard meant. For if our ears suddenly became deaf to the uncanny disruptions of would-be directedness, irony would inevitably come to seem an expression of detachment and lack of commitment rather than an expression of earnestness and commitment. One might think of Kierkegaardian and Socratic irony as a two-part movement of detachment and attachment: detachment from the social pretense in order to facilitate attachment to the more robust version of the ideal. But if one obliterates the second part of the two-part movement, all that remains is irony as a form of detachment. And it would make sense to experience the ironist as saying something other than he means.[50] It seems to me that Rorty's account of irony is symptomatic of something that has happened in modernity that has made it difficult to hear the resonances of the right-hand column.[51]

Appendix 2: Comment on James Conant's Interpretation of Kierkegaard's Method in the Pseudonymous Authorship

The subtle and deep work of James Conant on Kierkegaard's method deserves an essay of its own.[52] This is obviously beyond the scope of these lectures; but let me at least indicate in brief outline why I am not persuaded by his interpretation. I suspect that the key problems with Conant's interpretation flow from a mischaracterization of the pseudonymous author Johannes Climacus. Conant tells us that "Kierkegaard refers to the entire pseudonymous authorship as an aesthetic production."[53] And he thus treats Climacus as an aesthetic author. However, Kierkegaard distinguishes the "aesthetic productivity" of *almost* all of the pseudonymous works from *Concluding Unscientific Postscript,* of which Climacus is the pseudonymous author and which Kierkegaard, in his own voice, calls a "turning point" between the aesthetic works and the exclusively religious works. Kierkegaard continues: "The *Concluding Unscientific Postscript is not an aesthetic work,* but neither is it in the strictest sense religious. Hence it is by a pseudonym, though I add my name as editor."[54] That is, the pseudonym appears in this case because the work is not *in the strictest sense* religious. Thus it would seem open to regard the work as, *loosely* speaking, religious, or at the boundary of the religious. The pseudonymous author would then have to be someone capable of at least that level of religious seriousness.

The thought that Climacus is not an aesthetic author opens up serious challenges to Conant's interpretation as a whole. To give one example, Conant moves from "Johannes Climacus tells us he is not a Christian," which is true, to "Indeed, he is not even interested in becoming a Christian."[55] This inference would be valid if Climacus were an aesthetic author and if, as Conant thinks, the aesthetic is characterized by disinterestedness. But if Climacus is not an aesthetic author—or if the aesthetic is not characterized by disinterestedness—

then the inference is invalid. And I do not see any independent textual support for the claim that Climacus is not even interested in becoming a Christian. This matters because Conant wants to trap Climacus in a "performative contradiction" between his disinterested, objective consideration of Christianity and the essentially interested and subjective Christianity that he is investigating. It is that performative contradiction we are then supposed to see in ourselves—and *that* is purportedly the key to Kierkegaard's method. Conant refers to this method as holding up a mirror by which the reader can recognize his own confusions.[56] However, if Climacus is not an aesthetic author, then the performative contradiction, *if there is one,* is not as Conant describes. A further problem, but in the same vein, is that Climacus describes himself as a humorist; and gives an account of a humorist as one who tends to the boundary between the ethical and the religious.[57] That is, the humorist is not an aesthetic figure. Indeed, Climacus seems to leave open the possibility of a religious humorist, one who might protect his religiousness by *saying* that he is not a Christian: "The religious person does the same [as the humorist] . . . Therefore religiousness *with humor as the incognito* is the unity of absolute religious passion . . . and spiritual maturity."[58] Either way—Climacus as mere humorist or Climacus as religious person with humor as his incognito—he is not an aesthetic author. Thus I do not think one can find here a performative contradiction of an aesthetic author's disinterested objectivity with the subjectivity of Christianity.[59]

It thus becomes difficult to see what the efficacy of Kierkegaard's method consists in. We no longer have evidence that Climacus is engaged in performative contradiction. But even if there were performative contradiction and recognition, why should this make a difference? How does it make the difference it purportedly does make? Conant argues that the method achieves its efficacy via reflection: "If forced to reflect upon their lives, Kierkegaard thinks his readers can be brought to see that, if pressed, they would be at a loss to say what licenses the claim that they are Christians (unless the claim is based on something like their citizenship)."[60] I am concerned that Conant is here zeroing in on too narrow a field of readers. He gives us an image of the efficacy of the method by assuming that it targets relatively unreflective people who are nevertheless willing or forced on this occasion to reflect. They quickly come to see that they are at a loss, or they state some objective criterion that can then be dialectically undermined. Kierkegaard did diagnose—and lampoon—such figures. But if such relatively unreflective people are the ultimate targets, then Kierkegaard's method looks unambitious in scope. As I have argued in this lecture, we do not get to the real power of Christendom as illusion unless we also recognize that there were serious, reflective figures who nevertheless remained bound by the illusion. That is why irony is so important: because being forced to reflect further on one's life is often not sufficient to break out of illusion. In a similar vein, it is possible to see practical contradiction in others, and through mirroring to see it in oneself, and nevertheless remain in illusion. I take it that this is what happened in serious sermons heard by serious people who, while provoked and disturbed in various ways by the sermons, were nevertheless *qua inhabitants of Christendom* undisturbed.

As a result, I do not see how Conant can be right when he claims that *all* the confusions that Kierkegaard's method brings to light are ultimately grammatical (in Wittgenstein's sense of that term).[61] No doubt, Conant has isolated a significant class of confusions and correctly diagnosed them as grammatical. This is an important contribution; for Conant is able to bring to light how confusion arises from trying to apply objective judgments to essentially subjective categories. But it is also important that Kierkegaard's irony is capable of hitting a target that eludes this characterization. As I have argued here, there might be someone who grasps that Christianity is a matter of subjective commitment (in some nontrivial understanding of that term), grasps that it is not to be understood in aesthetic or objective terms, who even manifests a certain seriousness about his subjective commitment—and yet is *still* vulnerable to ironic disruption. (See my remarks on teaching, and on the two students above.) Irony matters, at least in part, because even people who are grammatically unconfused are nevertheless susceptible to its disruptive, uncanny powers.

2

Ironic Soul

In the previous lecture I argued that the experience of irony is an experience of erotic uncanniness. It is a significant form of pretense-transcending aspiring. Thus insofar as it is important to understand our capacity to aspire in ways that transcend the aspirations already embedded in social pretense, we need to understand better how this peculiar form of uncanniness works. I also claimed that it is possible to develop a capacity for irony: that is, a capacity to occasion an experience of irony (in oneself or another). One might have thought that since ironic experience is uncanny disruption, we must be passive sufferers. Indeed, in the first instance we are; but it is possible to become active with respect to one's own ironic experience. I also claimed that ironic existence is a peculiar human excellence: the capacity to deploy irony in the right sort of way at the right time in living a distinctively human life. In this lecture I would like to ask the question: What are we like such that all of this is possible? This is not a Kantian transcendental inquiry—what *must* we be like for irony to be possible?—so much as a Platonic inquiry: What *are* we like such that a purported virtue—ironic existence—is a possibility for us?

Aside from its intrinsic interest, there are two related reasons for me to take up this question. First, I want to correct a widespread assumption about the psychic shape that pretense-transcending aspiring must take. We have, I think, overlooked a significant possibility because it does not fit into the familiar range of possibilities. We tend to assume *either,* Plato-fashion, that one posits a special faculty of the soul—reason—whose special job it is to break us out of appearances and enable us to grasp reality as it really is; *or,* following Nietzsche and Freud, that one adopts a hermeneutics of suspicion in which aspirations to transcendence are diagnosed as hidden expressions of resentment, envy, or aggression turned on the self. This is an impoverished range of options. I want to open up room for a plausible moral psychology that in allowing us to see how irony works will also legitimate ironic activity. Second, getting the proper psychology in view will require us to rethink what it is to be a unified self. The unity that is genuinely available to us is, I think, marked by disruption and division. This is not the well-known view that whatever psychic unity we achieve will always be vulnerable to disruption, but rather a view that whatever unity is genuinely available *partially consists* in certain forms of disruption. The aim of unity should not be to overcome these disruptions, but to find ways to live well with them. Ironically, the unity that is available to us is a peculiar form of disunity. In trying to work out the family of concepts that include *rational will, action,* and *agency,* philosophers have tended to rely on an idealized conception of unity that does not really fit the human soul. I want to get clear on what this lack of fit consists in and why it should matter.

§1. The Possibility of a Nonmoralized Moral Psychology

It would be easy enough if we could simply posit a pretending part of the soul—that part which takes up social meanings and crafts a sense of identity around available social roles—and posit also a pretense-transcending part—a part that effectively calls into question the activities of the pretending part by using the very same terms. There then would be intrapsychic activity that was a fairly direct correlate of irony: the activity of these two opposed parts on one another. We could then question whether psychic unity was feasible, and what its costs and benefits were. But grasping how irony works is not that straightforward.

One broad-scale way to read Plato's psychology—as it emerges in different ways in the *Republic, Symposium, and Phaedrus*—is as an attempt to explain how irony is possible. Plato, of course, posits a pretense-transcendent good—The Good—which organizes the other pretense-transcendent forms. So the main question for his psychology is why it is that we are creatures who, for the most part, do not grasp the real situation we are in; and how it is that on occasion an individual is able to break free of appearances and engage in genuine acts of pretense-transcendent aspiring. On occasion he attributes this to our erotic natures—our capacity to be stunned by beauty and overcome by pretense-transcendent longing; on occasion he attributes this to what he calls "summoners of thought"—situations in which there is an apparent contradiction or no easy way to give an answer in terms of appearances; on occasion he attributes this to the instability of souls that are organized around the acquisition of honor or wealth.[1] There are various ways in which the world of social pretenses can break down for special inhabitants. And that breakdown, for Plato, opens up the possibility of aspiring to an ideal that is more true, better, than any finite socially embedded conception. Thus if there is some part of us that naturally does such aspiring, then there is some part of us that is naturally oriented toward and fulfilled in the real, the true, and the good.

Plato's accounts of psychological breakdown are astonishingly astute, but both Christine Korsgaard and Bernard Williams have argued that his positive account of how pretense-transcending aspiring occurs begs the question.[2] The fact that the breakdown should result in pretense-transcendent aspiring is guaranteed, for Plato, by positing a faculty that can grasp a transcendent object that is the source of value. This is not an explanation, Korsgaard argues, but a placeholder for where an explanation ought to go. And Williams claims that Plato has built into his psychology the morality he wants to get out of it. The task, according to Williams, is to formulate a nonmoralized moral psychology: one that is sufficiently rich to give us insight into ethically rich human activities, motivations, and emotions, while also making clear that these are natural phenomena.

These are powerful criticisms. Perhaps someday a great Platonist will come along to answer them, but for now the prudent strategy is to give an alternative and more modest account of how such pretense-transcending aspiring might occur. The way to do this, I think, is to notice *another* problem with Plato's psychology that has escaped notice—largely because the philosophical tradition has accepted Plato's assumption. From the beginning of philosophy's attempt to ground ethics in the unity of the soul, the "lower" part of the soul has been assumed to be disparate, heterogeneous, multifarious, lacking in unity. In the *Republic,* Plato says that the part of the soul that he calls appetite is so multiform (πολυειδῦαν) that it doesn't really have a name that is proper to it.[3] It is given the name *appetite* because of its paradigmatic examples: hunger, thirst and sexual desire. But appetitive desire can spread out to include desire for money, as well as desire for all the things that money can buy. This diffuseness is, of course, central to Plato's argument: the life of the tyrant, "ruled" as it is by appetite, is portrayed as a disorganized mess. Although much of Plato's psychology and metaphysics has been discarded, the presumption remains that the "lower" part of the soul, however conceived, is lacking in unity and organization. In this lecture I will question that assumption: I believe that unconscious fantasy provides an alternative source of unity for the self,. And the fact that each of us has an unconscious unifying principle has significant philosophical consequences.

But for the moment, notice that if one does become suspicious of pretense-transcending aspiring as Plato describes it, it is natural to become suspicious of pretense-transcending aspiring itself. Deflationary accounts and unmasking accounts have gone hand in hand. Nietzsche and Freud are, of course, two prominent examples. To take Freud: he was intensely suspicious of the claims that morality made on us—above all the idea that we should transcend our nature in the name of a higher ideal. And while the ego may be considered a faculty of pretense—governing how we put ourselves forward in the world—the idea that the superego in any of its guises might be a faculty for pretense-transcending aspiring would be met by Freud with skepticism bordering on derision. Far from being a faculty of pretense-transcendence, the superego is dedicated to keeping us in line. Especially in *Civilization and Its Discontents,* the superego is portrayed as a faculty of surveillance and punishment: keeping us on the straight and narrow when it comes to the demands of morality and civilization.[4] If anything, the superego is, on this characterization, a pretense-*enforcer*. It is, Freud tells us, a defensive structure (an heir of the Oedipus complex) that arose to resist the transgressive wishes of the id. It basically has the structure of response: a "No!" to the id's "Yes!" The guilty, unhappy, discontented individual who *thereby* manages a "civilized" life, a life of social pretense, is the outcome.

And this psychically unhappy-making structure does have an instance that looks a lot like irony. A punitive superego can painfully attack ordinary attempts to put oneself forward—claiming "You are a fraud!" or "You are guilty!"—in relation to which one experiences oneself falling abysmally short. Clearly, this is a significant source of human suffering; and if the irony I am trying to isolate were just a version of this structure, we would be better off without it. However, I do not think this is the end of the story.

§2. Unconscious Fantasy as a Source of Psychic Unity

There is more to be learned from psychoanalysis than Freud's initial diagnosis of the superego might suggest. If ironic experience is a peculiar form of un-canniness, then perhaps we can take a different clue from Freud. He famously claimed that "the uncanny [*unheimlich*] is something which is secretly familiar [*heimlich-heimisch*], which has undergone repression and then returned from it."[5] A repressed thought comes back to disrupt the present with an experi-ence that is at once weirdly familiar and unfamiliar. The claim I would like to add—and this is crucial—is that unconscious motivations are not simply a disparate hodgepodge of one-off desires, fantasies, and emotions that occa-sionally disrupt consciousness, but they can supply alternative unifying sources of the self. Indeed, it is not too much of a stretch to talk of uncon-scious practical identity. So what is breaking through in an uncanny experi-ence need not be just some rejected wish; it may be *me* coming back to haunt myself. To take this thought seriously will have an impact on what we take to be the philosophical significance of our conscious sense of practical identity, on what kind of psychic unity, *if any*, is available to us, and on what is in-volved in making the unconscious conscious.

To start at the beginning, the basic idea is that unconscious fantasies (of-ten referred to as "phantasies") are emotionally laden, motivationally charged structures of meaning that tend toward formal organization.[6] They tend toward the expression of an unconscious worldview, whereby all experience is interpreted in its terms. Correlatively, there is a subject who is at the center of this (unconsciously organized) world. The core fantasy has great organiz-ing power and provides an imaginative answer to the question: Who am I? The claim then is that the self tends to have a formal cause, unrecognized as such, which stands at significant odds with the conscious sense of practical identity.

I have come to believe this because, in addition to reading and teaching philosophy, I have over the past twenty years been seeing people in psychoanalysis. Over and over again I have watched these structures come into view. That is not *all* there is, of course; and I do not subscribe to the view that anything answers to the description *"the* unconscious." There are unconscious strategies, modes of thought, conflicting fantasies, ideation, and so on. The only important points are, first, that among the disparate forms of unconscious mental activity there is a subclass of disparate forms that are *kept* out of consciousness via a disparate group of motivated strategies. Second, in the analysis of adults there tends to emerge a core unconscious fantasy that has great organizing power. (I am not making any universal claim about human nature, but am commenting on a wide swath of human experience that Freud called neurotic.)

Here is a brief example. Ms. A., an attractive young woman in her mid-twenties from the West Coast, came into analysis because of lack of sexual feelings for her husband. She thought it was due to acne he had—which she attributed to his desire for greasy, fast food, but she wasn't really sure. In any case, the acne turned her off. Or maybe it was his slight paunch. According to Ms. A., her husband was upset by their lack sexual relations: he felt frustrated, ashamed, and inadequate. She entered analysis with the conscious desire to solve this specific problem. As the analysis progressed, it turned out that as she was growing up, she was a tomboy: she liked wearing boys' clothes and having her hair cropped short. She liked climbing trees, hanging out in a tree house. From first grade on she liked playing (as the only girl) on boys' athletic teams, and she grew up at a time and in a local culture (and at a particular moment in American history) that praised lack of stereotyping in respect of gender, race, or ethnic identity. She stayed on the (basically) boys' team through high school. She was not able to play on a the varsity team in college, but the university she attended was organized in such a way that there were intramural teams, and she played on one of the boys' teams. Even now, as a young professional, Ms. A. enjoys playing on an officially coed team, but the team has only two women on it, and the other woman rarely plays. It is in the heat of a competitive game that she feels most alive. Afterward, she glows with pleasure in recounting the most challenging moments. She likes hanging out with her teammates after the game—still suited up in uniform—and going to the bar afterward with them to talk about the game. This pattern of behavior drives her husband wildly jealous—he thinks she is flirting—but she doesn't understand what he is talking about. For her, this is the teammates having a beer.

Ms. A. mentioned an involuntary association. When she was thinking about her husband's acne an image of her stepfather came into her mind. Her husband's acne reminded her of some markings on her stepfather's skin. Might he have something to do with her inhibition? Ms. A. never really understood why her stepfather replaced her father. At some point during her ruminations and associations, a memory came back to her: at around seven years old, she got out of bed one night and wandered by her mother and stepfather's bedroom. The door was ajar, and the light of the television screen illuminated them. They were in an unusual physical position—one that disturbed her and made her anxious. The mother's position looked awkward. She hurried away, never mentioned it to anyone, and, indeed, forgot all about it until this moment in analysis about two decades later.

She also remembered something she was told in childhood: that when she was still in the womb, her parents thought she was going to be a boy. According to the story, the mother had visited the midwife, who, using ultrasound, thought she saw a penis. The parents had spent months expecting a boy and had picked out a boy's name for her. Here is the remembered content of a dream: she is at a party in the backyard of a house overlooking the Pacific Ocean. Everyone is busy talking, drinking beer. There is a little boy there about ten years old (whose hair color is the opposite of the dreamer's). While she is in animated conversation with others, the little boy falls down a sharp drop at the edge of the property. No one at the party notices. Suddenly she notices and runs over to jump off the edge herself—and then wakes up, with a vague sense that maybe she rescued him.

There is obviously much more to this story, but perhaps I have said enough to make it plausible that certain images of *boyishness* are providing *a* source of unity to Ms. A.'s life. For the most part, the manifestations of boyishness are not recognized as such. The love of a particular sport, for example, was certainly recognized, but it was not initially linked to anything else in the person's life other than a love of exercise. The memories of having been a tomboy—

where boyishness was explicitly recognized—were not deeply repressed, but they were not anything she thought about until coming into analysis. But once *boyishness* came into view as an unconscious source of identity an enormous amount of other behavior started to make sense. She was the one who paid the bills. Indeed, she was the income-earner in the family. She enjoyed being "competitive" in the workplace. The husband stayed at home. He is an artisan. She admired his ability as a maker of fine things, but she wondered why he rarely left the house, why he found it so difficult to put himself for ward professionally. On the rare occasions when they did have sex, she had to be "on top." She was successful in the business world, whereas he stayed home, sleeping late, often remaining in the same comfortable clothes he slept in. Her dress tended toward extremes in terms of images of culturally established gender identities, though on different occasions she would wear "masculine" or "feminine" outfits. As we saw, she enjoyed going out to the bar to hang out with the boys. She wore sports bras that tended to flatten her breasts. She talked a lot about responsibility, about paying her bills on time. She took pride in her self-reliance. She felt she could move anywhere and get a good job and do well. *For her,* these professional images were associated with masculinity; and they were, for her, a source of pride. There was also a lot in her dream-life in which young boys and their mothers and fathers played a significant role. And so on.

Three points command our attention. First, as we have begun to see, her image of boyishness is functioning as a kind of formal cause: there is nothing else that would otherwise hold together myriad and pervasive activities and features of her life: the way she pays her bills, stands at a bar, daydreams when she looks at trees, what she consciously imagines while having sex. Life is being organized and maintained around fantasies of boyishness. Second, the fact that there is an underlying, motivated unity amongst these disparate phenomena is itself kept hidden from view—because Ms. A. *herself* is anxious that the fantasies of boyishness significantly conflict with her conscious practical identity, which is markedly feminine. The point is not about any inherent conflict between boyishness and femininity. Third, because the fantasies of boyishness are held at bay, the images of boyishness *and* of femininity tend to depend on social images: soccer, beer, bars; dramatically feminine shoes, suggestively cut dresses, and so on. Note that this reliance on social stereotypes does not mean that Ms. A. was unreflective about her practical identity.

On the contrary, she had read feminist literature, and she took her feminine dress to be an expression of her version. However, her reflective activity of stepping back from received images seemed to be in the service of sticking with them. It allowed her to participate in received images even after having subjected them to, as she put it, "feminist critique."

§3. Making the Unconscious Conscious

I hope that if there is anything strange about the example above, it is its sense of familiarity.[7] I would guess that many of you, if you let your minds wander, will be able to think of someone who lives with a tension like this, or some other one that has a similar shape. We are not dealing here with anything exotic—for example, a biological male who is certain he is a woman trapped in a man's body. Rather, this is an example of the extraordinary stuff of ordinary life. It is a mark of the human that we do not quite fit into our own skins. That is, we do not fit without remainder into socially available practical identities. By now, this is a familiar thought. The unfamiliar thought is that this remainder should not be thought of as the flotsam and jetsam of life. What I have found over and over again is that if one allows a person—who, for all the world, looks like a healthy human being with some problems to discuss—to lie down on a couch and say whatever comes into his or her mind, one will find not only that the person does not quite fit into his or her skin, but that what lies "outside" is a basic organizing principle, working around primordial human challenges: for example, what it means to be the first-born or second-born, what it means to lose a parent early in life, what it is to be the child of divorced parents; how one could trust or be faithful to another person or, to take the classic case, what it is to be a person who is, for a while, a child, but who then must grow into adulthood, old age, and die. Unconscious motivations are not simply this or that temptation to break a socially accepted norm; they are also organized attempts to form an identity around the solution to a primordial human problem. At the same time, and in uncanny ways, the unconscious uses received social pretenses to both express and attempt solutions to these problems.

Notice, too, that all of the phenomena I mentioned in the case of Ms. A. are right there on the surface of life. I have not tried to provide a deep interpretation of anything, including the remembered dream. The only suggestion

I have made is that these myriad phenomena fit together: that they manifest a formal unity that is itself the manifestation and expression of unconscious fantasy. The fantasy thus serves as a source of unity of the self. *This* is what is unconscious. And there is another thought of which she was unaware, though it was manifest throughout her life: namely, that she *values* her boyish life. Even if she is not in a position reflectively to endorse it, the evidence is everywhere that *this* boy's life matters to her. These would seem to be acts that are paradigmatically coming *from her,* though the source of the self from which they come remains obscure to her.

But what, then, would it be to make this unconscious source of the self conscious? I am going to argue that the answer involves facilitating the development of a capacity for irony. This may at first seem like an odd answer, and it will take us a few steps to get there. Let us begin with the thought that the psychoanalytic understanding of what it means to make the unconscious conscious must be internal to psychoanalysis. Psychoanalysis is essentially a therapeutic technique. It aims to make people better (along some dimension of psychic well-being that needs to be spelled out), and its sense of what it is to make the unconscious conscious is essentially linked to that process. Thus we cannot understand the psychoanalytic meaning of "making the unconscious conscious" independently of understanding what is possible and desirable as an outcome of psychoanalytic therapy. Obviously, the process is misdirected if the major cognitive achievement is located in the analyst. The analyst listens and observes the analysand for a while, makes some remarkable connections, and shares her conclusion with the analysand, "You have an unconscious fantasy of being a boy." Even if the analysand "accepts" the expert's judgment, such "acceptance" need have no effect on the workings of the fantasy itself. The situation is somewhat improved if the analysand carries out the bulk of that observational work herself: she observes her own behavior, her memories, the flow of her thoughts, what she says, and so on, and, perhaps with some assistance from her analyst, draws her own conclusion that she must be organizing her life around boyish fantasies. She can sincerely say, on the basis of self-observation, "I realize I've been living with boyish fantasies all my life." And her sincere avowal can, for her, sum up myriad activities, daydreams, and dream-memories. Such a moment might be significant in a person's life, but it can also function defensively, to keep one detached from the fantasy precisely by the ostensible act of naming and recognizing it. The fantasy can find other routes of expression; and nothing significant need shift. Thus neither of these images of therapy can be an adequate account of the psychoanalytic meaning of making the unconscious conscious. What, then, would an adequate account look like?

§3.1. The Expression of Unconscious Emotion

To answer this question, we need to proceed in stages. Consider, first, a relatively simple act: the making conscious of a hitherto unconscious emotion, say anger. Here I am indebted to the work of my colleague David Finkelstein, especially his book *Expression and the Inner.*[8] There are two distinct ways, Finkelstein points out, in which one might be said to become conscious of one's anger. One way does not depend on my consciously feeling anger. Certain things I am doing strike my attention: I have started coming late to our meetings; I find myself making a spontaneous sarcastic remark; although I don't usually gossip, I have started to talk behind your back; and so on. I wonder about my own behavior, and then I remember something you did a few weeks ago that irked me at the time. I come to the conclusion that I am angry, though I have been unaware of it. I might even say to you, "You know, I can see in my behavior that I must have been angry at you." Or even: "I realize I'm angry at you" or "I'm angry at you." I might thus sincerely avow my anger in this familiar sense: I am sincerely making a true assertion about my anger, based on the evidence. But, in Finkelstein's sense, I am not thereby *expressing* my anger. For my anger is not *there,* present in the utterance; even though I am sincere and my judgment is responsible. In such a case, to use Finkelstein's terminology, I have become conscious *of* my anger, but I am not yet *consciously* angry.

Now consider this alternative scene: in the midst of boiling rage, I say "I'm *furious* with you!" In this case, the anger itself is present in the verbal self-ascription of anger that is directed at you. In this case, the self-ascription *of* anger is itself an *angry* expression. Unlike the former case, I do not have to observe myself to know that I am angry. I just *am angry;* and the form my anger at you takes on this occasion is the angry verbal self-ascription of anger directed at you. In this case, the utterance "I am *furious* with you!" may replace other forms of angry expression such as shaking with rage or impulsively striking out; or getting depressed or feeling guilty. This is a case, in Finkelstein's terms, in which I am not only conscious *of* my anger; I am *con-*

sciously angry. It is this sense of becoming conscious that is our central concern. In the occasion, I have nonobservational, first-personal authority for my anger—*not* because I have some private, inner-directed perceptual faculty, but because I have acquired the capacity *to express my anger* directly and spontaneously in a verbal self-ascription of anger, or in some other self-consciously angry statement. In this case, the verbal expression of anger is making a truth-claim about my anger that, in the instance, is a manifestation of the very anger about which the truth-claim makes its claim.[9]

To use a locution from Aristotle, in this expression *the what* and *the how* have come together. On occasion I can say *that* I am angry; on occasion, I can speak angrily; but on this occasion I angrily say that I am angry. The anger is manifest in the utterance; and the utterance is simultaneously saying something true about the anger, namely, that *I* am the one who is angry *at you.* Finkelstein's point is that it is in these special moments of coincidence that we can, inspired by Wittgenstein, talk about the verbal expression of anger *replacing* a natural expression. (Wittgenstein concentrated on the verbal expression of a sensation such as pain replacing natural expressions such as crying; Finkelstein extends that treatment to the expression of emotions.)

§3.2. THE PSYCHOANALYTIC HYPOTHESIS

So far, we have not introduced any particularly psychoanalytic idea. But now, suppose that the angry thought that is coming into consciousness has, until this moment, been held out of conscious awareness via various motivated strategies. It is somehow held to conflict with one's consciously held understanding of one's identity and emotional life.[10] On this assumption, there opens up a significant difference between these two cases of unconscious anger becoming conscious. In the first case, I notice that I have been behaving in not-altogether-nice ways to you and infer that I must be angry with you. I then reflect on possible reasons, realize that my actions are out of proportion, and resolve to try to get over my anger. This is an exemplification of the standard model of reflection, but there is this problem: what grounds my confidence that my resolution to get over my anger will have any impact on my anger? Obviously, there are cases in which my emotional life does follow my reflective assessment; and when it does, hooray for reflective criticism, and hooray for me as rational animal. But, on the assumption we are following—

namely, that the hitherto unconscious anger was unconscious because it was in some way rejected—it is equally possible that the reflective judgment, rather than abating the anger, serves to preserve and protect it by hiding it from awareness. The deployment of rational reflection in this case would look very similar to the case in which the judgment did abate the anger—only in this case, rational reflection would be in the service of hiding and preserving one's irrational emotional life. That is, a simulacrum of rational responsiveness would serve to protect an underlying irrationality.

The second model of making an unconscious emotion conscious poses a problem of a different order. Note, we need to examine a case not only in which I can say "I am angry at you" angrily, but one in which the anger has been *kept away* from consciousness. It is held out of consciousness not simply because it is painful, but because it violates one's sense of who one is. Thus the emergence of unconscious anger in this case has to be a *disruption* of one's conscious sense of self. How could this be therapeutic?

§3.3. REPLACEMENT

The question thus becomes whether there could be a process—not *too* disruptive—by which the verbal expression of anger actually *replaces* (in the Wittgenstein-Finkelstein sense) its unconscious manifestations. In which case a person might be able both to express her anger *and* to deal with it thoughtfully. This brings us to a second psychoanalytic idea, that concerns the functioning of repression: it doesn't work *that* well. As Freud famously put it,

> When I set myself the task of bringing to light what human beings keep hidden within them, not by the compelling power of hypnosis, but by observing what they say and what they show, I thought the task was a harder one than it really is. He who has eyes to see and ears to hear may convince himself that no mortal can keep a secret. If his lips are silent, he chatters with his finger tips; betrayal oozes out of him at every pore. And thus the task of making conscious the most hidden recesses of the mind is one which it is quite possible to accomplish.[11]

Thus the hiddenness of a repressed unconscious idea does not consist in its *lack* of manifestation, but rather in the *form* that manifestation takes. If one wants to provide an interpretation of psychoanalysis in the spirit of Wittgenstein, this, I think, is the point of entry. For now one can consider the conditions under which an appropriate verbalization can function as a genuine *replacement* for other manifestations such as coughing, upset stomach, irritable bowel, panic attacks, and rituals, as well as more sophisticated forms such as explicit disavowal or sincerely ascribing the opposite emotion to oneself.

The idea that the verbal expression of emotion or fantasy can serve as a significant therapeutic option is one that philosophers have not sufficiently explored. For example, Richard Moran's *Authority and Estrangement* is one of the most significant inquiries into the structure of self-knowledge in recent times. And it has the distinctive merit of taking the psychoanalytic situation seriously. Moran's account is rich and subtle, and covers a wide range of phenomena. Moreover, it is accurate in this sense: it gives a philosophical formulation of the actual practice of a wide range of therapists at work today. This is not just a philosopher's image of therapy: it is a philosophical characterization of actual forms of therapeutic practice. Yet, Moran draws the map of self-knowledge in such a way that there is no place in it for the form of making the unconscious conscious that I take to be central to psychoanalysis. In coming to see this, we can come to see something missing in the practice of a wide swath of therapists who have, in one way or another, overlooked this psychoanalytic insight. On one side Moran places the self-knowledge that one might acquire in a "theoretical manner" by taking an "empirical stance" toward oneself. A person observes her behavior, in this case with the help of an analyst, and comes to the conclusion, say, that she is angry at a dead parent. On the other side is avowal; but Moran uses this term in a special technical sense. Avowal, for Moran, is essentially linked to what he calls the transparency condition. A person avows her anger, in Moran's sense, only if she thereby commits herself to the rationality of her emotion: in this case, that anger is a fit response.[12] A person achieves transparency when, instead of looking inward to determine whether she is angry, she looks outward to consider whether the situation actually merits anger.[13] But the expression of anger *as replacement* need not occur on either side of this divide. Moran considers a case in which an analysand cannot avow her anger—because "she cannot learn of her attitude by reflection on the object of that attitude"—and he concludes: "She can *only* learn of it in a fully theoretical manner, taking an empirical stance toward herself as a particular psychological subject."[14] But this is not what happens when, in the midst of an analytic session, there is a moment of uncanny disruption and the anger breaks right through into conscious verbal expression.[15] Nor is it what happens when, in a tranferential outburst, the anger is expressed directly at the analyst. Such moments of unconscious emotions or fantasies breaking through into conscious verbal expression lie at the heart of psychoanalytic work, and, to put it mildly, they are not based on observation. Nor are they avowals in Moran's sense. Rather, the fantasy or emotion is getting openly, verbally *expressed*. And this is its own form of truthfulness—not transparency to external conditions that purportedly merit the response, nor correspondence to an internal reality inferred from observation by theoretical inference, but the direct *expression* of the emotion or fantasy in speech. That is, the speech not only acknowledges the content of the emotion or fantasy, but also expresses it; and it not only expresses the fantasy or emotion, but in its verbal form also acknowledges its content. In effect, Moran has given us an account of what might be involved in becoming conscious *of* a fantasy—derived from observation and inference, the advice of a therapist, and so on—but he has left no room for the peculiar case of *consciously fantasizing*—that is, giving the fantasy direct expression in speech that simultaneously and self-consciously gives its content. This ability to fantasize consciously is crucial to the psychoanalytic situation.

If one limits a therapeutic situation to the tools that Moran describes—observation, theoretical inference, and avowal that conforms to the transparency condition—one may well extend self-understanding. But, from a psychoanalytic point of view, such therapies run a significant danger of being used in the service of evading self-knowledge in the name of obtaining it—even facilitating the construction of a false self and self-deception. To use Moran's example: one discovers on the basis of self-observation and one's therapist's intervention that one must be angry with one's dead parent; one then decides that one does not have a good reason to be angry and resolves to get over it. Suppose one decides one has succeeded; and suppose the therapist agrees. The danger is that this purported therapeutic triumph is serving to hide and protect the anger that never got expressed in the first place. Obviously, if one were genuinely able to get over one's anger in this way, it would be a therapeutic gain—an instance of gaining rational control over one's emotional life. However, the danger is that the anger has not gone away, but has gone underground. How many furious people do you know who insist on their lack of anger and try to act as though they are not at all angry? From a psychoanalytic point of view, there are furious people who sincerely do not know this about themselves. But if one does open up room for consciously expressing hitherto unconscious emotions or fantasies, one thereby opens up room for uncanny disruption. Precisely because the emotion or fantasy has been repressed, it is likely that its initial recognition takes the form of uncanny disruption. It is the return of the unfamiliar as simultaneously familiar and unfamiliar. Thus it must disrupt the world that the analysand has consciously inhabited. And it does not fit the standard model of reflection on an item of consciousness that one is stepping back from; though such reflection may become appropriate later on.

§4. Making Unconscious Practical Identity Conscious

Now if we accept, first, that unconscious fantasy can function as something like an unconscious practical identity; and, second, that making the unconscious conscious necessarily involves the *expression* of the unconscious fantasy in the form of self-ascription, we seem to be led to a caricature for a conclusion: namely, that in addition to being able to notice the disparate manifestations of boyishness in her life, Ms. A. needs to be able to say "I am a boy!" *boyishly.* Obviously, such an exclamation need be no more than a camp gesture, or an embarrassing misfire. Still, the truth lies in what the caricature is a caricature of. Psychoanalysis facilitates a process by which one gains the capacity to *express* one's fantasies verbally: the fantasy is right there in the utterance, while the content of the utterance gives the content of the fantasy. Only then can the verbal expression of the fantasy *replace* (in the Wittgenstein-Finkelstein sense) other manifestations—such as bodily manifestations that arise with minimal self-conscious awareness, rituals that are poorly understood and not recognized as such, or motivated self-misunderstandings. And given that the core fantasy is something like an unconscious practical identity, making the unconscious conscious does consist in becoming able to *express* verbally a hitherto unconscious identity. In this section, I aim to drain the initial appearance of absurdity from this characterization. And I hope to show that the development of this capacity for replacement is itself the development of a capacity for irony.

To begin with, while we are familiar with certain images of social pretense, we are less familiar with the thought that social pretenses have their voices. I have a friend George, a young man in his twenties, who has a conscious practical identity that includes being "one of the guys." He was supposed to come over for dinner one evening right after he finished seeing an afternoon Chicago White Sox game. I realized I had a conflict and called him the night before to tell him we'd have to reschedule our dinner. His response: "That's *great.* Now I can get drunk with the guys at the game!" That was followed by a hearty laugh. It was not difficult to hear that in addition to the anticipation of typically "boyish" pleasures, there was boyish pleasure *in the anticipation.* This is one way in which the verbal expression of a conscious fantasy—a daydream or anticipated event—can provide its own gratification. And the verbal utterance was itself an *expression* of George's boyish practical identity. George's boyishness was right there in his utterance.[16]

As Ms. A. is lying on the couch reflecting on, say, the pleasures of suiting up in a team uniform—pleasures that she might not have thought of before—her out-loud thinking about her boyishness begins to become a boyish expression. Ironically, what is disturbing in this particular instance is not so much the content of the reflection as the vibrancy she experiences in her voice. Given the structure of the analytic situation, her expression is accompanied by apperceptive consciousness. The result is an uncanny jolt. This is a fractal moment: analysis is full of uncanny disruptions, in the microcosm and macrocosm. There are disrupting dreams, and disrupting associations to dreams, intrusive thoughts, associations that come to mind whether one likes it or not; and then, over time, in the transference, the core fantasy will attempt to take over and inform the entire analytic situation. The analysis becomes, say, a playing field in which the analyst is, on different occasions, coach, umpire, teammate, member of the opposing team, father in the stands yelling at the analysand to run faster!, mother crying for her lost daughter, and so on. As the core fantasy unfolds and its formal nature comes into view, the fantasy is right there in the utterance, getting itself expressed verbally. And as the expression is accompanied by apperceptive awareness this is tantamount to, or a half-step away from, self-ascription. In such a situation, to use Finkelstein's distinction, the analysand is not simply becoming conscious *of* a fantasy; she is *consciously fantasizing.*

Of course, there is plenty of room for reflection of the standard variety: stepping back and reflecting on what one believes, desires, the contents of one's dreams and fantasies. Such reflections can serve as important moments of consolidation and judgment. But from an analytic point of view they are derivative. Finkelstein has argued that as one acquires the ability to express one's emotions verbally, one thereby acquires first-person authority with respect to them. That is, I gain nonobservational authority precisely because, in the verbal act—"I'm *furious* with you!"—I am expressing the anger. Similarly, I want to claim, that as I acquire the ability to *express* this organizing fantasy verbally I also gain first-person authority with respect to it. I am *putting myself into words*. I am right there in the words that are expressing (as well as perhaps describing) who I am. Thus the verbal expression of what had hitherto functioned as an unconscious practical identity facilitates my ability to shape my practical identity.

This is a process that cannot occur without ironic disruption; and it characteristically occurs across four related dimensions. First, there is ironic disruption of one's conscious practical identity. As Ms. A., for example, comes to *express* her unconscious practical identity verbally, this expression cannot help but disrupt her conscious sense of practical identity. The analytic process aims to create a space in which the disruption can be playful, as opposed to scary, overwhelming, or traumatic. But there is a disruption of ordinary conscious life which, put into words, has this shape: "What does *any of this* have to do with *being a woman?*" The *"any of this"* stretches out in all directions, covering not only the boyish voice that is finding expression in the analytic session but also the feminine images that Ms. A. has, until now, lived by. This is the experience of erotic uncanniness that is irony. It is an uncanny doubling wherein Ms. A. is not only expressing herself (through her core fantasy); she is also looking over at herself as weirdly unfamiliar in her familiarity. Her question is urgent and practical, and it confronts her in the first person. It is disorienting in the sense that she can no longer *simply* appeal to received images or to standard reflections on her conscious practical identity—for that is precisely what is in question. Nor, correlatively, can anyone else answer her question for her.

Note that in terms of overt social manifestations, behavior, or even internal conscious stances about one's identity, there is no particular direction in which a person in Ms. A.'s position ought to go. She may consciously reaffirm the very shape of her conscious practical identity, stay with the received image of femininity she has lived with all along (only now it will be accompanied by an ironized sense of its possibilities); or she may decide to emphasize a more boyish identity; or she may opt for a playful mixture; she may decide she is bisexual, transsexual, cross-gendered, gay, or reenter heterosexual life. From the first-order perspective of establishing a gender identity, the analysis is not moving in any particular direction. It is simply facilitating a process by which cut-off parts of the self find their way into speech. This does not mean that the analysis itself is not moving in a direction; quite the contrary. When it is working well, analysis moves in the direction of freedom, truthfulness, and self-knowledge of the analysand. These concepts require philosophical reflection, particularly in the context of psychoanalysis. But I take it they are different ways of naming the formal and final cause of psychoanalysis.[17] And it is precisely because analysis is constituted by this aim that, at the level of conscious practical identity, it does not aim in any direction. But, for the moment, the important point to notice is that in facilitating the expression of hitherto hidden parts of the self, analysis simultaneously facilitates a process of ironic disruption.

The second dimension of ironic disruption concerns large-scale subjective questions that tend to unfold in an analysis. Ms. A., remember, did not come into the analysis with any conscious complaint about her practical identity; she was specifically concerned about sexual relations with her husband. But as an analysis deepens, broad-scale questions typically come into view: Am I able to love? to allow myself to be loved? to become a lover? Am I able to create in this world—something—before I die? Am I able to be a friend, a husband, a wife, a professor, an artist, a gardener, a journalist? And when such questions come into view, the available social pretenses themselves come into question. A person may know very well that he fulfills the social norms of being a husband— he's gone through the ritual, he's got the marriage certificate, he is cohabiting with the person with whom he went through the ritual, and so on. What he wants to know is: could he ever *be married*? It is precisely the disruptions of unconscious identity that disrupt any attempt to keep this questioning confined to what, in the previous lecture, I called left-column phenomena. The emergence of Ms. A.'s boyishness, for example, disrupts what might otherwise have been a standard-issue "therapeutic discussion" of whether she loves her husband. It opens up disruptive questioning of what loving, for her, could possibly mean.

In the previous lecture I concentrated on the experience of irony as an uncanny ballooning out of one's sense of practical identity. Here I have focused on the psychoanalytically familiar experience of not fitting comfortably into one's own psychic skin: in this case, one's practical identity comes to seem too small, too tight. We can now see how these experiences are related. The experience of one's *conscious* sense of practical identity being too constricted is occasioned by dynamic relations with an *unconscious* practical identity; and this may in certain circumstances be the occasion for an ironic disruption of one's conscious practical identity.

The third dimension of ironic disruption is in the transference. It is only when Ms. A.'s boyish fantasy enters the room, fills up her speech, and organizes her relationship to me—in effect, turns the analytic hour into a "late-night bull session," or the playing field I described—that psychoanalysis truly comes alive. Psychoanalysis cannot simply consist in a mutual conversation, based on observation and memory about how a person fits the masculine and feminine parts of herself together—even though such conversations may occur within a psychoanalytic context and can, of course, have some therapeutic value. An analysis will typically entangle the analyst in a disruptive drama: as, for example, when Ms. A. experiences the end of a session as me shoving her off the field. This has to be an ironic disruption of previous understandings of what it is to be an analyst, an analysand, in analysis—and it up-ends socially received images of therapy. In this regard, consider Freud's discussion of how what he calls the compulsion to repeat is replaced by remembering—though let me substitute "core fantasy" where he uses "compulsion":

> We render the [core fantasy] harmless, and indeed useful, by giving it the right to assert itself in a definite field. We admit it into the transference as a playground in which it is allowed to expand in almost complete freedom . . . The transference thus creates an intermediate region between illness and real life through which the transition from one to the other is made.[18]

I am not a fan of Freud's medical terminology, but his description of the analytic process as creating an intermediate region is exactly right.[19] This intermediate region is the region of the uncanny. For, from this perspective, "remembering" cannot be a purely cognitive process, as in remembering a certain forgotten content. Rather, it has got to be a playful disruption of the soul—which at the same time can give voice to what is happening.

The fourth dimension of ironic disruption may explicitly occur less often in an analysis, and pursuing it perhaps occurs rarely among humans; but one can now see how it arises out of the material we have been discussing. It is, in effect, an ironic questioning of the virtues. I am not claiming that all ironic questioning occurs in this way, but rather that this is one fascinating route. It arises with the practical question: How can I face *all of this* courageously? Or: How can I face *all of this* with integrity? But the *"all of this"* that emerges in analysis may on occasion put into question what, in this case, courage or integrity could be. Of course, the concept of courage has developed over time from its origins as a manly, warrior virtue;[20] and we are by now used to imagining all sorts of complex circumstances as occasions for courage. Still, the case that is envisaged here is not simply the difficulty of whether to apply a complex concept to a particularly tricky instance. If one acquires the virtues at all it is, as Plato and Aristotle emphasized, typically through a social education that begins in childhood. The education aims to instill a capacity to face *whatever comes one's way* virtuously; in this case, courageously. That is, one is being trained to face an expectable range of possibilities. Thus training in a virtue like courage—whatever its current historical manifestation—will be in relation to available social pretenses and conscious practical identities. These will assume ranges of possibilities that are themselves up-ended in ironic disruption. There thus arises the possibility of the question: How can one face courageously the disruption of the entire range of possibilities that was assumed in one's own training in courage? There is no obvious or automatic way to answer this question.[21] Thus one can see how, from this psychosocial turmoil, there might arise a question of what a virtue like courage consists in. In effect, this questioning imports a peculiar form of not knowing into one's life with the virtues. And in case you should think this an interesting story, but a million miles from Socrates, consider his account of how he came to focus on his characteristic activity:

> I am still unable, as the Delphic inscription orders, to know myself; and it really seems to me ridiculous to look into other things before I have really understood that. That is why I do not concern myself with them. I accept what is generally believed and, as I was just saying, I look not into them but into my own self: *Am I a*

beast more complicated and savage than Typhon, or am I a simpler ani-
mal with a share in a divine and gentle nature? (my emphasis)[22]

§5. Agency and Psychic Unity

I have been trying to show how our capacity for pretense-transcending aspiring can arise out of "lowly" psychic origins. We do not need to posit a special
faculty capable of breaking through the pretenses of ordinary life and grasping the true ethical value of one's identity. And we need not go in the direction of metaphysical extravagance to see how it works. Yet, as we try to give
a naturalistic, dynamic psychological account, we need not dismiss irony as
one more punitive function of the superego. It is certainly true that superego
functioning can make one feel that one is falling short in one's practical identity. But irony, as I understand it, emerges when the superego *relaxes* its punishing functions. These intrapsychic transformations have consequences for
our understanding of agency and of psychic unity.

Normally, we use the concepts of *action, agent,* and *agency* to describe a
distinctive form of life of which humans are capable: namely, that which is
typically thought of as rational self-governance. We are creatures who can
evaluate our desires and beliefs, ask what reasons we have for a proposed action; and often we can live in the light of our reasoning. In so acting, we constitute ourselves as agents. It is not simply that this or that desire—or this or
that psychic bit—causes this or that bodily movement; rather, I, in choosing
to act on this desire, constitute myself as the author of this action, and as an
agent I take charge of what I am doing. Obviously, the idea of responsibility
lies at the heart of this family of notions: as an agent acting, I open myself to
a challenge that is directed at *me:* "What are *you* doing!?" For this question to
be appropriate I have to have whatever unity is required to be the agent, the
author of that act. It is a familiar thought that this kind of unity is an achievement and a task. It is, as Korsgaard puts it, "the ongoing struggle for integrity,
the struggle for psychic unity, the struggle to be, in the face of psychic com-
plexity, a single unified agent." And she eloquently argues that it is precisely
the normative standards of practical identity that provide "the principles by
which we achieve the psychic unity that makes agency possible."[23] Thus, for
her, the psychic unity required for agency is simply the unity achieved by

living according to the norms of a practical identity that, by the same token, is the activity of self-constitution.

This is a plausible line of thought on the assumption that there are no other sources of psychic unity that are salient to agency or self-constitution. This is the assumption I have been calling into question. Consider how different the human scene will look depending on whether or not the assumption that rational judgment based on (conscious) practical identity is the only salient source of psychic unity in play.

Scene 1 is Ms. A. before analysis. And for the sake of argument, imagine that Ms. A. had been studying moral philosophy. The idea pops into her head that it would be nice to be having a beer with her friend Bruno down at the bar. (The fact that he is her teammate does not enter her mind.) She is somewhat surprised by the thought, and as she reflects on it she decides it would conflict with her sense of who she is. She is a wife who is loyal to her husband; and her sense of appropriate gender roles is such that a married woman does not call up a handsome, single man and ask him out to a bar. She judges that she will not act on this impulse. Morally speaking it looks to her as though she has done the right thing. She has rejected the "wayward" impulse by stepping back from it, judging it according to the norms of her practical identity—loyal spouse, mature woman, rational agent, principled person, faithful to her commitments, and so on—and thus this looks like the autonomous act of a rational agent, an act of self-constitution. On the assumption that there are no other relevant acts of psychic unification, such a judgment (and fidelity to it) can plausibly be thought of as an act of unification.

However, if we allow the possibility of unconscious unifying sources of the self, the scene looks different. For this impulse-emerging-into-consciousness is not the isolated atom that it appears to be. Far from this being a case in which the self is trying to maintain and preserve psychic unity in the face of a possible disruption "from outside," the very attempt to preserve psychic unity is in fact an act of psychic division in which a powerful and primordial source of psychic unity is treated as though it were just an impulse—or perhaps even a habitual one. In the name of rational agency, and in the name of practical identity, Ms. A. is ignoring—and thereby splitting off—a vibrant, organizing part of herself. The idea that her reflectively judged act is coming *from her* would be treated by Plato (as well as by Freud) as mere appearance.

Scene 2: Same as Scene 1, except that having made the decision not to call Bruno, she calls Bruno and invites him out for a drink. This of course looks akratic; but whether it is or not depends on what one takes *akrasia* (weakness of will) to be. It certainly is a case of deciding to do one thing and then doing another, of succumbing to temptation and so on. But it is not a case of Ms. A.'s understanding what her options are, making a rational decision, and then acting against it. It is not a case of her seeing clearly what the temptation is, deciding not to act on it, and then acting on it. In this sense, it is not so much a case of weakness of will as lack of self-knowledge—though perhaps this is what we call weakness of will turns out to be. But the important point for now is that, in this scene, Ms. A.'s conscious rational will, far from being the source of unity, is actively dividing the self by ignoring other unifying sources of the self.

Scene 3: Ms. A. is in analysis. If this is conceived on the standard model of reflection, it will look as though reflective consciousness is extending its reach: taking more and more mental items into account. And as the agent's reflective consciousness is able to judge these formerly unconscious items, the agent will increase the breadth and depth of her psychic unity. On this picture there is room for acknowledging conflicts, and for negotiating the insistent demands of fantasy with one's conscious commitment to a practical identity. Ms. A., for example, could reflect on how to fit together her boyish fantasies with her feminine identity. And she could take practical steps as a result of her deliberation. There is truth to this picture, and important truth. But to think that it gives us the whole truth—or even the essential truth—is to mislead ourselves about the kind of creatures we are. In the name of making the unconscious conscious one unwittingly collaborates in keeping it unconscious. For the unconscious is not some darkened realm of forbidden items over which a brave reflective consciousness casts its beacon. Indeed, it often makes itself manifest most clearly in moments when reflective consciousness is itself disrupted, thrown out of joint. By the time reflection can step back from this experience to consider it in its standard fashion, it has itself already been transformed by the disruption. This is a crucial point: the psychoanalytic process of making the unconscious conscious tends to be a radically nonconservative extension of one's conscious practical identity.[24] This is more than the straightforward point that as one discovers more about one's unconscious motivations one will have to go back and revise one's sense of who one is. In addition, there will be up-ending, uncanny moments such

[65]

that by the time one does go back to revise, revisions will have already occurred. The question then becomes one of learning how to live well with this unusual form of self-development. Ironically, there is an important form of psychic integration that consists in deploying well a capacity for ironic disruption. A deep form of integration can occur only when we find creative ways to disrupt and disturb ourselves.

Obviously, fidelity to our practical identity is an important human commitment; and reflection on the various temptations and incentives that come our way is one crucial way in which we maintain that fidelity. But that important truth can again lead us into error if we assume that our conscious practical identity is the only salient source of psychic unity available to us. What psychoanalysis has discovered is that one's conscious sense of practical identity is often achieved at great cost to other organizing parts of the self. Let us assume that every person has achieved an *ethically cleansed* practical identity in this sense: each person has been able to take on a set of social roles that do not interfere with the social roles chosen by other people; each person has been able to reflect on his or her practical identity and perform a reflective-endorsement test that conforms to the categorical imperative; and that reflective endorsement provides the grounds on which each person has the practical identity he or she has. In short, for some version of the kingdom of ends, we are in the kingdom of ends. No doubt, there is much to commend this world. In such a world each person will be respected by others and will respect other people—*if* what we mean by "person" and "people" is: inhabitant of an available conscious practical identity. This, of course, amounts to a maximally harmonious form of life in the left-hand lane. But, if the line of thinking I have been pursuing is correct, the problem with this kingdom of ends is that it is compatible with a dystopia pervaded by unfreedom.

The possibility for unhappiness is obvious: in the name of psychic unity, integrity, practical identity, and so on, the inhabitants of this kingdom would be splitting off a vibrant part of themselves—treating a deeply rooted source of psychic unity as though it were a mere disruption or distraction from the only unity we have. This would in effect be an act of repression and, as such, the occasion for psychic conflict. In the case of freedom, the language of "autonomy" would be deployed, among other things, to discredit and disavow other expressions of the self. In short, it would be possible to have a conscious practical identity, to have carried out successfully the categorical imperative test in reflective endorsement, to be a citizen of the kingdom of ends so described—and yet be a miserable failure as a human being. And here the issue is not simply that one might be unhappy even though one is an autonomous moral agent. The worry is that the language of autonomy would be deployed misleadingly to disavow other sources of the self. Traditionally, we have understood an agent's action to be free if it could genuinely be understood as coming *from her*. The appeal of this thought depends on the assumption that what it is for an action to come from her is for it to issue from her rational will. Thus the principles of rationality, psychic unity, and agency have traditionally been thought to coincide. I do not wish to pull this trio apart, but I hope I have said enough in these lectures to call into question what each of the elements consists in. Above all, it would seem to be rational to call into question the ultimate rationality of the picture of rationality as simply consisting in my ability to step back and reflect on how well or badly items of consciousness conform to my conscious practical identity.

Appendix: Comment on Richard Moran's Conception of the Psychoanalytic Situation

As I said in the lecture, Richard Moran's *Authority and Estrangement* is not only an important philosophical inquiry into the structure of self-knowledge; it also accurately captures the actual practice of a wide range of talking cures. That is why it is important to get clear on what is left out. Consider one of Moran's paradigmatic characterizations of the therapeutic situation:

> In various familiar therapeutic contexts, for instance, the manner in which the analysand becomes aware of various of her beliefs and other attitudes does not necessarily conform to the Transparency Condition. The person who feels anger at the dead parent for having abandoned her, or who feels betrayed or deprived of something by another child, may only know of this attitude through the eliciting and interpreting of evidence of various kinds. She might become thoroughly convinced, both from the constructions of the analyst, as well as from her own appreciation of the evidence, that

this attitude must indeed by attributed to her. And yet, at the same time, when she reflects on the world-directed question itself, whether she has indeed been betrayed by this person, she may find that the answer is no or can't be settled one way or the other. So, transparency fails because she cannot learn of this attitude of hers by reflection on the object of that attitude. *She can only learn of it in a fully theoretical manner, taking an empirical stance toward herself as a particular psychological subject.*[25]

I do not think that this last claim is correct. At the heart of psychoanalysis—really, what distinguishes it from other forms of talking therapy—is the development and handling of transference. If, say, anger at the dead parent for having abandoned her is a part of the analysand's fantasy life, one would expect to find repetitions and variations on this theme within the analysand's current life (breakups with boyfriends, painful relations with the boss, depression at the end of the school year when a class ends, and so on)—as well as some kind of manifestation within the analytic context: for example, conflicted feelings about the analyst's taking a vacation or missing a session. If there is no living manifestation of the anger, then it is hard to know what it means to say that the analysand is angry. Conversely, if anger at abandonment is unconsciously informing daily life, or life within the analytic session, then the analyst ought not to rely on theoretical inferences, but should rather be attuned to moments when the fantasy is alive and getting actively expressed. Analyst and analysand can then work together to facilitate a process in which the analysand can express her angry fantasy verbally. As Freud, commenting on the handling of the transference, so memorably put it,

The unconscious impulses do not want to be remembered in the way the treatment desires them to be, but endeavor to reproduce themselves in accordance with the timelessness of the unconscious and its capacity for hallucination. Just as happens in dreams, the patient regards the products of the awakening of his unconscious impulses as contemporaneous and real; he seeks to put his passions into action without taking any account of the real situation. The doctor tries to compel him to fit these emotional impulses into the nexus of the treatment and of his life-history, to

submit them to intellectual consideration and to understand
them in the light of their psychical value. This struggle between
the doctor and the patient, between intellect and instinctual life,
between understanding and seeking to act, is played out almost
exclusively in the phenomena of transference. It cannot be disputed that controlling the phenomena of transference presents
the psychoanalyst with the greatest difficulties. But it should not
be forgotten that it is precisely they that do us the inestimable
service of *making the patient's hidden and forgotten impulses immediate and manifest.* For when all is said and done, *it is impossible to
destroy anyone in absentia or in effigy.*[26]

From a psychoanalytic perspective, if the anger at the dead parent is to be
transformed it must be *worked through* in the here-and-now. This is decidedly
not a process of making theoretical constructions based on empirical observations and inference. It bears more resemblance to the painful but ultimately
liberating activity of mourning.[27]

Moran makes claims about the psychoanalytic situation that on first reading look eminently plausible; for example:

It is virtually definitive of psychoanalytic treatment . . . that it does
not begin by taking first-person declarations as necessarily describing the truth about the analysand's actual attitudes. And this
might be taken to mean that the knowledge of oneself it seeks to
culminate in would ideally dispense with avowal as something
unsophisticated and unreliable, substituting for it something
more interpretive and theoretically grounded. But any such suggestion would neglect, at the very least, the crucial therapeutic
difference between the merely "intellectual" acceptance of an interpretation, which will itself normally be seen as a form of resistance, and the process of working-through that leads to a fully
internalized acknowledgment of some attitude which makes a
felt difference to the rest of the analysand's mental life. This goal
of treatment, however, requires that the attitude in question be
knowable by the person, not through a process of theoretical self-
interpretation but *by avowal* of how one thinks and feels.[28]

If Moran meant by "avowal" what we often mean—a general term for sincere expression, then I would have no quarrel with this paragraph. The only issue would be to try to explicate in more detail what this particular kind of avowal consists in—namely, the verbal *expression* of the fantasy. However, Moran does not mean this; as he makes explicit: "That is, what is to be restored to the person is not just knowledge of the facts about oneself, but self-knowledge that obeys the condition of transparency."[29]

Certainly, Moran is right that analysis aims at more than restoration of theoretical knowledge of the facts about oneself. But what grounds the thought that the aim is to restore self-knowledge that obeys the conditions of transparency? In the example Moran uses, this would consist in the analysand's anger at the dead parent abating when she realized that he did not abandon her, he just died. Obviously, if the analysand's anger did abate in this way, there would be much to be said in favor of such a movement: the analysand would be living in more realistic (and rational) relations to events that actually happened in the external world.

But, from a psychoanalytic point of view, there is a further challenge of how to take *internal* reality into account. By "internal reality" I do not simply mean the truths about one's inner life. Rather, as one probes one's inner life one comes up against a certain obduracy. So, as an analysand comes to recognize that she is angry at a dead parent for abandoning her, and she also comes to recognize that, in fact, he simply died, she may *also* come to recognize *that she is still angry!* Perhaps the anger and disappointment may diminish over time as she works through her anger; but there may be a significant residue that perdures. She may indeed feel her anger vividly, express it verbally, all the while knowing that—considered at the level of rational assessment—it is not warranted. Of course, the phenomenon of recalcitrant emotions is well known; but the psychoanalytic interpretation of the phenomenon is distinctive. For the aim of psychoanalytic therapy is not to make one's fantasy *go away* even when it becomes conscious, which in effect is what is being called for when one states that the goal of analysis is that one's emotional life should obey conditions of transparency. Rather, the goal is to find creative and life-fulfilling ways of living *with* fantasy. On occasion, this may involve transformation of the fantasy, and a correlative abating of emotions like anger or guilt. But on occasion, when the fantasy perdures, it may involve a transformation of how one lives with it. That is, the anger and disappointment at the dead parent might not go away, even after rational assessment that it is not ultimately warranted, even after analytic therapy. But it might become an occasion for humor, for poetry, for meditation on loss, for taking up moral causes, for writing critical book reviews, for spending more time with one's own children, for reading Shakespeare, for taking up canoeing. The success of the therapy does not necessarily depend on the anger's *going away* in the light of rational assessment (transparency), but rather on whether one ceases to be *stuck* with the anger in rigid routines that one does not understand.

It also must be said that there are huge swathes of fantasy-life in which it does not make sense to seek transparency conditions. While it does make sense to ask whether residual anger at a dead parent is called for, what could it be to ask whether a fantasy of boyishness is appropriate? Appropriate to what? But even in those cases in which it does make sense to inquire about appropriateness—say, anger at the dead parent—fantasy-life by its nature resists transparency. It is a part of imaginative life that feeds off of (and informs) real-life experiences in oblique ways, but is also insulated from them. In that sense, fantasy is essentially different from those familiar propositional attitudes that do aim to conform to transparency. In its isolation, in its insistence, and its obstinacy, fantasy-life has a reality of its own. The aim of analysis is not simply to make our emotions appropriate reactions to the external facts (that is, conform to the transparency condition), but to find creative and life-enhancing ways of negotiating internal and external realities.

II

Commentary

3

Self-Constitution and Irony

CHRISTINE M. KORSGAARD

I haven't thought much about the topic of irony before, and when I was asked to comment on these lectures, my first thought was that Kantians probably are not very good at it. Kantians, as we all know, are nothing if not earnest. But if irony is what Jonathan Lear says that it is, then it is more than compatible with Kantianism. If it is what Lear says, then irony is just a special manifestation of the general human capacity that I have called reflective distance: the ability to get your own attitudes—in the practical case, your desires and other motives—into reflective view, to call them into question, and to ask whether you should allow yourself to be moved by them or not.

As Lear has told you, I have argued that when we reflect on our own practical attitudes, and decide whether to act on them or not, we assess them in terms of what I call our "practical identities": the various roles and relationships in terms of which we value ourselves, and find our lives to be worth living and our actions to be worth undertaking.[1] Motives that spring *from* our practical identities offer themselves as possible reasons; motives that are incompatible with them alert us to our obligations. In ratifying and rejecting our potential motives, which we do whenever we act, we give shape to our own identities and become the authors of ourselves. In the course of doing so, a part of our aim is to give ourselves the unity that is necessary for agency.[2] Unity is required for agency because in order to see our movements as actions, we have to see those movements as arising from ourselves as a whole, rather than from something merely working in us or on us. To act is, as it were, to put yourself fully behind your own movements, and you can do that only to the extent that you are unified. And finally, drawing on both Kant and Plato, I have also argued that in order for you to achieve this unity, your actions must be in accord with morality. Integrity in the moral sense and, for persons, integrity in the metaphysical sense are one and the same thing.[3]

But having a practical identity, valuing yourself under a certain description, is obviously *itself* a kind of attitude, and therefore it, like anything else, can come up for reflective review. Sometimes, the occasion for review is an incompatibility between two roles that we value, as when a woman comes to wonder whether the demands of being a dedicated professional are compatible with those of being a good mother.[4] What's special about moments of irony, in Lear's account, is that a form of practical identity in a sense comes up for review as measured against *itself*: that is, as measured against the standards that are inherent in that very form of identification. An agent finds himself wondering how being a Christian can be compatible with the standards of being a Christian, or how being a teacher can be compatible with the standards of being a teacher. Seen that way, Learian irony is very nearly a form of what Kant would call critique. And just as the point of critique, as Kant famously tells us, is to curb the pretensions of knowledge in order to make room for faith, so the point of Socratic irony, according to Lear, is "to inject a certain form of not-knowing into polis life." A certain kind of modesty, about the reach of human knowledge and know-how, is the aim of both.

In the moment of irony, we find that we have no real idea how to perform well in some role that gives our life such meaning as it has. Nowhere is this experience more poignant or more possible than when the identity in question is that of *philosopher*, and the form of the ironic moment is the realization that you have no idea whether the questions you have been trying to answer are anything like the right questions, or exactly what finding answers to them is supposed to do for you even if you can. Indeed, such moments are especially troubling to philosophers. Whatever is or isn't really going on in the sciences—whether their pretensions to tell us what the universe is really like are true or not—they at least give us technology. But philosophy, like a movie star, has nothing to offer to the world but herself. Yet no philosopher who doesn't experience such moments is worthy of the name.

That isn't so with psychoanalysis, which, whatever the fate of *its* theoretical pretensions, at least sometimes appears to help people get well, or be happier, or something like that. But in his second lecture, Lear claims something more for it, which is that it can uncover what Lear calls "sources of unity" in the self—a discovery without which even the best of us might be a "miserable failure as a human being." And Lear takes this to be a challenge to my own view, that the unity of agency must be produced by autonomous acts of self-conscious rational self-constitution.

To illustrate: A unifying fantasy is found to underlie various otherwise seemingly disconnected or poorly understood impulses in the life of Lear's exemplar, Ms. A. Ms. A. consciously identifies as feminine, but her motives and impulses reveal a pattern that suggests that she has not only has, but values herself under, an identity as boyish. Bringing Ms. A.'s boyish identity to consciousness, according to Lear, "involves facilitating the development of a capacity for irony." The work of the analyst is to produce an ironic moment, one in which Ms. A.'s practical identity is called into question in its own terms. She is brought to wonder, about her own behavior and motives, "What does *any of this* have to do with *being a woman?*"

Why is this supposed to be a problem for a view like mine? One might reply—and ultimately I will reply—that no special problem is posed by the fact that sometimes a kind of practical identity is at work in us of which we are not conscious, or even that we deliberately repress. The initial materials with which we work in constructing our particular identities come to us in all sorts of random ways. The genetic lottery assigns you a family, as well as the basic abilities and capacities that determine which activities you will be drawn to. The accidents of geographical and cultural proximity determine who your friends and associates are, and they in turn determine which groups you regard yourself as a member of, which causes you ally yourself with, and so forth. Our identities are our own to make, but the material from which we make them floats in from all over. Practical identity, as I understand it, is at once the material from which we work, and the output of our self-constituting activity. So why shouldn't it be the case that some of our practical identities, *in their role as the materials with which we work,* are the result of psychic forces working on us in ways of which we are unaware, and over which we consequently have no control? So what? Once the psychoanalyst brings the resulting forms of identity to consciousness, it is for us to decide whether we really value ourselves under those descriptions or not, just as it is in any other case. The case shows how self-knowledge can be an aid to conscious self-constitution, but, as I will argue, it does not show that conscious self-constitution can be replaced by anything else.

Lear thinks that such cases pose a problem because of something either that we disagree about or that he misunderstands about my view—I am not sure which. Lear thinks that the fact that we discover unity in Ms. A.'s various impulses challenges an assumption that is clearest in Plato's moral psychology: namely that the "lower" part of the soul is "disparate, heterogeneous, multifarious, lacking in unity." The appetitive part of the soul in Plato's famous metaphor is a many-headed beast.[5] In contrast, Lear characterizes Ms. A.'s unconscious identity as a "deeply rooted source of psychic unity." And he says that therefore we should call into question "the picture of rationality as simply consisting in my ability to step back and reflect on how well or badly items of consciousness conform to my *conscious* practical identity" (my emphasis).

But this isn't my picture of rationality. That description suggests that you simply *have* a practical identity, as a kind of given, and that rationality consists solely in checking whether your actions cohere with that identity or not.[6] But that is not consistent with the idea that we constitute ourselves, and differs from my conception in several ways.

First of all, on my view, there is certainly heterogeneity in the materials from which we construct ourselves. We have many forms of practical identity, and they are a jumble: much of the work of self-constitution is pulling them together into a coherent whole. I do think that there is a problem in the way that both Plato and Kant presented their ideas about the "lower" part of the soul; but it isn't heterogeneity. The problem is that views like Plato's and Kant's can make it seem wholly mysterious why we ever allow ourselves to be motivated by our nonmoral desires and impulses at all. Kant tends to characterize our everyday inclinations as caused in us, without much in the way of our own participation.[7] At a notorious moment in the *Groundwork of the Metaphysics of Morals,* he announces that we should prefer to be rid of them;

at another moment he says that they are not a part of our proper self.[8] Yet he thinks that absent moral reasons why not, we will act on them; and we are rational to do so. If our ordinary desires are just so much random debris blowing in from the causal network, we might wonder why it's rational to act on them at all. Plato, in a similar way, seems to suggest that we should identify with reason but not with our appetites; if appetite is like a many-headed beast, he proposes, reason is like a human being.[9] The idea that our desires and impulses are grounded in our practical identities is intended to address this problem. Now I have already admitted that I do think there is something *right* about the idea that we come to occupy the roles and relationships that give rise to our nonmoral desires in rather random and contingent ways. But still, those are the roles and relationships that give our lives meaning, and we identify with the desires arising from them for that reason.

But the idea of practical identity is not supposed to solve the problem of unity: unity, in my view, is the result of the unifying activity of the agent herself. That is, it is the result of the activity of making decisions in a way that preserves your integrity, so that you will count as the author of the resulting actions. In my view, we do not just compare our motives to the demands of a preexisting identity. We do check to see whether our motives are consistent with our practical identities, and probably we act accordingly. But I think that every time you decide to act in a way that conforms to your practical identity, you count as *re-endorsing* that form of identity and making it your own, and you can always reject it. Your identity is never just a given, but something you are always at work at constructing, and—within the limits of the demand for integrity—how you construct it is really up to you.

The reason why we have to see it this way, the reason why this matters, is because of something important about the nature of *human* agency. Any agent, even a nonhuman animal, must be seen as the cause of certain effects in the world. But a human agent *determines herself* to be the cause of the effects she produces: that is to say, she self-consciously undertakes to *make* herself the cause of those effects. Lear says that an agent's action is free if it can genuinely be understood as coming from her, and insists that Ms. A.'s various boyish acts "would seem to be acts that are paradigmatically coming *from her*, though the source of the self from which they come remains obscure to her." But Ms. A.'s boyish acts—considered as expressions of a boyish practical identity—come from her only in the same sense that a squirrel's act of burying an acorn comes from the squirrel: they are expressions of her nature.[10] Human actions must "come *from us*" in a different, richer sense, because they come from an agency or identity that we constitute ourselves. And we constitute ourselves as the agents from whom our actions spring by endorsing the identities from which they spring. But Ms. A. cannot perform any actions from an endorsement of her boyish nature until it comes into her own reflective view. So until Ms. A. consciously incorporates her boyish nature into her unified identity, she cannot fully be the author of any actions to which it gives rise.

I have some other worries about whether Ms. A.'s case really is a case of ironic experience in the sense laid out in Lear's first lecture. Lear's claim that it is rests on an analogy between Ms. A.'s envisioned response and the responses of the Christian and the teacher whom we met in lecture one. Lear characterizes Ms. A.'s therapeutic experience this way: "there is a disruption of ordinary conscious life which, put into words, has this shape: 'What does *any of this* have to do with *being a woman?*'"

This is supposed to be like the way in which the teacher wondered what any of his activities have to do with teaching. But Learian irony is supposed to involve the realization that it is essential to you to live up to a certain standard, while you don't really know what counts as meeting that standard: what counts as being a Christian or a teacher? Does Ms. A. realize that it is essential to her be *a woman,* but that she doesn't know what counts as being a woman?

That doesn't seem obvious, for consider what happens next. Lear says:

> there is no particular direction in which a person in Ms. A.'s position ought to go. She may consciously reaffirm the very shape of her conscious practical identity, stay with the received image of femininity she has lived with all along (only now it will be accompanied by the ironized sense of its possibilities); or she may decide to emphasize a more boyish identity; or she may may opt for a playful mixture; she may decide she is bisexual, transsexual, cross-gendered, gay, or reenter heterosexual life. From the first-

order perspective of establishing a gender identity, the analysis is not moving in any particular direction.

These alternatives—being gay, bisexual, transsexual, and so forth—aren't naturally understood as alternative ways of being a woman. Some of them might seem more naturally described as ways of realizing that it isn't important to her identity as a sexual being *that* she is a woman. And what Lear says suggests that it is her identity as a sexual being, or more broadly her gender identity, which is the subject of the ironic experience. But having some form of gender identity or other—as opposed to having a particular one—is not, in itself, a form of practical identity. At one point in the first lecture, Lear characterizes ironic experience this way: "we seem to be called to an ideal that, on the one hand, transcends our ordinary understanding, but to which we now experience ourselves as already committed." So perhaps his idea is that Ms. A. experiences herself as called to boyishness, and as responding to that in one of the specified ways. But I think it would be bizarre to think that a revision of her identity as a sexual being was an acceptable outcome of Ms. A.'s call to boyishness, even if it is a perfectly acceptable thing in itself. Let me explain.

I am more than willing to grant that there is no particular direction in which Ms. A. ought to go—in the sense that nothing counts as simply getting it right about one's "gender identity." But surely there are things that count as getting it wrong. Hitherto, it seems, both Ms. A.'s conscious and unconscious identities have been governed by the most banal gender stereotypes—or, as Lear puts it more kindly, "received images."[11] Ms. A. herself, if I've understood the story rightly, considers it to be boyish to be the one who pays the bills, to be the one who is on top during sex, to be professionally successful, and to like sports. But we have been offered no evidence that Ms. A. is sexually attracted to women, unless that is supposed to be somehow implied by her lack of interest in her husband. Yet we are offered the possibility that, even in the absence of such attraction, Ms. A. might conclude that she is bisexual or gay—or decide to be bisexual or gay, however you want to put that. Surely a woman who spots a pattern of "boyishness" in her liking to pay the bills and be successful and so forth, and concludes that therefore she is or should be bisexual or gay, even in the absence of any attraction to members of her own sex, has simply got things wrong. Liking to pay the bills and be successful has nothing whatever to do with how you should construct your sexual identity. So if this is her response to the analysis, then she seems to have come out of the analysis even more weirdly enslaved to the banal gender stereotypes than she was before. How can that be the result of ironic insight?

Leaving that aside, I am left with a question about the relation between irony and self-constitution. As I mentioned earlier, Lear claims that one may be a law-abiding member of the Kingdom of Ends, with a consciously constructed identity of one's own, and yet be "a miserable failure as a human being." But is the failure supposed to rest in the lack of ironic insight itself, or in the failure to draw on unconscious sources of the self that supposedly can result from ironic experience? What Lear says in his second lecture suggests it is the second.

Let me try to say why that seems wrong to me. Socrates is Kierkegaard's and Lear's exemplar of irony, and he is Plato's and Korsgaard's exemplar of successful self-constitution.[12] If we are right to cast Socrates in both of those roles, we can ask: What is the connection between his irony and his successful self-constitution? In his first lecture, Lear rewrote a famous story told by Alcibiades, in which Socrates stands still out of doors all night, while his bemused companions move their bedding outside, in order to watch and see how long he will carry it on. Alcibiades says that Socrates stands still because "he's thinking about a problem" and "he won't give it up." Lear disagrees. He says: "Socrates is standing still not because he is too busy thinking, but because he *cannot walk,* not knowing what his next step should be."

I think Alcibiades is right here and Lear is wrong. To me, the arresting thing about Socrates is his utter self-possession. He is always so completely himself, in any sort of circumstance: in battle, while being tried by the Athenians for his life, on the day of his death. Self-constitution is a process that takes place from the inside, but most of us are hampered in our efforts to shape our own identities by forces from outside. Anyone else would have become embarrassed and moved off if those around him made a spectacle of him in the way that Socrates' companions did on that night. And Ms. A.'s lack of self-possession—her enslavement to banal sexual stereotypes—probably reflects the effect of social pressure in a similar if deeper way. But neither the elementary pressures of social embarrassment nor the threat of death can deter Socrates from doing what he decides to do, or being who he has decided to be. How is his irony related to his integrity? Although it's paradoxical, it seems plausible to me to say that Socrates' awareness of the possibility that none of us quite knows what we are doing is part of what enables him to proceed with such confidence. He's not measuring himself against an artificial standard, or against others' imagined superior know-how. He knows that *every* human action is a kind of leap of faith, but he also knows that the condition is so utterly universal that it *can't* be a reason for hesitation or half-heartedness.[13] But if something like that is right, it's Socrates' ironic insight itself that contributes to his integrity, not his ability to draw on unconscious sources of the self. So while I am sympathetic to the view that irony and integrity may be related, I do not see the relation as one that challenges the self-constitution view.

4

Irony, Reflection, and Psychic Unity

A Response to Christine Korsgaard

§1. Socratic Irony

I am amused by Professor Korsgaard's claim that I "rewrote" the famous story Alcibiades tells of Socrates standing still. It puts me in mind of Bertrand Russell–inspired conjugations: "I interpret; You take liberties; He re-writes." Actually, there is one excellent reason for preferring my interpretation to hers. And this is a way of opening up our more basic differences: over the nature of psychic unity and over the adequacy of her account of self-consciousness in terms of reflective distance.

Let me first clear up a misunderstanding. Korsgaard says that Alcibiades says that Socrates stands still because "he's thinking about a problem" and "he won't give it up." She says, "Lear disagrees." That is not correct. I agree that in this scene Alcibiades describes, Socrates is thinking about a problem, that he won't give up, and that that explains his standing still. My claim that Alcibiades "just doesn't get it" flows from his claim that Socrates is thinking about *some problem or other* (220c). There is a sense in which what Alcibiades says is true: Socrates *is* thinking about *a* problem; but Alcibiades completely misses what that truth is. This is, I think, an instance of Platonic irony: there is a meaning of Alcibiades' utterance that transcends the particular meaning that Alcibiades intends. Alas, most interpreters, Korsgaard included, stick with Alcibiades' own understanding of his words—his pretense—and they thereby miss the irony. By using the Greek particle *ti* Alcibiades suggests that Socrates is thinking about some problem or other— that the peculiar nature of the problem is not what is at issue. This has suggested to readers that the reason Socrates comes to a halt is that the problem he happens to be thinking about is particularly difficult and requires *a lot* of thought. Standing still is the way Socrates manifests that he is utterly absorbed in thought.

This interpretation is inelegant—and, if I am right, it misses the irony. If Socrates is coming to a halt simply because he is absorbed in thinking about a difficult problem, then the fact of his coming to a halt is utterly contingent. Another Socrates—a person just like Socrates except that this one can think and walk at the same time—would have kept on walking. A person can be utterly absorbed in thought and walk at the same time: Einstein could do it! Many brilliant people go for a walk *in order to* absorb themselves in thought. The fact that the actual Socrates (as reported by Alcibiades) stands still for long stretches might be a charming curiosity about him—it puts on display what an eccentric fellow he is—but it would be no more than that. It would have no philosophical significance.

By contrast, on my interpretation, Socrates' coming to a halt is a necessary outcome and manifestation of the situation he is in. Socrates' thinking is practical thinking: it is focused directly on himself and what he will do. It literally concerns the next step he will take. This is the crucial issue that Alcibiades overlooks when he says that Socrates is thinking about *some* problem (or other). If Socrates is aware that he does not yet know what his next step should be, then, practically speaking, he *cannot* take a next step. Standing still is the form that his knowing that he does not know takes. In this interpretation, standing still is not just a contingent fact about eccentric Socrates; it is the practical manifestation of his understanding of his own ignorance. It is a form of self-knowledge. So, on my interpretation, the fact that Socrates comes to a halt is practically required of him—it is not just a charming curiosity—and thus it is philosophically illuminating in a way that the Alcibiades' flat-footed interpretation is not.

Alcibiades is a marvelously unreliable narrator, I think, precisely because there is a sense in which the words he utters are true and yet, as Plato dramatizes him, he misses the point. For all Alcibiades cares, Socrates might have been thinking about a difficult problem in geometry, or, worse, he might have been thinking about what virtue is, but in an intellectual, theoretical manner. Alcibiades is oblivious to the *form* of question Socrates is confronting—that it is eminently and immediately practical—and this obliviousness puts on display a crucial flaw in Alcibiades' character: that while he may love *talking* to Socrates, all that talking does not actually make a difference to how he acts. As he drunkenly confesses:

> I am only too aware that I have no answer to [Socrates'] arguments. I know I should do as he tells me, but when I leave him I have no defense against my own ambition and desire for recognition. So I run for my life, and avoid him, and when I see him, I'm embarrassed, when I remember conclusions we've reached in the past. (*Symposium* 216b–c)[1]

Korsgaard thinks that I "rewrote" the famous story; I think that she, in following Alcibiades' lead ("I think Alcibiades is right here and Lear is wrong") has missed the irony of the situation.

Korsgaard says, "the arresting thing about Socrates is his utter self-possession. He is always so completely himself, in any sort of circumstance: in battle, while being tried by the Athenians for his life, on the day of his death." I agree with this assessment. But I worry that it might foster a false image of psychic unity: as though Socrates never experienced psychic conflicts, momentary crises, or experiences of disruption. What is astonishing about Plato's depiction of Socrates is that it puts on display a person who is an exemplar of self-possession—paradigmatically himself in all his acts—and yet who regularly experiences crises, disruptions, and moments of conflict. Socrates is no Zen Master (for whom nothing is a conflict).[2] The unity that Socrates manifests is not one in which there are no crises, but one in which the crises ultimately serve to nourish him in his pursuit of wisdom.

Let me mention one example: Socrates giving a speech all the while draping a cloak over his head (*Phaedrus* 237–242). The origin of this speech deserves an interpretive essay of its own, but in brief: Socrates is tempted, threatened, and cajoled into giving a speech the performance of which requires him to fight off feelings of shame. Phaedrus wants Socrates to give a speech in competition with one he has just heard, according to standards of which he, Soc-rates, disapproves. There is to-ing and fro-ing between them, and then Phaedrus makes an oath: that if Socrates doesn't make his speech, he, Phae-drus, will never again recount a speech to him. "You devil, you!" Socrates says. "How cleverly you've found the way to force a lover of speeches to do what you tell him . . . Now that you've sworn that, how would I have been able to keep myself away from feasts of that sort?" (236e). He continues:

> Do you know what I shall do, then? . . . I shall speak with my
> head covered, so that I can rush through my speech as quickly as
> I can and not lose my way through shame, from looking at
> you. (237a)[3]

He gives his speech, and, as he then tries to leave, he receives what he takes to be a divine sign: "a voice from this very spot, which forbids me to leave until I have made expiation, because I have committed an offense against what be-longs to the gods." He continues: *"for something certainly troubled me some while ago as I was making the speech, and I had a certain feeling of unease"* (242c; my emphasis).

It is difficult to capture the nuance of this situation precisely because Korsgaard is right that Socrates is a model of self-possession: "He is always so completely himself, in any sort of circumstance." This moment is not a counterexample: Socrates is quintessentially himself. And yet this is a mo-ment in which Socrates is conflicted between his desire to feast on speeches and feelings of shame in giving the speech. He puts that conflict on display by both giving the speech and covering his head in shame; he is disrupted by voices he hears; and he treats the whole experience as a crisis that requires reparative response.[4] Participation in this vibrant jumble is precisely what it is for Socrates to be "completely himself." His self-possession does not flow from lack of psychic conflict—and here I worry that moral philosophers fix on overly idealized conceptions of harmony—but from the gusto with which he lives through the conflict and his determination to find an adequate reso-lution. Socrates says of himself that, in trying to follow the Delphic inscrip-tion to know oneself, he recognizes that he does not know "whether I am actually a beast more complex and more violent than Typhon, or both a tamer and simpler creature, sharing some divine and un-Typhonic portion by nature."[5] It is *that* ignorance, he says, that is driving his inquiry.

§2. Why the Unconscious Makes a Philosophical Difference

It does not surprise me that a Kantian like Korsgaard thinks that she can take the unconscious in stride. If one is starting out in a Kantian frame of mind, it is easy to think that the fact of unconscious mental phenomena poses no special philosophical problem. I hope I will not caricature the issue by putting it into broad relief. After all, if some desire pops into my conscious awareness, why should it matter where it comes from—whether it comes from my "unconscious" or anywhere else? On occasion I become aware that I am hungry and desire a pizza; on another occasion, perhaps with help from my analyst, I become aware of longings for a relationship with my father of which I was hitherto unaware. The same question confronts me in both cases: What am *I* going *to do* about *that?* And the fact that an unconscious desire's becoming conscious tends to be somehow disturbing does not significantly alter the situation: I may be disturbed by reading a good book, dipping a cookie into tea, stumbling upon the sidewalk, filling my car with gasoline. Whatever the disturbance, it is all just grist for the Kantian mill: What *am I* going *to do* about *that?* And, Korsgaard claims, the same strategy applies even if one accepts my claim in the second lecture that the Freudian unconscious includes not just isolated desires, but structures of practical identity. As she puts it: "So what? Once the psychoanalyst brings the resulting forms of identity to consciousness, it is for us to decide whether we really value ourselves under those descriptions or not, just as in any other case."

This argument looks persuasive because it assumes a particular division of form and matter. *Whatever* it is that comes into conscious awareness—whether it was previously unconscious or not—that is the matter on which reflective consciousness can impose its form. And insofar as reflective consciousness succeeds in imposing a form, it succeeds in crafting or authoring unity. As Korsgaard says, "the idea of practical identity is not supposed to solve the problem of unity: unity, in my view, is the result of the unifying activity of the agent herself. That is, it is the result of the activity of making decisions in a way that preserves your integrity, so that you will count as the author of the resulting actions."

It is precisely this picture of form and matter that the Freudian unconscious calls into question. Basically, I want to make three claims. First, the Freudian unconscious is its own form of thinking: differing in form from reflective self-conscious thinking. Freud himself insisted upon this. Thus the unconscious cannot be understood in terms of repressed contents—or contents that become available for self-conscious reflection of the standard type. "Making the unconscious conscious" properly understood cannot exclusively consist in bringing items—desires, wishes, fantasies whether isolated or elaborately linked—before the self-conscious mind according to the model of reflective distance. It also crucially consists in a kind of self-conscious participation in the "item" itself—the expression of fantasy. This self-conscious participation in the fantasy is what, I claim, the model of reflective distance fails to capture. Second, any genuine psychic unity available to humans must be a unity that encompasses these very different forms of thinking. This unity cannot be achieved by reflective self-consciousness' deciding what it thinks about this other form of activity—as though it were judging whether or not to act on a desire or on some other "incentive." The direct and effective act of will resulting from self-conscious consideration along the lines of reflective distance will not achieve the unity it purports to achieve. Although self-conscious reflection and decision will continue to play a crucial role in authoring psychic unity, it requires a more complicated dance than can be accommodated by the Kantian picture of reflective distance. One important reason for this is, third, that, in its own peculiar and weird way, the unconscious acts as its own formal principle, treating self-conscious mental activity as *its* matter. Thus the philosophically significant conflict between reflective self-consciousness and unconscious mental activity is not about repressed contents—which to allow into consciousness or which, once allowed into conscious awareness, to act upon or consciously to reject. Rather, the conflict is between two distinct forms of mental activity each of which seeks to take the other as its matter. To achieve true psychic unity, then, cannot be a matter of imposing self-conscious form on (hitherto) unconscious matter; it must consist in finding routes of accommodation between differing forms of mental activity.

To make the case for these three claims is a life's work. Here I can only point in the direction that a defense should take. But I hope I shall say enough to show that, *if* these claims are true, Korsgaard's Kantian attempt to accommodate the phenomena will not work.

The first point is fairly straightforward. From early on Freud insists that the unconscious cannot be understood in terms of repressed contents, but must be grasped as an alternative form of mental activity. In his essay "The Unconscious" there is a section, "The Special Characteristics of the System Unconscious"—and these characteristics all concern forms of thinking. So, the unconscious works according to a "primary psychical process" in which there are (from the perspective of conscious thought) loose and weird associations among ideas, and transfer of psychic energy across these connections.[6] Unconscious processes are, he says, timeless: they pay no attention to passage of time, are not ordered temporally—there are, as it were, no tenses to the verbs. The processes also pay little regard to reality: in particular, they are not particularly influenced by that primary principle of self-conscious thought, the law of noncontradiction. "To sum up: *exemption from mutual contradiction, primary process* (mobility of cathexes), *timelessness,* and *replacement of external by psychical reality*—these are the characteristics which we may expect to find in processes belonging to the system *Ucs.*"[7] And in a footnote in the *Interpretation of Dreams,* he warns analysts against thinking of the unconscious in terms of repressed content: "At bottom, dreams are nothing other than a particular *form* of thinking, made possible by the conditions of the state of sleep. It is the *dream-work* which creates that form, and it alone is the essence of dreaming."[8]

Freud was a pioneer in showing that it really was legitimate to conceive of the unconscious as a different form of thinking. It could regularly be seen as trying to think through a problem that confronted the person in daily life, and to offer an alternative, if wishful, solution. In the second lecture and in other writings, I have tried to show how unconscious fantasies are organizing, structuring, unifying activities that take on the most fundamental questions of conscious life and offer their own form of answer.[9] Obviously, the unity these structures display is not subject to the same normative standards as in normal self-conscious reflection. (A person may dream he is attending his own funeral; he is there as a little boy watching as his old corpse is lowered into the ground. The contradictory images may on occasion enhance rather than undo the sense that one person is in view.)

Now the reason Freud thinks he needs to warn analysts is that, as creatures who are familiar with the self-consciousness of reflective distance, it is tempting to conceive of the process of "making the unconscious conscious" in terms of bringing hitherto unavailable contents into view. That is, analysts themselves often describe the process in terms that fit Korsgaard's model. Once we can reflect on the forbidden wish, we can decide what to do about it. And around that decision (and our ability to live with it) lies the unity we might achieve. But if the unconscious is primarily its own form of mental activity, then reflecting on any particular content (however forbidden, wishful, hitherto hidden from view) is not going to capture it. Even more important: the very activity of reflecting on and judging the various incentives, thoughts, desires that present themselves to self-conscious awareness is not itself sufficient to achieve psychic unity. (This is so even if we grant all the sophisticated variants that Korsgaard brings to our attention). What does it even mean to accept or reject the unconscious as a form of my own mental activity? Even if I take it into consideration according to the model of reflective distance and, say, accept it—what difference does that make? Or if I reject it, what difference does that make? The unconscious as mental activity is going to keep on doing its thing harmoniously or disharmoniously *regardless* of my self-conscious judgment. Genuine harmony is not a matter of acting only on those desires and thoughts, whatever their origin, which I can endorse from the standpoint of my reflective identity. It is, rather, a matter of being able to think unconsciously in ways that nourish my reflective decisionmaking; and of being able to reflect consciously in ways that take up and make use of the unconscious thinking which I am engaged in (no matter what).

An image that comes to mind is of the impotent judge in a B Western movie. He judges the drunken cowboy to be in contempt of court, but it makes no difference: there is no one there to haul the cowboy off to jail. Or, for strategic purposes he may decide to make the cowboy the sheriff. It still makes no difference. Now we just have a drunk and disorderly sheriff. The point is that if you genuinely want to restore harmony to Last Gulch, you have to employ different methods from those that the judge has at his disposal. Indeed, the situation is even more dire. Unbeknownst to the judge, someone has slipped him a mickey. The judge does not realize it, but himself is drunk. As he attempts to render sober judgment on this drunken cowboy who stands before him, the judge manifests his own drunkenness. This is the comedy of the unconscious: it undermines the attempt to achieve reflective distance on it by, as it were, coming up from behind and manifesting itself in the very attempt to achieve reflective distance. The unconscious, in its pervasive, ever-present activity, never quite allows itself to be the object of reflective consideration. This does not mean that reflective consideration is not of value—I am engaging in such reflection right now, and I hope effectively—but I think that the proper conclusion of reflection is to recognize the limitations of the model of reflective distance when it comes to making the unconscious conscious. Insofar as the process of becoming consciously aware genuinely promotes psychic harmony we are going to have to conceive of it in terms of a different model.

Let us consider the claim that the unconscious treats self-conscious mental activity as its own matter upon which it tries to impose its form. For the sake of argument, let us assume that the unconscious is at work in the production of the experience of irony (as I have described it in the lectures). I have elsewhere argued that it is a mistake to think of the Freudian unconscious as Another Mind, with the same structure as reflective self-consciousness, only hidden from conscious view.[10] Thus to claim that self-consciousness is matter for the unconscious is not to claim that the two forms of mental activity are structurally mirror images of each other. Still, if we think of those moments of irony we have been considering—where I am trying to take myself seriously as a Christian, as a teacher, as a student, as a neighbor, as someone who respects human dignity—a familiar pattern of mental activity comes into view. At the level of self-conscious reflection, I am earnestly engaged in trying to think through how, say, to respect the human dignity of my neighbor. I experience myself to be taking the available alternatives into consideration. I reflect on the various "incentives" as they present themselves: perhaps I have to think about how I am going to respond to a beggar who has just accosted me. Now this encounter may trigger a flurry of superego activity: I experience myself as falling short—perhaps wildly short—of my own commitment to human dignity. *All of this*—including the experience of falling short—becomes the occasion for unconscious working over of the same topic. It may come up in dreams of alligators coming at me, in stomachaches, feelings of being bloated, in constipation or pains in my foot that make taking a step difficult—and it may come up in an experience of irony. And when it does—when the ghostly twin of human dignity comes to haunt and disrupt my self-conscious musings about human dignity—in this moment, my reflective musings (in all their variety) *all* come to seem so minor. It is *as though* it is the unconscious that is taking human dignity *really* seriously. It is *as though* the unconscious is taking a "step back" from all of my conscious stepping back (including my superego experience of falling short of my own ideals) and "judging" that the self-consciousness of reflective distance has in its complex entirety fallen short. Obviously, unconscious mental activity does not literally have that form. It does not have the structure of reflective distance. But that is one way of formulating the significance of the experience of uncanny, anxious longing that is the experience of irony.

It is in the context of this reflection that we can, I think, see Korsgaard's remarks about Ms. A. as too severe—and, in their severity, missing the point. Korsgaard says that Ms. A.'s conscious and unconscious practical identities "have been governed by the most banal gender stereotypes," that her consideration of various alternative possibilities is confused (and that I don't seem to do anything to correct it), and that her boyish acts "considered as expressions of a boyish practical identity—come from her only in the same sense that a squirrel's act of burying an acorn comes from the squirrel: they are expressions of her nature." I both admire and am amused by Korsgaard's forthrightness. But in this case, I think her example is a reductio ad absurdum of her own position. Do I really need to say that, in comparison to the squirrel, it is a different kind of question where Ms. A. has buried her nuts? I am struck by the discrepancy between the uncompromising stand Korsgaard takes here and the more nuanced view expressed in her book *Self-Constitution:* "action," Korsgaard tells us there, "is an idea that admits of degrees."[11] I am limited by considerations of confidentiality (and mutual agreement with Ms. A.) in how much I can say about this particular case. But when Korsgaard says that Ms. A. is "governed by the most banal gender stereotypes" it is her use of the word "governed" that distorts the situation. It is as though Korsgaard is taking up a superego voice judging Ms. A. as banal because she is "governed" by banal stereotypes. The clinical reality seems to me precisely the opposite. Simply by growing up in contemporary society we have all been influenced by banal gender stereotypes. It is part of the process of freeing ourselves from governance by them that we allow them to come into full, vibrant view within the analytic situation. From a psychoanalytic perspective, those who seem to us most sophisticated when it comes to gender identity may be under the influence of banal stereotypes of which they are unaware; whereas those who are giving loud vocalization of the banal may thereby be in the process of freeing themselves from it. And when any analysand considers her alternatives—and here I am not talking about an intellectualizing defense—her discourse might seem confused, banal, mixing categories that do not properly go together. It seems to me that the proper response to this is humility and patience. At any given moment in the analysis, the analyst does not know whether what he hears as confused (or banal) really is such or whether it is a moment of poetic re-creation, in which things are starting to be put together in new and unusual ways. It is precisely the playfulness of unconscious mental activity that may facilitate new forms or organization (and unity) that, from the perspective of contemporary judgment, seem confused, politically incorrect, or even against the analysand's own best interests. I agree with Korsgaard that mistakes—terrible mistakes—can be made. As she puts it, "surely there are things that count as getting it wrong." But the criteria by which one would come to adequate judgment about this are, in my opinion, importantly different from those that Korsgaard deploys in her comments.

§3. Reflective Distance Is Insufficient

"Learian irony," Professor Korsgaard tells us, "is very nearly a form of what Kant would call critique." Compliments don't come better than that—at least, coming from a Kantian. (And I do thank Korsgaard for taking my work so seriously.) But she continues, "If [irony] is what Lear says, then irony is just a special manifestation of the general human capacity that I have called reflective distance." This interpretation is not correct. There is no way to account for irony as a manifestation of reflective distance, no matter how special. The experience of irony is a peculiar form of *breakdown* of the reflective structure that Korsgaard describes. And the breakdown of a structure is not another instance of it.

In trying to accommodate irony to her model of self-consciousness as reflective distance, Korsgaard does not address one of my central theses: that the experience of irony is a peculiar species of uncanny anxiety. But it is only when one takes this uncanny anxiousness seriously that one can see that the experience of irony cannot fit the model of reflective distance. There is no doubt that Korsgaard's model of self-consciousness is robust.[12] It has great flexibility and covers a wide range of phenomena. So, when I confront that beggar on 57th Street there are all sorts of reflections I might go through—how much to give him, a critique of my own principles, wondering what my principles are, questioning the social fabric, a recognition that I have not really begun to live up to my own principles, and so on. I completely accept Korsgaard's point that "we do not just compare our motives to the demands of a preexisting identity." The model of reflective distance of course has this kind of flexibility, and I did not in any of my remarks mean to suggest otherwise. The model of reflective distance can accommodate a wide range of self-conscious phenomena—and that is why it is such a powerful model.

The problem is: it leaves irony out of account. I am concerned with a moment of anxious breakdown of my capacity to achieve reflective distance which is nevertheless a moment of excruciating self-conscious awareness. On other occasions the glance of a beggar might be the occasion for all sorts of reflections (on what to do, who to be, what principles to live by, what the meaning of the principles are, and so on), but *this time* eye contact unsettles my ability to make *any* such use of the moment. This is something that happens to me; it is not something I do. It is an uncanny, anxious haunting in which I am called to a halt seemingly by my own principles, or, perhaps, by their ghostly twins. This is not simply a moment in which I do not know what to do; it is a moment when my capacity to reflect on not knowing what to do has itself momentarily broken down in anxiety.

So, when Korsgaard says, "What's special about moments of irony, in Lear's account, is that a form of practical identity in a sense comes up for review as measured against *itself*: that is, as measured against the standards that are inherent in that very form of identification," her words can be used to describe two very different phenomena. One reading of her words fits her model: by reflecting on Christian principles, I come to see that I have not been living up to those principles, and perhaps I have not even previously understood the rigorous demands of those principles. I come to revise my understanding of what neighborliness consists in, by measuring the principle against its own demands. A Kantian can accommodate this form of reflection, just as Korsgaard says. But, on another reading, the nature of the "review" is itself uncanny: it consists in a breakdown of the standard processes of review. The uncanny anxiety *is* the "review."

§4. Disruption and Unity

My aim is not to valorize disruption. Rather, I would like to come to a realistic philosophical understanding of what the psychic unity available to creatures like us consists in. It is one thing to say that, for humans, true psychic unity is a difficult accomplishment, and that it is only rarely realized in very special people; it is quite another to fix on an image of unity that is not a genuine human possibility. The danger that concerns me is that of falling in love with a false image of unity and then idealizing it, when, in fact, there is no good reason for thinking that such an image ought to be an ideal.

The expression "psychic unity" functions for us as a signifier: it points us in the direction of a phenomenon we do not well understand. It is a mistake to assume that we already know what psychic unity is; that the only issues are to explain how to achieve it or why it matters. The danger of assuming that we know what we are talking about when we speak of psychic unity is that we will not be able to distinguish simulacra of unity from the real thing. To give just one salient example, we tend to assume that psychic disruption must stand opposed to psychic unity: that a moment of disruption is a moment of disruption of the unity we have achieved. Why think that? Perhaps certain types of psychic disruption are constitutive moments of the type of unity that is genuinely available to us.

The experience of uncanny anxiety is not in itself of any ethical value. But it may be the occasion for making a profound difference to ethical life. In her comments, Korsgaard does not address what I take to be the central problem confronting Kierkegaard in his polemical writings: *the problem of illusion.* The problem is essentially practical, not theoretical. Kierkegaard took it to be a Christian requirement upon him to somehow get through to his neighbors about the Christian requirements confronting them. From Kierkegaard's perspective (as I understand the problem): What it would be for him to love his neighbor as himself would, in part, be to help them grasp what it is *for them* to love their neighbors as themselves. The problem that confronted Kierkegaard was not merely that his neighbors already took themselves to be Christian and thought that they already understood the requirements of loving one's neighbor; it was that there was no way to reach them via standard forms of reflective argument or critique. Their entire form of life—*Christendom*—was an illusion. It was *illusory* in the sense that it offered stunted images of Christian life as though they were the real thing; and it was *illusion* in the sense that it was able to metabolize and contain efforts to achieve reflective distance. That is, if one were already an inhabitant of Christendom, any attempt to "step back" from Christian teaching and achieve some "reflective distance" would be yet another move within Christendom.

To grasp the problem in a neo-Kantian context let us secularize the example. Let us imagine for the sake of argument that we are, unbeknownst to ourselves, inhabitants of a secular counterpart to the illusion that Kierkegaard tackled: I will call it *Liberaldom*. Liberaldom is a form of life that takes itself to have many strands—to embody a variety of political conflicts and outlooks—but to be essentially concerned with human dignity and human rights. The familiar conflicts between liberals and conservatives are themselves contained within Liberaldom. So, for instance, some within Liberaldom focus on the rights of the unborn (and are considered "conservative"); others focus on the rights of women, or on the right to privacy (and are considered "liberal"). The conflicts are bitter; on occasion they become violent; and the conflicting perspectives are considered irreconcilable. The conflicts and debates, the "polarization" of positions, the sense of intractability all contribute to a sense that the bases are covered. Nevertheless, each side thinks it is justified in terms of the dignity and rights that befit human life. Although this is an imagined example—I am not prepared to argue that we actually are living in Liberaldom—it is crucial (just as it was in the case of Christendom) not to caricature it. So we should imagine Liberaldom to include the political and social debates, the reflections on liberal society that one finds in contemporary Western discourse. It is easy to caricature Liberaldom: those espresso-drinking, Starbucks-inhabiting readers of the *New York Times*. But, wait a second: *that includes me!* There are serious thinkers and actors within Liberaldom: indeed, Liberaldom aspires to be a self-reflective and self-critical form of life. Let us suppose that—just like the Christendom that preceded it—it has a certain success in containing reflection upon it. That is, Liberaldom aims to be and for the most part is closed under reflection. So, here I am again: walking down 57th Street, in front of the Medici, confronted by a beggar. What am I to do? I take myself to be seriously committed to respecting the dignity of all human beings. Such an ideal represents who I want to be, who I think I am, who I want to become: it is constitutive of my practical identity. So imagine that I am seriously reflecting on what to do. The beggar is providing me with an "incentive" to achieve some reflective distance—and I am making full use of the occasion. I want to claim that it is possible for me at once to pass the neo-Kantian test of morality and to flunk the Socratic test of ethics.

I pass the neo-Kantian test because I will that the maxim upon which I act be a universal law. I will that respect for human dignity be a universal law, and I take my particular act—whatever it happens to be, and however complex the deliberation—to be a manifestation of appropriate respect.

But then I start to get anxious. Here I am not concerned with the anxiety providing an occasion for subsequent reflection on what to do—though this is of course important. I am concerned with capturing the quality of the anxious moment itself. Anxiety is by its very nature a disturbance of our ability to achieve reflective distance. It is difficult to describe the phenomenon because the structure of the sentences has subject-object form, and this tends to reinforce a picture of reflective distance. Heidegger, who tried to capture the phenomenon of anxiety in *Being and Time,* says, for example, "That in the face of which one has anxiety is not an entity within-the-world . . . That in the face of which one is anxious is completely indefinite . . . the world has the character of completely lacking significance."[13] It is a misunderstanding of what he is saying to picture me, in my anxiety, as stepping back from the world and reflectively deciding that it lacks significance. Rather, my anxiety is an emotively laden inability (in the moment) to take a step back from any object and consider it reflectively—and *all of that* is a manifestation of the world's lacking significance. It is in this indirect way, Heidegger argues, that the world comes into view.

Now Heidegger wanted to keep his philosophical inquiries rigidly separate from more empirical inquiries into ethics and psychology; so he would not concern himself with the peculiar species of anxiety that is irony.[14] But the phenomenon fits the large-scale structure he describes (though it has surprising features of its own). So, in that moment with the beggar, I may start out trying to treat our meeting as an occasion for reflective consideration (à la Korsgaard), but in the anxiety things break down. The breaking down in this case has a local focus: it is not (à la Heidegger) that all my worldly involvements fall away; it is that all my worldly involvements *with human dignity* fall away: the world of social pretense, the world of Liberaldom, the world of knowing what to do, or, at least, knowing how to question what to do, and so on. The crucial point is that this very moment of anxious breakdown manifests that human dignity both does and does not matter (to me). The anxiety is itself a manifestation of human dignity mattering to me—*hugely*, enough to disrupt my normal ways of going on. But the anxiety is *also* a withdrawing of significance from my worldly involvements with human dignity. What used to feel so important now feels empty; yet there is also intense desire that it should somehow feel genuinely full. Thus the anxiety is experienced as an uncanny doubling: it is as though my life with human dignity is suddenly haunted by its ghostly twin. (Heidegger himself characterizes anxiety in terms of uncanniness, and I think this is what he is getting at.)[15]

Such a moment may, as I said, be of no value: it might just be a passing moment that is forgotten about. But, in the imaginary example I am pursuing, it could also serve as an occasion to break through the false unity of Liberaldom. By hypothesis, this false unity is not going to be broken through by yet another act of reflection on liberalism. Indeed, the unity of Liberaldom is in part constituted by the myriad acts of critical reflection upon it. Now if we can imagine Liberaldom as a possibility for us—the secular equivalent to Kierkegaard's Christendom—then I think we can see that Korsgaard's approach to identity, self-constitution, and morality can be at once too strict and too lax with respect to unity's requirements.

It is relatively easy for a well-meaning person who wishes to follow morality's requirements to develop a punishing superego with respect to a false image of human dignity. In trying to become a person who respects human dignity, I end up trapped in a punishing self-surveillance that constricts my possibilities in the name of autonomy. In describing the pull of the normative, Korsgaard uses language that, however true on some reading, can be put to severe uses.

> Consider the astonishing but familiar *"I couldn't live with myself if I did that."* Clearly there are two selves here, me and the one I must live with and so *must not fail* . . . It is the conceptions of ourselves that are most important to us that give rise to unconditional obligation. For to violate them is to violate your integrity and so your identity, and to no longer be who you are. That is, *it is to no longer be able to think of yourself under the description under which you value yourself and to find your life to be worth living and your actions to be worth undertaking. It is to be for all practical purposes dead or worse than dead.* When an action cannot be performed

without loss of some fundamental part of one's identity, and *the agent could just as well be dead,* then the obligation not to do it is unconditional and complete.[16]

I do not dispute the truth of what Korsgaard is saying here—at least, under one understanding of these claims—but I am concerned with the uses to which these claims can be put. "I couldn't live with myself if I did that!" "I might just as well be dead!" These are the sorts of thing a person with a cruel superego says to himself—and they may serve to keep him on the straight and narrow in his adherence to a pinched conception of human dignity. Note that these psychic structures can tolerate, even encourage, a high degree of reflective awareness. It is precisely my hypervigilant concern about being a person who respects the dignity of others that motivates me to reflect on what dignity is, to engage in critique of established conceptions, to read the current debates, and so on. I will no doubt be in the business of universalizing the maxims on which I act—especially when it comes to respect for human dignity. And yet, if we allow ourselves the imagined thought that we are, unbeknownst to ourselves, inhabitants of Liberaldom, then all of this reflection, all of this vigilance, all of these threats of self-punishment, all of these purportedly noble attempts at universalization—all of this ultimately serves the purpose of shoring up the illusion of Liberaldom. If we are living, unbeknownst to ourselves, with a constricted conception of what respect for human dignity requires, then in the name of morality we will be perpetuating a simulacrum.

It is the experience of irony that can serve to break these ersatz unities apart. And thus it can serve as a constituent moment in the developmental effort to achieve a more genuine unity. It is in a moment of uncanny anxiety that a sense of the possibilities of human dignity starts to open up that had hitherto been foreclosed in all my attempts to achieve reflective distance. Indeed, as I have suggested, they may have been foreclosed *by* my attempts to achieve reflective distance. It is only in this moment of uncanny anxiety that I have a glimmer that all my previous attempts to grasp human dignity fall wildly short of its requirements.

It is worth dwelling a moment with the conception of *falling short*, because two very different sorts of phenomena can be described with this expression. On the one hand, there is the experience of falling short that is, broadly speaking, a superego phenomenon. A person with a punishing superego may be living within Liberaldom and experience himself as falling wildly short of its requirements. The superego, in Freud's analysis, is a psychic structure—an internalized representation of civilization's demands—that is deployed to keep us in line.[17] One manifestation of the superego is a sense of guilt or shame that one is falling short. The superego-experience of falling short is experienced as punishment for falling short. It is from the perspective of the ideal that one's own efforts are held to be so paltry. By contrast, with irony, my experience is not that my act falls miserably short of my principle; rather, my experience is of my principle falling weirdly short of itself. It is as though there is an internal instability in the signifier *human dignity*. This is not a case in which civilization gets its hooks into me (the superego phenomenon); it is a case in which the hooks already in me are coming undone. The principle of human dignity—as it has been inculcated in me by training by teachers, parents, by the culture at large—is coming to be haunted, seemingly by itself.

§5. A Different Kantian Inheritance

I have taken issue with Korsgaard's neo-Kantian approach to irony. I do not mean to suggest that a Kantian approach is impossible. But we need a different choice of inheritance from Kant than that of reflective distance. The appropriate place to look, I think, is Kant's insistence that for a self-conscious human agent *there is no distance at all* to be had between the thought that represents the causality of the action and the thought that is the causality. As Stephen Engstrom puts it, "the efficacy of practical thinking is integral to the thinking itself, so that the self-consciousness essential to thinking in general also pertains, in the case of practical thinking, to that thinking's efficacy, its productive power, and hence that the efficacy depends on the consciousness of it. Thus practical thinking *can* make its object actual through and only through its *consciousness* that it can do so."[18] This is a form of self-consciousness that is not at any distance from that of which it is conscious. On the contrary: the self-consciousness of the efficacy of practical thinking is constitutive of that very efficacy. Now when an agent is deliberating about what to do, she is deliberating about what is to be done (by her). That is, her practical reasoning gives the ground her action. But then, as Sebastian Rödl puts it, "*the same thing* is the cause of her doing it and the ground of her thinking that she should do it. This identity is *no accident;* rather, it character-izes *the form* of action explanation."[19]

The experience of irony is a self-conscious experience of the disruption of the efficacy of practical thinking. Since the efficacy of practical thinking is constituted by a self-conscious awareness of its efficacy, the experience of disruption of efficacy is itself a disruption of the efficacy. But it is not any old experience of disruption of efficacy—such as the shooting pain of a headache, or a sudden attack of hiccups. Rather, my experience is of the ground of my practical thinking weirdly haunting itself. So, I am still on 57th Street, facing the beggar: My self-conscious awareness of my efficacy is there, present in the practical thinking of what to do. But my awareness of efficacy is also an aware-ness of the ground of my thinking: it is the principle of respect for the dignity of my fellow human beings that is directing the course of my thinking. If things were going normally, my practical thinking would issue in action. But this is what gets disrupted in the experience of anxiety. It is at once an experi-ence of disruption in the ground of my thinking, a self-conscious experience of disruption of the efficacy of my thought and thus a genuine disruption in the efficacy of my practical thinking. I am called to a halt.

And this brings us back to where we began: Socrates' coming to a halt. In a practical context, this experience of ironic anxiety is one significant way in which we come to know that we do not know. In his exposition of Kant, Eng-strom has argued that one of the hallmarks of practical knowledge is an awareness of itself as self-sustaining.[20] Just as we expect our acts of theoreti-cal cognition to fit together in an intelligible and thus self-sustaining whole, it is internal to each of our acts of practical cognition that we expect them to fit together and support each other. We expect each act of practical knowledge to agree with itself and with every other. Practical knowledge is not only self-sustaining; it is aware of itself as self-sustaining: the awareness of itself as self-sustaining is constitutive of its being self-sustaining. All of this comes apart in the experience of irony. The experience can be described as a self-conscious awareness that the practical judgment I am in the midst of making is *not* self-sustaining. And this is tantamount to self-conscious awareness that I do not have practical knowledge. In trying to act from respect for human dignity, the very idea of human dignity becomes unstable for me: and this is a significant way in which I come to know that I do not know. The outward manifestation of this practical awareness is: I come to a halt.

5

Psychoanalysis and the Limits of Reflection

RICHARD MORAN

In an 1896 letter to Wilhelm Fliess, the first and primary confidant for his fledgling ideas, the young Sigmund Freud wrote: "I see that you are using the circuitous route of medicine to attain your first ideal, the physiological understanding of man, while I secretly nurse the hope of arriving by the same route at my own original objective, philosophy. For that was my original ambition, before I knew what I was intended to do in the world."[1] When philosophy is mentioned in his later, published, writings, it is normally an occasion for Freud to disavow any such connection with the enterprise of psychoanalysis, a repeated gesture of denial that naturally only goes to show how profound the relationship must really be. For many years now, Jonathan Lear has been one of the great mediators between the worlds of philosophy and psychoanalysis, showing us what they have to learn from each other, and what they have difficulty accepting from each other. In these lectures he explores a connection between a stance toward oneself that is furthered in the psychoanalytic session, and a stance toward one's life to which Kierkegaard gives the name "irony." I will begin my remarks with some thoughts about the general picture of irony presented in Lear's lectures, and its relation to certain philosophical claims for the role of what is variously called "critical reflection," "self-consciousness," or the metaphor of "stepping back" from some aspect of one's thought or engagement in the world. I will then focus on the idea of self-knowledge at play in the lectures and the role of something called "expression" in this context.

Given the topic of irony and the forging of an identity, I hope it will seem appropriate that I start with a depiction of the dramaturgical aspect of the lectures, the narrative composed out of the contending forces he describes so vividly. In many ways we are presented with a narrative of confinement and illusion, and the hoped-for liberation from both. We may begin with the thought that, as he puts it, "It is a mark of the human that we do not quite fit into our own skins. That is, we do not fit without remainder into socially available practical identities." This is said to be a "familiar thought," and indeed it is. The idea of a "remainder" that doesn't fit in finds expression in various guises in philosophy, and Lear himself has explored one of these themes in his 2000 book *Happiness, Death, and the Remainder of Life,* and more recently in his 2003 book *Therapeutic Action: An Earnest Plea for Irony.*

In the present context, this remainder is contrasted with what are called "socially available practical identities," and their role can be seen in the familiar forming and deforming activities of the social world and its institutions. These formations precede the individual, and the anarchic self can never fit entirely comfortably within these structures, which nonetheless present themselves as the only available sources of meaning or companionship. In the civilizing labor of fitting the emerging self into the available social categories, much of the original material will be left out, will find no recognized place in the practical identity as inhabited and recognized by the world. But of course, what it means for these "remainders" to be "left out" is itself a large question. Being "left out" certainly does *not* mean that the remainders of the self cease to exist. They do persist, and exert their force, and shape the experience and values and desire of the person, even if they are unrecognized as such. Being "left out," then, means something more like being *disavowed,* denied recognition.

If, in this picture, the socially available categories are cast as the confining containers, and the social institutions of the family, school, job, and state are cast as the enforcers of these identities, then the philosophers, as presented here, occupy an interestingly equivocal role. For philosophers beginning with Plato have promised liberation from illusion, and philosophers at least since Kant (but going back to the Stoics) have promised freedom in the form of *autonomy* or self-rule. Now it is true that what *gnōthi seauton* meant for the Greeks is surely something different from what "self-consciousness" means in Kant, but in both traditions, and many others besides, the liberation or *self-rule* in question is pictured as in the closest possible connection to self-knowledge or a capacity for *critical reflection*.

And it is here that philosophy's role is shown to be equivocal with respect to the narrative of confinement. For although it presents itself as representing an *outside* perspective, one not confined to the socially available categories, it is not only just as much an agent of repression as any of the other figures in this story, but in addition is ironically blind to its own complicity in these structures. For the stance of critical reflection that it promotes is not, in fact, a perspective genuinely *outside* the "socially available identities" after all, but fully within them, serving their interests. One way the philosophical appeal to critical reflection is shown to fail is when it is reduced to an impotent recommendation to get a grip, and assert rational control over oneself. Lear describes this in the following terms: "I then reflect on possible reasons, realize that my actions are out of proportion, and resolve to try to get over my anger." As he goes on to note, this depiction invites the question: "what grounds my confidence that my resolution to get over my anger will have any impact on my anger?" If the philosopher pictured here really thought that the sheer realization that one's anger is out of proportion were sufficient to transform it into something better, he is shown to have a naive faith in the power of reason alone.

A second form of failure is less innocent, and closer to a traditional understanding of the idea of irony, for in this scenario the philosopher's procedures of critical reflection, being part of the very structures being reflected upon, turn out to be simply another form of repression itself. This threat is described in relation to the Kantian picture of freedom as expressing a "kingdom of ends." Lear says: "In the name of psychic unity, integrity, practical identity, and so on, the inhabitants of this kingdom would be splitting off a vibrant part of themselves—treating a deeply rooted source of psychic unity as though it were a mere disruption or distraction from the only unity we have. This would in effect be an act of repression and, as such, the occasion for psychic conflict." We are reminded that *any* of the procedures of critical reflection can be co-opted and pressed into the service of the very illusion or bondage they purport to be independent of. As Lear says, "It is equally possible that the reflective judgment, rather than abating the anger, serves to preserve and protect it by hiding it from awareness." In relation to the Kierkegaardian problem of "Christendom" in the first lecture, Lear puts this fact into relation with irony in the following way: "The problem would not be so difficult and irony would not be so important, if reflection and criticism were not already part of the social practice."

Reflection and criticism are thus revealed to be elements of the very same structures that they present themselves as providing an independent perspective on. By contrast, "irony," trauma, disruption, and the uncanny are various names for the something that can arrive only from *outside* these structures. In these ways, then, the narrative of inside and outside here is a narrative of the supplement, the excess, the unstable element outside the system.

I'm not sure just how we are to understand Lear's specific point that reflective judgment may serve to protect and preserve the anger or fear in question, for it seems to me that this is a general liability for *any* stance or procedure one may adopt with respect to some part of oneself, and is not restricted to a particular philosophy or therapeutic practice. Even in those traditions of philosophy that *are* explicitly therapeutic, such as the practices of Socrates, or Nietzsche, or Wittgenstein, such a risk is endemic to their procedures. Socratic elenchus can itself be pressed into the service of preserving ignorance, Nietzschean genealogy can be practiced in the spirit of the ascetic ideal, and the practice of Wittgensteinian therapeutic reminders can be distorted into the constructions of new orthodoxies, fully as constraining as any picture that held us captive. And of course, we are all familiar with the phenomenon of the analysand who exploits the process of psychoanalysis itself to evade rather than confront the demands of his life. So while it may indeed be therapeutic in the ways Lear describes to cultivate a capacity for irony, this cultivation will necessarily be subject to these very same risks. And, on the other hand, if the charge is that philosophers have been blind to these risks, it will be important to the convincingness of this charge that it not rest on characterizing them as traditionally assuming that something called reflection alone *was* sufficient for radical self-change, that there was no need here for such things as courage, accidents of history, the creation and destruction of new forms of life, or conversion experiences, for one would have to search far in the tradition to find philosophers who would fit that description.

This, however, belongs with the fact that along with the inside and outside of structures and identities, there are also *figures* who are depicted as either inside or outside of the perspective disclosed by irony or the remainder. (This much of the traditional dramatic/rhetorical meaning of irony, in terms of an implied division within an audience, is, I take it, retained in Lear's account.) So, on the one hand, there are the figures of irony like Socrates and Kierkegaard who see the infinite questionability of our lives and our identities. And on the other hand, there are the figures, like Alcibiades, who "don't get it" or who are complacently inhabiting their practical identities as though they were matters of simple membership in a group, the kind of accreditation that comes with simply having a driver's license, valid for driving in the left-hand lane of life, perhaps, but hopeless for travel in the right-hand lane of irony. As a narrative of uncapturability, then, it requires a few philosophers to play the role of straight man, or straight woman, as the foil to the ironic figure who brings the structures into question. We are introduced to them early in the lectures as the mere pretenders, those who are *"perfectly sure* of being human and knowing what it means to be a human being."

In the drama of confinement and exclusion, these figures are depicted as located comfortably *within* a structure that, from the perspective of irony, is shown to be less complete, less assured than they imagine. The requirements of conflict for a drama of this sort also exert a pressure on the narrative to cast different figures as antagonists, and to depict one of them as denying or repressing the possibilities of the other. The specifically spatial language of confinement and exclusion asserts itself here as well, and in the case of some work of mine, for example, we are told that "Moran draws the map of self-knowledge in such a way that there is no place in it for the form of making the unconscious conscious that I take to be central to psychoanalysis," and in particular that he has "left no room for the peculiar case of *consciously fantasizing.*" From this and other critical remarks, one would receive the impression that I had presented a theory of psychoanalytic practice, and inexplicably left out of account such things as transference, fantasy, construction, resistance, projection, and the like. I'll say just a few things here to correct that impression.

Since there is much in Lear's account of psychoanalytic practice that I find myself in agreement with, or to which I must defer, I would if possible like to resist the role of opponent here. I would like to think that nothing I say in that book or elsewhere *excludes* the phenomenon that Lear is concerned with here. I had not presented an account of unconscious fantasy or the interpretation of transference in psychoanalytic practice in my book, and I would be impressed if he thought I was capable of that. Very briefly, what I *am* concerned with there, under the heading of the notion of avowal, is the ordinary phenomenon that a person can come to know, for instance, whether he resents his sister by thinking about *his sister,* or that he is dreading the holidays by thinking about *the holidays.* In some other cases, however, this first-person access to myself might be blocked, and I might be able to know about my dread or my resentment *only* by the same sort of observations that another person could make of me, by seeing how I tend to act or respond in certain situations, and *not* by attending to the *objects* of these attitudes of mine. What I try to account for in the book is why the former kind of access to my own attitudes, self-knowledge in that sense, should be seen as fundamental; the capacity to know how I think or feel about something in thinking about that very thing. Now the relevant idea of "thinking about" here is a deliberately capacious notion, and is something that will vary greatly from context to context, very much including such things as musing on some possibility, dwelling on some hurtful remark, or retelling the incident to one's analyst. All of these can count as the sort of thinking about the object of one of my attitudes that puts me in touch with my attitude itself. This is not simply a matter of telling oneself (or being told) to be reasonable, but rather of having the world that my moods, feelings, and attitudes are directed upon be available to me in my relation to my moods, feelings, and attitudes themselves. If my reflection on the world that my attitudes are directed upon (for example, my sister, the holidays) is unrelated to the shape of my attitudes themselves, and my access to my resentment or dread, then these are conditions I am merely assailed by rather than attitudes of mine that I am participant in. Psychoanalysis, particularly in the conducting of the transference, engages with the subject in quite different ways, but restoring that capacity belongs with the very idea of the therapeutic, and the understanding of why self-knowledge should matter at all, beyond satisfying the absorbing interest we tend to take in ourselves.

One thing that may separate us is my own sense of the enormous heterogeneity in the idea of self-knowledge that has attracted philosophical attention. The form, and meaning, and import of self-knowledge varies enormously across the terrain spanned by the idea of "first-personal," or "subject position," or "self-knowledge," and features or problems associated with one of them cannot be simply carried over to another one. My relation to my fantasy life, for instance, though indeed a matter of my subjectivity, and my understanding of myself and my world, is something deeply *unlike* my relation to the sensation of pain in my knee, which in turn is something deeply unlike my relation to what I know as an agent about what I am doing now, or how I know what it is that I believe about something, which is different again from all the ways in which my knowledge of myself is a matter of embodied orientation, so that I know myself in much the same way that I know my surroundings, practically and tacitly.

These are all modes of subjectivity, in one way or another, and there are of course conceptual relations among all of them and more, but at the same time the very idea of "immediacy" in self-knowledge, or the idea that the subject enjoys some sort of "authority" with respect to them, will either mean very different things in these different contexts, or indeed will not apply at all.

It is not yet clear to me how to make good sense of the idea, but if there *is* a notion of "first-person authority" that describes something real in our relation to our fantasy lives, especially as these are indeed structuring with respect to our experience, this will have to be something *very* different from related notions, as discussed by myself and others. Consider two ways in which philosophers have approached the distinctiveness of the first person:

> One is Wittgenstein's thought that, for certain first-person present-tense thoughts there is no *logical room* for doubt (as is sometimes claimed about the case of pain; see *Philosophical Investigations* §§ 246 and 247).

>Another is the idea that a person can *know* what she is doing or
>what she thinks about something in virtue of her being *active* or
>*committed* with respect to an action or a thought (something ex-
>plored in my book and elsewhere).[2]

The very possibilities of knowledge or authority in these two cases are enormously different, and differently contested. (And indeed, in those cases in
which doubt is logically excluded, Wittgenstein will argue that there is no application for the idea of self-*knowledge* either.) The present point, however, is
that *neither* of these thoughts would apply to various other elements of my
subjectivity, for instance, my knowing whether some current experience of
mine is a memory or not. And one or another of the ideas of knowledge or
authority may have no application at all to my relation to my dreams, my
moods, or my deeper motivations. In response to the charge that I have formulated a notion of self-knowledge or first-person authority that fails to
transfer to the case of unconscious fantasy, I would have to embrace the
charge and say that these notions cannot be simply transferred from one region to another, but need to be defined anew in each different context if they
are to mean anything. Whatever might be meant, for instance, by speaking
of the "transparency condition" as applied to unconscious fantasy will need
its own specific motivation and defense. I don't see this as having been provided here, but it could well be something worth developing.

In spelling out what will count for him as making "an unconscious practical identity" "conscious," Lear appeals to a notion of "expression" as the "replacement" of some nonverbal behavior with a piece of speech. This is seen
as related to another distinction, between merely reporting on one's anger
(from the outside, as it were), and the full-blooded *expression* of one's anger.
This is a distinction important to early work of mine,[3] but David Finkelstein
and later Lear take it to be best understood in connection with a remark of
Wittgenstein's about the "replacement" of a natural expression of pain with
a verbal utterance such as "I've got a slight headache today" (*Philosophical Investigations* § 244).

As with the ideas of "transparency" and "first-person authority," I doubt
that this thought of Wittgenstein's can be adopted in this way. Even in the
context of the *Philosophical Investigations* § 244, his remark that in some cases
"the verbal expression of pain replaces crying" is presented as merely "one

possibility," and is restricted to a special case of physical pain or other sensations. The context is one in which he is asking how words come to refer to sensations in the first place, and *not* one in which the question is what makes one form of expression more fully present than another, or how someone might progress from merely reporting to a more fully felt self-expression.

It is out of the grammatical variety and heterogeneity described above that Wittgenstein distills a particularly pure and primitive form of purported subjective unchallengeability, the case of immediate sensations, of knowing that I am in pain. This notion is not meant to be representative of the first-personal generally, but is rather constructed by Wittgenstein to fit the requirements of the picture he is *opposing*, the picture of the inner realm's containing inner objects that I can observe and name. The strategic point at this stage of *Philosophical Investigations* is to apply pressure to this picture of the inner by examination of what should be the very best case, the most vivid instantiation of the picture of "object and designation": the throbbing pain seizing my attention right now. The idea is that, if the picture of our subjectivity as an inner realm could make sense *anywhere*, it would have to be here. Hence if it can be made to fail *here*, the picture of the inner realm will be fatally undermined. This is a special case, in several ways.

Consider the case of pain in contrast with other forms of knowing oneself, or not knowing oneself, that make their appearance in Wittgenstein:

- My knowing what I or *we* would mean by a certain expression in my language, the whole question of the first-person *plural* in Wittgenstein[4]
- My knowing my way around a city
- My knowing whether it was really love that I felt, which is different from identifying a feeling, Wittgenstein tells us, *beca*use *love* is put to the test, whereas a sensation or a headache is not
- The way I can say that it's *King's College,* and not another just like it, that I am imagining to be on fire[5]
- The difference between feeling pain and feeling grief, and whether one *could* feel profound grief for just one second
- How I may know, but not really know, my own fear, and how my utterances of fear run the entire spectrum of cases

from the instinctive shriek to the statement "I'm still a bit
afraid, but no longer so much as before"

Wittgenstein uses the discussion of expressions of fear to explicitly disavow
any general "expressivist" account of the first-personal discourse:

> A cry is not a description. But there are transitions. And the words
> "I am afraid" may approximate more, or less, to being a cry. They
> may come quite close to this and also be *far* removed from it.[6]

It is the special features of the case of *"pain"* that suggest the idea of "expression" at work in the thought about teaching the child "pain behavior," so
that the natural response of crying is "replaced" by the *utterance* "That hurts!"
or perhaps "It still hurts, but it's not as bad as the day before." This comparison suggests itself to Wittgenstein because the case of pain seems to be one
in which the very idea of doubt or uncertainty in one's own case is difficult to
make sense of. His opponent in the argument interprets this fact as evidence
for the excellence of our detection of an "inner state," and hence as representing our best case for a piece of knowledge that is absolutely certain, im-
mune to challenge. Wittgenstein turns this thought on its head and argues
that if doubt or uncertainty is logically excluded, then so is knowledge or
certainty. On these assumptions the first-person statements of pain cannot,
for logical reasons, be seen as reports on something independent of themselves that they aim to describe accurately. Hence the comparison with a cry,
which does not play that kind of role in discourse, though as we have seen an
utterance such as "I am afraid" can lie anywhere at all on the spectrum from
cry to description. And this spectrum itself does not represent anything like
the transition from forms of self-expression that are more fully experienced
to those that are less so; so it is unclear how this thought of Wittgenstein's
could be applied to the case of, say, the acknowledgement of one's anger
within the context of transference.

The more important point for our present purposes, however, is that very
little in this context of argument can be applied to the case of practical identities or unconscious fantasies. No one, I take it, would want to say of either of
these aspects of our lives that "here the expression of doubt or uncertainty is
senseless." If anything, given how buried and/or pervasive either uncon-

scious fantasy or practical identity can be in one's life, it would be closer to the truth to say that it is the expression of anything approaching *certainty* that would be absurd. And similar differences would show up from elsewhere in the range of forms of subjectivity and self-knowledge. For instance, nothing more characterizes my relation to my *intentions* than the fact that here the expression of uncertainty, of my being more or less certain, and so on is fully at home if anywhere in life. And yet my relation to my intentions is surely a first-person phenomenon as well, and a matter of my knowing or not knowing my own mind.

The idea of "replacing" one mode of expression for another is not perfectly clear to me, particularly in the therapeutic context into which Lear is importing the idea. On a basic level, we might ask: If the two modes of expression are really doing the same work, then what is the *point* of "replacing" one with the other? If we take the notion of replacement literally, then what is gained, for instance, by substituting some words for some tears? Does that mean that the tears are now unnecessary, having been replaced by something else?[7] And on the other hand, if the verbal expression and the nonverbal expression are *not* doing the same work, so that the verbal expression, for instance, means that the person can now *tell us* about her pain or her anger and what it means to her, then this seems to reassert all the old problems about *how* such a remarkable transition is possible, how a person can be in a position to know these things without having to observe herself in the way *we* would have to observe her to know her condition.

Despite these differences, Lear and I want several of the same things from an understanding of the first person and its relation to self-expression. We share the view, which is not universal among contemporary philosophers, that a philosophical account of self-knowledge is obliged to make understandable why it should matter, why it should be so difficult, and why it should be different in form from our knowledge of other things, including knowledge of other people. We both share a concern with the connections between philosophy, self-knowledge, and certain ideas of the therapeutic. Anyone with these commitments will need to account for why, out of all the ways in which we do express ourselves, the expression of ourselves in *words* should be privileged in any way at all; why finding words for ourselves, and a context for their utterance, should have anything in particular to do with the forms of self-knowledge that have something to do with psychic health. I think that about this question in particular, philosophers and others still have very far to go. I take it that an unconscious fantasy can indeed be a structuring of one's life, and hence a source of psychic unity in that sense, and hence can *express* itself in one's life, without itself needing to be *verbalized* at all, and may indeed be all the healthier for that. So we will need to say more about just where and when a part of the self can be said to be not fully owned when one is unable to give voice to it in speech, or how bringing it to words alters its character. It is an ancient idea, and surely part of what Freud took from the philosophical tradition in formulating the theory and practice of psychoanalysis, the "talking cure"; but, as with the task of becoming human, we are still far from understanding what that means.

6

The Immanence of Irony and the Efficacy of Fantasy

A Response to Richard Moran

Richard Moran's writing on self-consciousness, avowal, and expression has illuminated the field. We share a core belief, not common these days, that understanding psychoanalysis is of crucial importance if we are to grasp such philosophically significant concepts as self-knowledge and human freedom. Thus I am not surprised that we are in broad agreement. And when he says, in conclusion, that we still need to account for why the ability to express ourselves in words should have a privileged position when it comes to the forms of self-knowledge that have something to do with psychic health, I want to cheer. Let me engage with the points he makes, in the hope of taking the conversation forward.

§1. Irony and Narrative

Moran interprets me as offering a familiar narrative structure: "In many ways we are presented with a narrative of confinement and illusion, and the hoped-for liberation from both." "'Irony,' trauma, disruption, and the uncanny are various names for the something that can arrive only from *outside* these structures. In these ways, then, the narrative of inside and outside here is a narrative of the supplement, the excess, the unstable element outside the system." For two reasons, I do not accept this characterization. First, I am not trying to provide a narrative, but to bring certain phenomena—primarily, the experience of irony, but also the capacity for irony and ironic existence—into view. The reason I keep returning to the beggar on 57th Street is not because I need to elaborate his story, but because the repetition in imagination may cause discomfort in some readers. The internal recognition of a rising level of discomfort in oneself may be of greater value in getting a glimpse of the experience of irony then any narrative about the rising level of discomfort. The choice of literary form had a surprising effect on me: I had no idea when I began writing these lectures that I would end up donating the royalties of this book to the Chicago Food Depository. (And I want to thank all the commentators for agreeing to this.) I do not think that this happened because of a narrative about the beggar; it happened because, in imagination, I repeatedly brought myself before his visage. And the reason I chose to publish a book with this form—lectures, followed by comments and responses—is not because it has been done before, but because the to-and-fro of philosophical conversation provides an alternative to a straightforward narrative structure. I suspect that this form is better suited than narrative to bring irony to light for a certain sort of reader.

Second, insofar as there is a narrative here, I do not think it is captured by the image of inside and outside. Rather, the image is of a form of life and a moment of breakdown *internal* to that form of life. So, to pursue an example from earlier discussion, as an inhabitant of Liberaldom I take myself to be concerned with human dignity.[1] Of course, it is Liberaldom itself that has instilled conceptions of human dignity in me—through education, acquaintance with the history of the culture's reflections on dignity, and its travails, the conflicted visions, the self-conscious variants, and so on. On the one hand, Liberaldom seeks to metabolize and contain reflections on human dignity; and yet, on the other hand, there is an instability within the form of life. My life with the concept of dignity suffers ironic disruption when, say, I make eye contact with a beggar.

I am interested in the case in which my own outbreak of ironic anxiety is symptomatic of the form of life I inhabit. The fact that *I* cannot go on—here and now—is not just an idiosyncratic psychological fact about me; it manifests an instability in the form of life's own commitments. We normally take a form of life's values to be manifest in its practices—in its implicit and explicit commitments, as well as in its reflections, constructions of history, and so on. On occasion, though, a form of life's values is revealed in a peculiar sort of breakdown, an inability to go on as usual. Sometimes they are revealed in broad-scale social phenomena—a society's inability to maintain its ways; but there can be occasions when the fact that *I* cannot go on in certain ways— with respect to human dignity, say—manifests an instability in the form of life. So, my own concern with respect for human dignity is a result of the form of life's having had its influence on me. My own ego ideal or superego is a psychic site where the form of life's value is lodged within me. Thus the anxious ironic disruption of normal superego and ego functioning may be symptomatic of an ideal's really mattering to me in ways that differ from my normal ways of expressing that an ideal really matters (via normal ego and superego forms). (See, for example, my discussion in the first lecture of the ways in which teaching matters to me. In that case, an intimation that the goodness of teaching outstrips my self-consious understanding up-ends my ability to go on as usual.) This anxious form of expressing what matters may be so unfamiliar to me that I do not self-consciously recognize it as an expression of things' mattering to me. Morevoer, my own travails psychically speaking may be emblematic of something going on in the form of life: that is, in my anxious irony I might *be* the form of life's instability manifesting itself. I may in some weird way be manifesting instability *on behalf of* the form of life. We see this on occasion in the anxious instabilities of certain artists, prophets, and other witnesses. The experience of irony may be possible because there is a certain instability in a master signifier that has been installed within me. We do not need to understand this in terms of the call of a Platonic Idea or even a Kantian idea: the signifier *human dignity* is manifesting its own instability. With irony, the instability has a peculiar form: anxious, uncanny longing. That is, my longing to respect human dignity is, in the moment, undermining my understanding of what it would be to do that. But, in a peculiar way, I manifest a commitment to the values of the form of life—in this case, by *not* being able to go along with them in their normal forms.

Anxious irony is an immanent form of longing for transcendence. We do not need to posit a metaphysical or transcendent form in order to understand the longing for transcendence. Nor do we even need to think of something coming "from outside." In the moment of anxious breakdown, it is precisely because the ironized category matters to me that I am detached from the ordinary worldly manifestations of that category. In the moment, those ordinary forms (however complex and sophisticated in themselves) feel wildly inadequate to the category, though I lack a sense of how to go on. In this sense, the experience of irony can serve as a prolegomenon to a more authentic engagement with the ironized category. The opportunity for a more authentic engagement may be taken up or declined, but in the moment of irony it is there in the form of *immanent* longing for transcendence.

Moran is concerned about simulacra, and so am I. He says he is "not sure just how we are to understand Lear's specific point that reflective judgment may serve to protect and preserve the anger or fear in question, for it seems to me that this is a general liability for *any* stance or procedure one may adopt with respect to some part of oneself, and is not restricted to a particular philosophy or therapeutic practice." He points out that Nietzschean genealogy can be used in the service of promoting an ascetic ideal, that Socratic elenchus can be deployed to preserve ignorance, and so on. And he concludes: "So while it may indeed be therapeutic in the ways Lear describes to cultivate a capacity for irony, this cultivation will be necessarily subject to these very same risks." These are important points; but there is something to be said in response.

The point about reflecting on one's anger is not that the situation is unique in having the pitfalls it happens to have, but that the example is particularly well suited for exposing the falsity of a familiar narrative about reflection. The mode is humorous self-recognition. It is not uncommon for us to recognize that we were at some earlier point deceived by our own resolutions. I recognize that I am angry with someone, realize that there are good reasons to get over it, and resolve to do so. My anger seems to go away. And then I find myself striking out at this person at some later time. Perhaps I am surprised; perhaps I am not all *that* surprised. Not all instances that have this structure are exactly alike. But in some cases, the very idea that reflection on my anger allows me to gain distance from it plays a role in my coming to think I have achieved such distance. Perhaps *that* is why I am spending so much time thinking about reflective distance!

§2. Uses and Misuses of Irony

Now when it comes to irony, I agree that there are all sorts of risks of misappropriation, misunderstanding, and misfire. Indeed, it has been one of the aims of these lectures to argue that the contemporary philosophical reception of irony has largely been off target. In that sense, irony is not a magic bullet. That being said, it is *also* true that, on certain occasions and when well deployed, irony can be of invaluable use in calling forms of living into question. It is not that it always does the trick; but when it does do the trick nothing else is likely to have been able to do it in its stead.

In the lectures, I distinguish *the experience of irony* from *the capacity for irony* and from *ironic existence*. It is only ironic existence that is a human virtue: it is a capacity for putting irony to excellent use in the living of a distinctively human life. Kierkegaard thought it occurred rarely: he took Socrates and himself to be exemplars. The experience of irony, by contrast, does not point in any particular direction. It is the outbreak of a particular species of anxiety—a species that it has been the aim of these lectures to articulate. It is true that, in its paradigm form, it is a manifestation of some principle, identity, or commitment mattering to me. It is an expression of pretense-transcendant aspiring. And yet, in itself, that is all it is. It *might* serve as an occasion for a deeper engagement with the ironically disrupted principle; it might serve as an occasion for a more authentic appropriation of my own identity. But it might not. It might be forgotten as soon as it's over. Or it might be an occasion for *flight* from irony.

To my eyes, that is what the contemporary cultural reception of irony looks like. The image of the "ironist" as someone who is detached from (the vulgarity of) commitment: this is a complacent ideal. There is a "knowingness" here that if only I can remain detached *nothing* is going to rattle me. This is irony-as-defense: the defense against getting rattled by one's own commitments. By contrast, the capacity for irony, as I understand it, is partially constituted by an openness to getting rattled by one's own commitments. A question I have is whether the contemporary cultural reception of irony is a motivated attempt to cover over the possibility of irony. One symptom, I suspect, is the tendency in the culture to treat irony as satire.

I have a similar concern with the contemporary philosophical interpretation of irony. As I discuss in the appendix on Rorty in the first lecture: his ironist is someone who remains metaphysically detached as she investigates the myriad cultural forms in which others have found a path to commitment. Ostensibly, this is a comforting image. The ironist so described is able to hold herself aloof from the unfounded dogmatism. On offer is a kind of *ataraxia*.

If we can only be ironists, our philosophical problems will be over. Instead, we can spend our time in "philosophy" as aesthetic discernment: making fine discriminations among positions, working out the arguments, enjoying the brilliance, laughing at the stupidity—all without risking the instability of commitment. Calling this ideal of detachment "irony" keeps from view the thought that anything is missing—the thought that there is a phenomenon that is getting left out of account, namely, irony.

All this is by way of saying, yes!—I agree with Moran that "irony" can be put to all sorts of uses.[2]

§3. The Therapeutic Stance

It now seems to me that Moran and I agree about a broad range of psychoanalytic phenomena and their relation to issues concerning self-knowledge. He is, I think, right that a fundamental form of access to one's own attitudes is to be had by focusing on the object of those attitudes. As he puts it, an excellent way to figure out whether I resent my sister is to think about my sister. And I certainly agree with him that the notion of "thinking about" is a "deliberately capacious notion" that "will vary greatly from context to context." And I accept his claim that he did not mean anything he said in his book *Authority and Estrangement* to exclude the psychoanalytic phenomena I discuss. So, *good!*

Still, there is a question of what a well-meaning reader might take away from *Authority and Estrangement*. I want to dwell on this for a moment—not to hold onto a disagreement with Moran, but because I think *Authority and Estrangement* provides the best articulation of a view that is prevalent in the psychotherapeutic profession. In *Authority and Estrangement,* Moran asks us to envisage a situation in which transparency fails: a person tries to reflect on whether she feels betrayed by a dead parent by reflecting on the parent, but she cannot settle the question in this way. Moran then *seems* to present us with a single alternative:

> She might become thoroughly convinced, both from the con-
> structions of the analyst as well as from her own appreciation of
> the evidence, that this attitude must indeed be attributed to her.
> And yet, at the same time, when she reflects on the world-directed
> question itself, whether she has indeed been betrayed by this per-

son, she may find that the answer is no or can't be settled one way or the other. So, transparency fails because she cannot learn of this attitude of hers by reflection on the object of that attitude. She can *only* learn of it in a fully theoretical manner, taking an empirical stance toward herself as a particular psychological subject.[3]

This passage seems to suggest an either/or: either transparent reflection on the worldly object of one's attitudes or taking up an empirical stance (perhaps with the encouragement and direction of one's analyst). It is this either/or that led me to say that Moran had not left room for the psychoanalytic phenomena that I think are crucial.[4]

This view is prevalent among nonpsychoanyytically-minded psychotherapists—and it contributes to the decline of interest in psychoanalysis. For if the alternative to ruminating on one's dead parent (in a transparent fashion) is taking an empirical stance toward oneself in a theoretical manner, why bother with all the time and effort of psychoanalysis? Why not just switch to cognitive behavioral therapy? It is faster, cheaper, and it can lead to modifications of behavior and self-conscious outlook—which are precisely the phenomena under review when one takes an empirical stance toward oneself. Psychoanalysis comes to seem like an extravagance of dubious value. In a sense, the profession is right: if the only routes to therapeutic insight are through transparent reflection on the people and events in one's life or through taking an empirical stance, then a lot of psychoanalytic technique does look like mumbo-jumbo. Why, for example, should the analyst spend so much time quiet, when she could be more active in helping the analysand come to an accurate empirical view of his situation? This stance can easily seem cold and remote, a shamanistic strategy to maintain power.

It is in the grip of this picture that therapists are led to talk too much. After all, if the analysand is stuck—if she cannot get to her feelings via transparent reflection—why not help her out with a construction based on the evidence? From this perspective, it seems churlish to keep silent if one has some insight. But, psychoanalytically speaking, we have no idea of what is involved in her becoming "thoroughly convinced" by the analyst's construction. And the problem is most difficult to detect when the analyst's construction is genuinely insightful and the analysand correctly sees that there are very good reasons to accept it. It is at such moments of insight and reasonableness that hidden dimensions get overlooked. For example, does she find the analyst's construction thoroughly convincing because, in fantasy, she is finally receiving advice from the dead father that she always longed for? Are the good reasons for the construction serving to cover over these nonrational forces at work? It is only when unconscious fantasy is taken seriously—its power to structure a life as well as the peculiarities necessarily involved in bringing it properly into view—that psychoanalytic practice can be justified. For the point of much psychoanalytic technique is to facilitate a process by which these fantastic forces come into view. By and large, this process requires abjuring constructions.

§4. Avowal, Expression, and Replacement

In my discussion of the expression of unconscious fantasy, I take inspiration from Wittgenstein's discussion of how the verbal expression of pain can replace its natural expression. Moran says, "I doubt that this thought of Wittgenstein's can be adopted in this way." I say: But I just *did* adopt it in this way![5] The aim of my account is not to give a detailed interpretation of Wittgenstein's reflections, but to take inspiration from them. The important question, then, is whether it is an illuminating adaptation. I think it is. Moran is right to insist on the heterogeneity of the phenomena under consideration. Indeed, I think the phenomena are far more heterogeneous than myriad examples he cites from Wittgenstein—which are all conscious phenomena.[6] As is well known, with psychotic patients, fantasies often take concrete, somatic forms.[7] I once had a patient who said to me, "Everything was all right until my life left me."[8] Had this been coming out of the mouth of a neurotic patient, it would have been a revealing slip of the tongue: perhaps his wife was metaphorically associated with the vibrancy of his life, and after she left, he became depressed. But for this psychotic patient things were more literal and concrete. He took his wife—her concrete, physical presence—to be the embodiment of his own life principle. It was as though his soul was located *over there,* in her. (Or: there was no firm conception of the boundary where he ended and she took up.) When she walked out on him he fell into a catatonic state and had to be taken to the hospital in an ambulance. It was days before he was able to regain any movement at all; and even after he became conscious, he could barely walk or speak. He could not organize himself in any effective way. So, yes, in coming to understand the value of expressing one's fantasies in words we do need to comprehend such heterogeneous phenomena as this person's coming to express his fantasy consciously in these words, rather than falling into catatonia. In using the term *replacement,* I did not mean to suggest a one-size-fits-all method, but rather a genus-category through which we could see a broad-scale similarity among myriad species of transformations—and transformations *for the better.*

One reason the image of replacement is useful is that humans are creatures who develop. The idea of development, as opposed to that of mere change, is teleologically organized. If we can understand certain types of response as coming to take the place of others along such a developmental trajectory, we can see that there is some value in the replacement. And if we can state in detail what that teleological trajectory is we can explain what the value of replacement is. I have elsewhere argued that if one looks at two of Freud's case studies—those of Dora and the Rat Man—one can see their emotional reactions as adults as resulting from a disruption of what should have been a developmental path of emotional life.[9] Their emotional lives were in various ways disrupted in childhood; and through the disruption the childish emotional strategies were preserved into (biological) adult life. Outbursts that can appear quite bizarre in the context of an adult life might be residues of infantile strategies for expressing fantasies and emotions. In *these* cases, at least, the development of the capacity to put the fantasies and emotions into words *might* be part of the process by which the (hitherto stalled) process of emotional development is resumed. In this sort of case, replacement would be of value because it would be a manifestation of the resumption of a teleologically organized process. Of course, one still needs to say what the teleological process is, why it is of value, and what the particular contribution of putting one's fantasies and emotions into words consists in. But I take it that insofar as human life is considered in terms of a developmental process, the final cause is human freedom. And I take it that *psychic freedom* is the formal and final cause of psychoanalysis: it is that which ought to structure psychoanalytic practice and be that toward which it aims. In saying that, though, I do not take myself to be doing more than gesturing in the direction in which an answer lies.[10] *Freedom* is functioning here as an open-ended signifier: we will come to know what it means as we come to answer the myriad questions of how to promote it.

Nevertheless, there are a number of points I make in the second lecture that, I think, point us in the right direction. First, there is a way of consciously expressing one's imaginative-emotional life, such that the fantasy is right there in the verbal expression that gives its content. In such a case, the verbal expression of the fantasy is the fantasy that it expresses. Psychically speaking, this is significantly different even from a sincere avowal that uses the very same words to ascribe exactly the same content to oneself and one's imaginative life. That is, it is possible for a person to avow sincerely that he is still angry at his dead father without thereby expressing his anger, in this special sense.[11] For such an avowal to occur the anger need not be *there*, informing the avowal itself. We need to understand better what this gap between consciously fantasizing and sincerely avowing a fantasy consists in. But even now, if one can see the possible gap that exists between avowal and expression—that is, not all avowals are expressions—then one can see that when it comes to the therapuetic potential of psychoanalysis this issue is not strictly about being able to put one's feelings or fantasies into words. Thus it is not, strictly speaking, about why putting one's feelings and fantasies into words should have a privileged position. It is, rather, about putting one's fantasies and feelings into words *in the right sort of way*. It concerns a peculiar form of verbal manifestation. Influenced by Wittgenstein, Finkelstein, and Moran, I have used the term "expression"; and in the second lecture I tried to give a preliminary indication of what this might mean when it comes to unconscious fantasies. This form opens up an unusual way to live with one's fantasies that should ultimately be understood as a manifestation of the freedom of self-consciousness. We are self-consciously intervening directly in the fantasy in a way that both promotes and manifests human freedom. Obviously, much more needs to be said about what this consists in. But I am convinced that it cannot be adequately grasped by our ordinary understanding of what it means to be self-consciously aware—and able to articulate verbally what our fantasies or emotions are. What we need to understand better is how this process opens up new possibilities for living, not simply through a better appreciation of what our possibilities are, but through a transformation of those possibilities via a direct, self-conscious intervention, in our imaginative life. In this peculiar case, the accurate verbal description of one's imaginative life can be an occasion for a practical transformation of its possibilities. This is possible not merely because one is putting one's imaginative life into words, but because one is putting one's imaginative life *into* words. Imaginative life, in this peculiar case, suffuses the words, and thus the self-conscious transformation of one's assessment will thereby be a transformation in the expression of the fantasy.

The second point I make in the lectures that is of particular relevance here: when the conscious expression of a fantasy concerns material that has hitherto been repressed (and thus unconscious), we should expect the material to come to light in the context of anxiety and disruption. The process of making the unconscious conscious—in the psychoanalytic understanding of those terms—is fraught, and is experienced as such. And since our fantasy life typically concerns the important figures in our lives, it should not be surprising that the process of making the unconscious conscious is often experienced as uncanny, anxious longing. Unconscious fantasies tend to be organized around important characters in one's life—albeit distorted by fantasy. It is difficult to capture the interplay between particularity and structure. On the one hand, a person will have very particular images of the peculiarities of *his own* mother, father, siblings, teachers, and friends. On the other hand, each will take up structural positions: as Mother, as Father, and so on. These internal figures are experienced as having uncanny authority with respect to *good* and *bad*. And yet they also seem to come with a historical account of the patient's early struggles with his own emerging sense of good and bad. And all of this is embedded in fantasies that include monsters, strange dark figures lurking outside doors, under beds, and, in my analytic experience, lots of cats. This all-in-the-family inner world seems to structure an unconscious sense of good and bad. Insofar as they have psychic influence, we can see how our conscious life with the categories of good and bad might be subject to uncanny disruption.

Third, psychoanalytic therapies tend in the direction of broad-scale subjective questions—from: Did my father love me? to Did my father abandon me? Did he betray me? leave me in the lurch? to What is it to have a father? What is it to be a child? What is it to grow up, to accept responsibility? and so on. All of these questions are ripe for irony—and the conditions of psychoanalysis are such that that ripeness is often brought to fruition. Psychoanalysis does facilitate ironic disruptions around life's most important questions. Obviously, this process can go astray in all sorts of ways. One can, for example, use the description I am giving here to construct an intellectualizing defense. One might go into one's analyst's office with the *theoretical* question: What is it to be a father, after all? Suffice it for the moment to say: that is not what I am talking about. I am interested in what it is for this question to come alive as anxious, uncanny longing, self-consciously recognized as such.

Thus I agree with Moran—and with the Wittgenstein he cites—in disavowing a general expressivist account of first-person discourse. The point I have been trying to make throughout the lectures and comments is that *there are sincere first-person avowals that do not count as expressions*. And I agree with Moran and Wittgenstein that "there are transitions. And the words 'I am afraid' may approximate more, or less, to being a cry. They may come quite close to this and also be *far* removed from it."[12] I am not sure what Moran means when he talks about "the transition from forms of self-expression that are more fully experienced to those that are less so." I do not take myself to be concerned with that. But I am concerned with the case in which in the utterance "I am afraid!" the fear is right there in the utterance. It is the presence of the fear *in* the utterance that gives it a certain similarity to a cry—*when,* that is, the fear is in the cry. There can, I think, be sincere cries of fear that are not themselves fearful cries. I accept that much more needs to be said about what this means, but I do not think it can be understood in terms of which expressions are more or less fully experienced.

Perhaps one way to focus the issue is to disagree with Moran in a way that might at first seem absurd. When it comes to practical identities and unconscious fantasies, Moran says, "No one, I take it, would want to say of either of these aspects of our lives that 'here the expression of doubt or uncertainty is senseless.'" Well, I do. Obviously, the expression of doubt or uncertainty will be always be possible when it comes to the large-scale structure and deeper meanings of fantasy life.[13] But, to take an example that is still ringing in my ears as I write this—a moment from an analytic session that occurred on the morning of writing this response: when the analysand exclaimed, "Who the fuck *was* my father?!" there is a sense in which the expression of doubt or uncertainty would have been senseless. In this case, the utterance was a cry: a cry of confusion and hurt. And I want to say that the hurt and confusion were right there in the utterance. In this case, the expression of doubt or uncertainty as to whether it was such a cry would have literally made no sense. That does not mean that there might not be other occasions—even in an analytic situation—when the analysand uses the same words, uses them sincerely and emotionally, and when the expression of doubt and uncertainty would make sense. But something similar is true of a cry of pain. The fact that there are occasions when it does make sense to express doubt or uncertainty about a cry of pain does not mean that there are not other occasions when the expression of doubt or uncertainty would make no sense.

7

Thoughts about Irony and Identity

Cora Diamond

My comments start from a very general claim that Jonathan Lear makes about our life with the concepts with which we understand ourselves. I wondered whether it applied to all the cases it was meant to cover. But my original answer to the question I was asking led to more questions than I have been able to answer. In the first section below, I give the question from which I started and what I took to be the answer. In the second and third sections, I give some reasons for thinking that that answer was too quick and simple. The fourth section approaches the issue from a different perspective, and shows that there were two distinct questions that I had failed to distinguish. One of my aims is to look further at the connection between the *Gorgias,* and the issues raised by Lear; and this is one of the topics of the fifth and final section.

§1. A Question and a First Answer

In the middle of the first lecture, Lear said that "it is constitutive of our life with the concepts with which we understand ourselves that they are subject to ironic disruption." Here I'd like to ask: Are there no concepts with which we understand ourselves which are not subject to disruption in the way Lear describes? My question can be asked in other ways. Are there any concepts with which we understand ourselves which are social pretense through and through? So that whatever aspiration is embedded in them, it is aspiration that remains within the realm of social pretense. Another possible way to get at the question would be to start with something Lear said just before the remark I quoted. He said that "developing a capacity for ironic disruption may be a manifestation of seriousness about one's practical identity." I'd like to ask: What about understandings of our practical identity that are unserious?—in the sense, that is, that there is no manifesting seriousness about *that sort* of identity through ironic disruption? Are there any practical identities that are, in his terms, left-hand only?

For an example of the sort of practical identity about which one might ask whether it is open to disruption in the way Lear describes, I shall look at Tolstoy's description of his attempt to become *un homme comme il faut.* In his late teens, he took being *comme il faut* to be, not just a great merit, an admirable quality, but "a necessary condition of life without which there could be no happiness, no glory, nor anything good in the world."[1] To make clearer how he had understood that identity, he considers someone who has successfully and apparently without any effort inhabited the identity throughout his life, dying and going to heaven. Asked in the next world who he was and what he had done down below, this man replies, *"Je fus un homme très comme il faut."* It is important to the story that even when he is dead the man speaks French. When Tolstoy much later wrote about his attempt to inhabit the identity of being *un homme comme il faut,* he took it to have an aspect of comic horror. But at the time, this was the identity through which he understood how he wanted to live.

Here one might ask whether the story does not merely show that Tolstoy attached great value to being *comme il faut.* The suggestion is that this is not the same as his actually having conceived his practical identity in such terms.[2] But my reason for choosing the example is that Tolstoy's language seems explicitly designed to push toward an understanding of the case in terms of practical identity, as comes out in the anecdote about the dead man who is asked to say who he was. That Tolstoy took being *un homme comme il faut* to be a practical identity emerges also in Henri Troyat's account of this period in Tolstoy's life. Being someone who is *comme il faut* is a possibility for Tolstoy that takes the place of seeing his life in terms of being a scholar, a poet, or a soldier; it is a practical identity that one can inhabit or try to inhabit as one might that of scholar, poet, or soldier. A further consideration is the resemblance between the concept of *l'homme comme il faut* and that of the dandy, where the latter is more clearly a concept of a practical identity. Dandyism is a complicated phenomenon, and there are differences between the dandy and *l'homme comme il faut*. But both practical identities involve the production of a social self-appearance of elegance and refinement, while the effort that goes into the production of that appearance is hidden from view. There are numerous varieties of practical identities of this general sort, involving this or that social appearance (which may leave more or less room for the development and expression of one's own tastes) and the performance of one or another style of social ease and elegance or anti-elegance (expressive of authenticity or rejection of bourgeois conventionality). The successful inhabitor of such an identity has a knack for *getting it right*. So, for example, the indie guy gets which thrift-store jeans are right and which aren't, and the *homme comme il faut* whom Tolstoy wanted to be gets which boots are absolutely correct. I am not suggesting, about the kinds of practical identity with which I am concerned, that they involve accepting what others take to be cool or hip or *comme il faut;* someone may, say by wearing some sort of shoes, *set* what is only then recognized to be cool. And that may be the intention with which the shoes were worn. My talk of "getting it right" anyway doesn't quite get things right, doesn't get the complex way in which rightness plays into the enacting of these identities. See, for example, the remark of Stringham to Templer (in *A Question of Upbringing*): "If you're not careful you will suffer the awful fate of the man who always knows the right clothes to wear and the right shop to buy them at." He will be snubbed for his vulgarity. There is an irony here that remains within the realm of social pretense: wearing the right clothes isn't wearing the right clothes.[3]

Someone might suggest that what Lear says about the possible ironic disruption of other practical identities holds also of the practical identity of being someone *comme il faut*. The suggestion would be that we might put weight on the place of the verb *falloir,* what is necessary, in the concept of *comme il faut*. Thus the idea is that the concept of being *how one has to be,* or of what is proper, might open up, as it were; the idea is that one might suddenly cease to know at all *how one must be,* or what it might be to move in the direction of being as one has to be. But what would ironic questioning be like in this case?

Might we ask: "Of those who are *comme il faut,* is anyone *comme il faut?*" But imagine Tolstoy asking this. Does he ask in French? Speaking correct and elegant French is part of being *comme il faut,* as Tolstoy had thought of it. So, if Tolstoy asks in French, "Of those who are *comme il faut,* is anyone *comme il faut?*," the very asking of the question in French marks it as a question that attends to social pretense and does not disrupt it. If it is asked in Russian, it may indeed remain within the realm of social pretense. The question might, however, reach beyond social pretense—but without opening up the practical identity of being *comme il faut.* It may, that is, open up a question about how to live, about living as a human being, without assistance (as it were) from aspiration embedded in the concept of *comme il faut.*

The question I am asking is whether practical identities of the sort I've mentioned are significantly unlike the practical identities that work so well as examples for Lear—those of politician, teacher, Christian, rhetorician, student, doctor, shepherd, wise person. In each of these cases the experience of irony can disrupt the social pretense associated with the identity, and leave one utterly without the sense one had had that living with that identity was available to one, that one knew what it involved. In each case, there is a kind of aspiration associated with the practical identity, where the aspiration goes beyond anything available within the realm of social pretense, including within that realm the variety of ways in which the social pretense itself can be modified and criticized and can develop new forms. Are there understandings of human excellence that are very different, though? I do want to emphasize that the sort of practical identities that I have in mind are (at least sometimes) understandings of human excellence. Certainly the teenage Tolstoy, as he later described himself, saw being perfectly *comme il faut* as human excellence, that on which true happiness depended. But then is it possible for conceptions of human excellence to be so tied to social pretense that they are not disruptable by irony *in the way Lear describes?* Let me try to put the question differently, in terms of a contrast between two ways in which ironic disruption might work. In the case of the teacher, the ironic disruption of practical identity as a teacher leaves the person utterly without any kind of idea what it is *to be a teacher;* whereas the ironic disruption of Tolstoy's understanding of human excellence as being perfectly *comme il faut* might be, not a sense that one had no idea what it really was *to be comme il faut,* but rather a sense that truly realizing being human could not be understood as being *comme il faut and* one had no idea what it was instead. What ironic disruption of the practical identity of being *comme il faut* brings out, then, is that whatever aspiration there might have been in taking being perfectly *comme il faut* to be human excellence, so far as the aspiration transcends social pretense, it is not an aspiration understandable as tied to being *comme il faut at all. Truly realizing being human* and *becoming très comme il faut* come apart in the interrogation by ironic disruption.

There are three points I should make, to clarify how I am approaching Lear's ideas.

A. In a note about "aesthetic" existence in his first lecture, Lear says that it is "a life organized around appearances: how things appear, seem, are given to one." He adds that the aesthetic "is the world of social pretense, the world of practical identity understood in terms of social role" (To Become Human, note. 45). There are very different ways in which a life might be said to be "organized around appearances," and that expression can cover very different sorts of practical identities. The identities that I have particularly in view, which I call identities of social appearance, are unlike identities understood in terms of social roles like that of the teacher, doctor, or politician, or other social roles like that of parent, spouse, or student. Tolstoy's criticism of the practical identity of *l'homme comme il faut* includes this: that the person who thinks of himself as such thinks it is quite sufficient; he need not have any social role in the usual sense: he needn't be an official, a teacher, a carriage-maker, a soldier, or anything else. It is enough for him to live elegantly; he needn't actually do anything. Lear's phrase "a life organized around appearances" can be used so that it includes at least two different sorts of practical identities: those which are understood in terms of social roles like that of teacher or parent or soldier or student, and those in which the production of a self-appearance worthy of esteem is the whole point. While there is no reason why "social role" should not also be given a use in connection with such cases, what is meant by it in reference to them would be quite different. Indeed, critics of the sorts of practical identities that I called identities of social appearance have often phrased their criticisms in terms of the failure of those with such identities to take part in "the world's work." The practical identity of the Christian, a central example for Kierkegaard and for Lear, has significant differences from practical identities like that of the teacher and doctor and also from practical identities of social appearance, like that of the dandy and *l'homme comme il faut*. And there are other sorts of practical identity, with differences from all those I have mentioned, including those of friend and lover. There isn't any general model of how a life may be "organized around appearances." I return to the distinctions touched on in this paragraph in section 4, but I do not consider further any practical identities other than those like the teacher and the doctor on the one hand, and those like *l'homme comme il faut* on the other.

B. Even in a case in which we may speak of two people who inhabit the "same" practical identity, there may be great differences in what this comes to, within the realm of social pretense and beyond it as well. Thus, for example, even if we speak of two people both of whom might be described as having, as their practical identity, that of the *gentleman*, they may differ both in what they take to be the social pretense of that identity and in what aspirations might be embedded in it. What might be involved in the disruption of such an identity by irony may be quite different in the two cases.

C. Some remarks that Lear made a few years ago are connected with my question. In his book *Freud*, he discussed living a life keeping up with the fashions of the day.[4] Although a person living such a life may think of it as a good way to live, Lear says that we should not assume that the "elusive" question "How should one live?" has in fact been raised by the person. But, as far as I can see, Lear did not think that the case would necessarily be different for someone whose practical identity was that of a teacher; for such a person, too, the question "How should one live?" may not arise. While there is an important contrast between the case of someone for whom the question arises and that of someone for whom it does not arise, the contrast that I have been developing here is different. My contrast is between two kinds of ways in which practical identity may be ironically disrupted, a contrast that depends upon the underlying differences between the case of inhabiting a practical identity like that of the teacher and that of inhabiting a practical identity like that of *l'homme comme il faut*.[5] One aim of the rest of this chapter is to make these differences clearer. It is worth pointing out here that the kinds of cases I have been considering, while they include people who live a life keeping up with fashion, also include people who are not keeping up with fashion but whose relation to dress is far more complex. Beau Brummel is an obvious sort of case. However one understands his sort of dandyism, it was not a matter of keeping up with what was fashionable. I shall return to this point in section three.

§2. Two Sorts of Rhetorician

In this section I look at the argument of the *Gorgias*. I shall suggest that the treatment of the rhetorician by Socrates can be seen to raise doubts about my argument in section 1. But I shall begin my account with some of the things Lear says about the "fundamental ironic question" of Kierkegaard. This fundamental ironic question is given by Lear in two forms: "In all of Christendom, is there a Christian?" and "Among all Christians, is there a Christian?" This is the question that can be taken to open up a gap between social pretense (as made available in a social practice) and an aspiration that transcends the practice. In section 4 of his first Tanner lecture, Lear notes that Kierkegaard's inspiration comes from Plato's Socrates, and that ironic questioning of the sort expressed by Kierkegaard can be seen in the dialogues. Several of his examples come from the *Gorgias*. The example to which I want particularly to draw attention comes from *Gorgias* 502d–504a. Lear puts the Socratic question this way: "Among all rhetoricians, is there a single rhetorician?" Here is Lear's comment on Socrates' answer to the question:

> His answer again is that no one who puts himself forward, or anyone so reputed from earlier times, has been engaged in anything more than shameful flattery and gratification. (503a–d) The true rhetorician looks to the structure and form of the soul, and crafts his speech so as to lead souls toward virtue and away from vice (504d–e, 503e–504a). Plato's implication is that if there is a single rhetorician in all of Athens, it is Socrates.

In this part of the *Gorgias,* Socrates holds that there are two kinds of rhetoric, and the good rhetorician will seek to bring righteousness and other virtues to birth in the souls of his fellow citizens. What is striking about the parts of the *Gorgias* to which Lear refers is the contrast with earlier parts of the dialogue, where Socrates, in conversation with Polus, had spoken as if there were not any kind of rhetoric other than that which engages in shameful flattery and gratification (462–466). In this part of the dialogue, rhetoric is said by Socrates to be to the soul what cookery is to the body: the practitioners of rhetoric and cookery have enough empirical know-how to provide pleasure to the consumers of what they purvey. There is a condition of soul which gives the appearance of health, just as there are bodily conditions in which there is the appearance of health. The pseudo-art of cooking gives us pleasant things to eat, but does not provide what is genuinely nourishing, and the trickery and gimmickry of rhetoric also provide pleasure but not what nourishes the soul. Rhetoric, Socrates tells us, is dishonorable; and in this part of the dialogue, we are not told anything about there being a good as well as a bad sort of rhetoric. It is possible, after reading the latter part of the dialogue, in which Socrates allows for a good and a bad sort of rhetoric, to reread the conversation with Polus, and to see points at which Socrates can be read as allowing that his account of rhetoric might be challenged, but the dramatic character of the dialogue requires that in this part of the conversation he give an apparently straightforward condemnation of rhetoric as manipulative flattery.

When Socrates, speaking to Callicles, distinguishes true rhetoric from the rhetoric which is mere flattery, he adds that Callicles hasn't ever seen the genuine variety. We can say, then, that Socrates' description of rhetoric, earlier in the dialogue, as just plain dishonorable, just plain flattery, just plain purveying of gratification, was meant to apply simply to rhetoric as it is generally experienced. That's why it was possible to characterize it as like cooking in being concerned with the production of appearances, of what merely pretends to be good for one. The existence, then, of rhetoric as we are familiar with it in experience (and as it is described by Socrates in speaking to Polus), as concerned with flattery and gratification, leaves it open for Socrates to give a transformed account of rhetoric later in the dialogue, in terms of a contrast between such rhetoric and true rhetoric, about the latter of which it can be asked whether there is any exemplar.[6]

Might one then suggest that my account in section 1 of practical identities like that of *l'homme comme il faut* resembles Socrates' account of rhetoric in the conversation with Polus? I argued that such identities were social pretense through and through, and that whatever aspiration is embedded in them is aspiration that remains within the realm of social pretense. While such identities can (I argued) be disrupted by ironic questioning, the result of such questioning would be, not that one loses any sense that one knows what it is to inhabit that identity (as in Lear's description of ironic disruption of the practical identity of *teacher*), but rather that one is thrown out of the sense that *that is one's practical identity*. To suggest that my account of such identities resembles Socrates' account of rhetoric at *Gorgias* 462–466 is to suggest two things: (1) that my account is based entirely on cases of which we have experience, and fits those cases, in the way that Socrates' description of rhetoric in conversation with Polus fits the cases of rhetoric which we come across in experience; and (2) that there is room for a distinction between the kinds of cases that I focused on and deeply contrasting cases, just as there is room for a distinction between the kind of cases of rhetoric with which we are familiar in experience and true rhetoric, which is the distinction Socrates makes in speaking of rhetoric to Callicles. So even if my argument in section 1 is correct for the cases that I had in mind, it is at least worth considering whether I was leaving out a vital kind of case which my argument would not fit, a kind of case the existence of which I did not see.

Let me put my question another way. There are some profound transformations of thought to which the *Gorgias* can lead the reader. But the dialogue has been read and read; it is no longer new. It no longer takes us anywhere unsuspected, because we are quite familiar with where it takes us. If it was ever possible for us to be startled at the idea of rhetoric's being wholly unlike rhetoric as we have seen it, it isn't any more. But if we think our way back to the point at which it *takes a lot* to imagine rhetoric as being something quite other than everything that Polus, Gorgias, and Callicles, and we ourselves, have seen, then maybe it is possible also to think of being *comme il faut* (say) as being quite other than what I have described it as being; maybe it is possible to think of it as being quite other than what we have seen it to be. This would be a transformation as unexpected as the transformation of thought about rhetoric that Socrates carries out in conversation with Callicles. And so the criticism that I am working toward of my argument in section 1 is that in that section I am wholly unaware of the possibility of such a transformation. I remain stuck with an understanding of practical identities like that of *l'homme comme il faut* based entirely on what one comes across in experience and in stories (like Tolstoy's account of his youth) based on experience. If we recognize that it is quite weird to suggest that Socrates is the only rhetorician in Athens, we can perhaps contemplate the possibility of things equally weird, as would be (say) the possibility that he is the only *homme comme il faut* in Athens. (That Socrates does not behave as a well-bred person would be expected to is in fact clear at several points; he gives the conversation with Gorgias a turn that can be described as "boorish" (461), and with Callicles (494) he brings up things that are too disgusting to be the subject of polite conversation). Within the context of Lear's understanding of irony, what makes possible the idea that being a rhetorician may be quite different from what it has always been in our experience is that there is an aspiration that transcends the social realm embedded in the identity of the rhetorician. If there is indeed a possibility of understanding what it is to be *un homme comme il faut* totally differently from the way it has been understood, that would depend upon there being an aspiration embedded in such a practical identity, an aspiration going beyond social pretense. If the *Gorgias* invites us not to dismiss the possibility of such an aspiration in the case of the rhetorician, we may learn from it that we should not dismiss too easily the possibility of such an aspiration embodied in the practical identity of *l'homme comme il faut*.

My argument in section 2 has consisted largely in the claim that I may well have overlooked a significant sort of possibility in section 1, but it hardly makes clear what grounds there might be for taking such a possibility to be more than merely not positively ruled out. In section 3, I give further reasons for thinking that I overlooked important possibilities in section 1; I start by going back to Tolstoy's account of his desire to be *un homme comme il faut*.

§3. Anxieties and Aspirations

Tolstoy's description of the period during which he desired more than anything to be *un homme comme il faut* is highly comic, as he lays out for the reader his combination of contempt for everyone who is not *comme il faut* and his recognition of the inadequacy of his own attempts to become *comme il faut*. We see him surreptitiously working away at his French, trying to get his nails cut in the desired shape, practicing dance steps or the control of eye movements as he bows, and attempting to develop the necessary air of indifference to everything. He is envious of others who seem to have it all down without apparent effort, and makes the mistake of actually asking one of his brother's friends how he gets his nails to their fine elegant shape. This distinctive kind of anxiety about being *comme il faut* is reflected in the existence of handbooks for those who want to become *comme il faut*. Recent writers on such handbooks take the readership to have been the growing bourgeoisie of the nineteenth century. The books may indeed have been bought by members of the bourgeoisie, but accounts like Tolstoy's show that the anxieties that provided a readership for the books could afflict adolescents regardless of whether they were or weren't members of the aristocracy, and could afflict Russians because they weren't French.

While such handbooks were meant to enable their readers to achieve a kind of social identity, no handbook could really do this. For one thing, the natural capacities involved are very unequally distributed—a point that Tolstoy is evidently aware of and that some of the handbooks state quite explicitly. They further make clear that a kind of individuality was essential to the man of smart society, and that merely mastering the conventions cannot make one into a person of any social distinction.[7] Disdain for the vulgar includes disdain for those who, in attempting to be *comme il faut,* manage to be nothing more than just like everyone else with the same ambitions. A striking expression of this contempt can be found even years after Tolstoy had (to his own satisfaction) abandoned his earlier desire to become *un homme comme il faut.* In *The Death of Ivan Ilyich,* Ivan Ilyich picks out for his house antiques that he considers to be particularly *comme il faut;* and although Ivan Ilyich is very happy with the result, Tolstoy allows himself a sneer at the furnishings as merely what is typical for middling people trying to look rich. Far from being genuinely smart, the furnishings are just what people of that class "have in order to resemble other people of that class."[8] Tolstoy's judgment here is entirely from within the standards of the kind of man he once wanted to be. The whole range of practical identities with which I am concerned, identities of one or another kind of smart or cool or elegant or anti-elegant social appearance, share with the identity of *l'homme* or *la femme comme il faut* a particular combination of features: (1) one can attempt to inhabit the identity by doing as those do who seem obviously and easily to inhabit the identity, and (2) there is nevertheless an insistence that really to inhabit the identity cannot be a matter of doing as others do, but must come from oneself, one's own instincts, desires, loves, and hates. If you are enacting a self that is to be seen, appreciated, admired, and envied, you are not going to be successful if what you appear to be is a copy of everyone else. The dandy and the scenester (to take two very different examples) have in common a contempt for what is merely conventional in the societies around them, but equally for what has become conventional in those attempting to exhibit those identities. (One form which such contempt takes is that forms of uncool can come to be the new cool, since it is only by distance from what has counted as cool that one can be cool.)

I have laid out these features of identities of social appearance in order to bring out that people can have quite different relations to such identities. Tolstoy's relation to being *un homme comme il faut* is just one possibility: of anxiety and desire, a sense that one hasn't *got* it as those around one seem to have, that one hasn't picked it up as they have and doesn't know how to do so. Then there are those who, unlike Tolstoy, have got it all, but have got it just a little too well. There is the quite different relation to that identity of someone who actually buys and attempts to put into practice the rules of a handbook to being *un homme comme il faut*. There is again the relation to the identity of someone who has indeed picked it up quite brilliantly from those around him. Although there is not a wrong note in his performance, he feels nevertheless alienated from the identity: it is all for him a matter of his own clever mimicry, and is not real. And then there are those who shape the identity by their own talents and instincts, who inhabit the identity, or seem to do so, with an unselfconscious ease; in some cases at least one might say that the particularity of their being makes or seems to make their version of the identity a kind of revelation of human possibility. It seems plain that I was oversimplifying in section 1 in suggesting that, whatever aspirations may be embedded in identities of social appearance, the aspirations remain within the realm of social pretense. Contrary to what I said, it is not obvious what aspirations may be embedded in such identities. The recognition of the variety of ways in which someone may stand to such an identity makes clear that no simple generalization can be drawn about what aspirations the identity may or may not have embedded in it.

There is an argument by Harry Berger Jr. that will help me to make the point in a different way. His argument is made with reference to Castiglione's *The Book of the Courtier* and those to whom it is addressed, but I shall rephrase it as an argument about Tolstoy's adolescent self and his desire to be a member of the circle of those who count (in comparison with all the rest of humanity)—the community, as it were, of the *comme il faut*. With the wording slightly changed to fit that context, here is a question that I have taken from Berger: "Doesn't such a community cast about itself a permanent shadow of representation anxiety? Can it avoid being haunted by its construction and representation of the unrepresented—by the specter of an unrepresented community of hidden and less worthy selves that its commitment to the culture of *comme il faut* conjures up?"[9] Tolstoy's anxiety about his own "less worthy self" is in fact hardly unrepresented, to himself anyway; it is enacted all too well in his attempts at dancing better, conversing in more elegant French, cutting his nails right, and so on. But the point about the spectral selves that haunt the culture of *le comme il faut* is that it enables us to see in the culture an aspiration that does not have to be taken to lie entirely at the level of social pretense. The sense of a "less than worthy" self leaves unsettled what it would be for the self to be *worthy*. There is here no way to rule out aspirations that may be quite inchoate but that implicitly transcend social pretense.

Astonishingly successful performances of identities of social appearance, like that of Beau Brummell, and notably anxious and hapless performances of such identities, like that of the narrator of Tolstoy's *Youth*, in different ways bring out the impossibility of generalizing about the aspirations embedded in such identities.

§4. Knowing How to Live

The modes of behavior of people in fashionable society may be learned to some degree from handbooks, or may be picked up by the young from relatives and friends and others whom they are in a position to observe or who intend to teach the behavior, just as methods of cooking food may be learned to some degree from cookery books, or may be picked up from relatives and others whom one is in a position to observe or whom one assists, or from those who teach cooking. In the *Gorgias*, Socrates characterizes cookery as not a *technē* but an empirically based know-how. It would be irrelevant whether the know-how were picked up by trial and error, by apprenticeship, by observation of accomplished cooks, or by reading cookery books. If we imagine how the capacities exhibited by *un homme comme il faut* would look from the point of view of the Socrates of the *Gorgias*, it seems that they would similarly constitute an empirical know-how, not a *technê*, irrespective of how the capacities have been picked up. Someone who has the capacities is admired and accepted in smart society, envied and imitated. But from the point of view of the *Gorgias,* the important thing to note would be that the esteem given to such people resembles the esteem given to pastry chefs by those who lack any sense of what is genuinely wholesome food. Tolstoy's admiration for the apparently effortless elegance of his brother's friend Dubkov would thus be similar to the admiration that children (or those with no more sense than children) have for the splendid productions of a pastry cook, but what such admiration shows (according to Socrates in the *Gorgias*) is how easily we can be caught by the trickeries of those who produce a kind of illusion of good.

If we consider the empirical know-how of *comme il faut,* its value to someone who (like the young Tolstoy) seeks it is not simply that it makes possible the kind of elegance demonstrated by the Dubkovs of the world but also that it establishes one's distance from everyone who doesn't count. Tolstoy had himself taken there to be a fundamental division of mankind into those who were *comme il faut* and those who were not. The latter he despised; and despite the inadequacy of his own efforts at becoming *comme il faut,* he took only those who were *comme il faut* to be worthy of being on terms of equality with himself. In section 1, I quoted Tolstoy on being *comme il faut* as a necessary condition of any genuine goods in life. Those on the wrong side of the line between those who count and those who don't were distinguished not only by their vulgarity and ineptitude, but also by their lives themselves' being (as Tolstoy thought) hardly human. Life as it is meant to be lived *is* life as lived in smart society. Thus what is needed in order to become *comme il faut* can be identified with *l'art de vivre.*[10] The connection comes out, for example, if one considers *eating.* What it is to know how to eat (what is involved in that part of *l'art de vivre*) can be taken to be knowing how to eat in a way that does justice to the high idea of one's own social value, that puts into view one's tastes and habits, one's delicacies of appreciation, or one's disdain for what is generally or vulgarly taken to be good. While expressions like *l'art de vivre* and *savoir-vivre* have some uses in which they are quite narrowly limited, the latter often being used simply to mean good manners, the background idea is of good society as the site of *living.* What I have spoken of as practical identities of social appearance are identities in which one shows how splendidly one knows how to live, and with what ease one does so. The process through which one comes to inhabit such an identity gives one, or seems to, "access to everything which defines those human beings who are truly human."[11]

My argument in this section has been intended to lead back to the beginning of Lear's first lecture, where he speaks of "becoming human" as a difficult task. I've suggested that the difficult task of becoming human may, in some forms of thought, be identified with the task of living well in smart society, the task of living elegantly, of becoming *un homme* or *une femme comme il faut*. But, if that is true, it reveals the mistake I was making in section 1. For, if inhabiting a practical identity like that of *l'homme comme il faut* enables one, or seems to enable one, to *become truly human*, then I was quite wrong in suggesting that such identities do not have embedded in them an aspiration that implicitly transcends social pretense, for the aspiration to *become truly human* can be taken to transcend social pretense. The same point comes out if one considers another remark of Lear's from his introductory discussion of irony. Irony, he says, is a form of not being perfectly sure about being human—an insecurity about being human. This insecurity, he adds, is at one and the same time constitutive of being human and yet embodied, in Athens, only by Socrates. I have tried to bring out in section 3 Tolstoy's anxiety about becoming *comme il faut*. So far as the task of "becoming human" has been, for Tolstoy, identified with that of living as those do who are entitled to be members of smart society, anxiety about his ability to do so is the expression of what Lear describes as the insecurity about being human that is constitutive of being human. The idea I mentioned in section 3, of the "community of the *comme il faut*" as haunted by the excluded unworthy selves, expresses the same insecurity about being human.

In section 1, I raised two questions that I failed to see were quite distinct: whether there are practical identities that do not have embedded in them any aspiration that goes beyond social pretense, and whether there are practical identities that, if disruptable by irony, are not so in the way Lear describes. I have tried to show in this section that identities of social appearance can be taken to have embedded in them an aspiration that implicitly goes beyond social pretense, the aspiration to *become human*. But this does not mean that Lear's description of ironic disruption fits these identities. Their difference from identities like that of teacher or doctor comes out in various ways.

In the case of someone whose practical identity is that of a teacher, irony (as Lear describes it) opens up for her the question of what it is *to be a teacher*, where that question reaches beyond social pretense. The difficult task of *becoming human* can for her take the form of the difficult task of *becoming a teacher*—a task that confronts her without her knowing what it involves. But the task depends upon her aspiration *to be a teacher*, which does not lie entirely within the realm of social pretense. Even within the realm of social pretense, the conception of what it is to be a teacher involves some understanding of what teachers do, what they aim at, distinct from simply producing some appearance of being a superior sort of person. This is what makes it possible for her to have an aspiration of which it is true both that it goes beyond the realm of social pretense *and* that it is not barely the aspiration to *become human*. I have suggested that, in the contrasting sort of case, that of the practical identities of social appearance, there may well be an embedded aspiration that transcends the realm of social pretense, but, if so, the aspiration is nothing but the aspiration to *become human*. If the practical identity of the teacher provides a kind of content to the embedded aspiration, so that it is not barely the aspiration to become human, the practical identity of *l'homme comme il faut* provides no such content, since there is nothing to it within the realm of social pretense but an enacting of an appearance of human excellence. A fine example is that of Gilbert Osmond in James's *The Portrait of a Lady*. Osmond's pretensions to being a superior sort of human being are all there is; he has never done anything.[12] Identities of social appearance do not tie the aspiration to become human to any form of human activity with anything to it beyond appearance. And indeed the idea that the dandy or *l'homme comme il faut* or the Victorian aesthete doesn't actually *do* anything beyond the enacting of superiority is the basis of much of the criticism directed toward them, as is clear in Tolstoy's later discussion of his own case, the criticisms of Osmond expressed by other characters in *The Portrait of a Lady*, and Carlyle's criticism of the dandy.[13]

A further important difference between identities of social appearance and the identities that Lear uses as his examples comes out if one considers the significance of apparent ease, indifference, nonchalance, *disinvoltura*, or cool in identities of social appearance. In the case of the practical identities that Lear takes as examples, irony introduces a form of ignorance, of not-knowing, into one's understanding of what it is to inhabit the identity in question. But, in the

case of the practical identities of social appearance, what irony does is intro-
duce a form of insecurity into one's relation to the identity in question. Irony
undercuts the *ease* that is an essential element of the performance of these
identities. The title of Lear's first lecture is 'Becoming human does not come
that easily'; whereas the performance of any of the identities of social appearance is a performance of ease-in-being-truly-human. Irony, Lear says, is a form
of insecurity about being human; and irony is thus in a sense at war with the
varieties of nonchalance, elegant *désinvolture,* and cool that, for the possessors
of these identities, show or are meant to show how far they are from any such
insecurity.[14] Such insecurity belongs only to a banished or excluded self; and
here we see the connection with Lear's description of the uncanniness of
ironic experience as a matter of *me* coming back to haunt myself.

There is an astonishing portrayal of such insecurity in *The Portrait of a
Lady,* in the great scene in which Isabel Archer, Mrs. Osmond, reflects on the
character of her husband. Osmond's practical identity is, as one might put it,
that of *a perfectly unvulgar man.* He takes himself to be a greatly superior person; he has "a sovereign contempt for every one but some three or four very
exalted people whom he envied"; and the people whom he envies are those
with absolute power, owed consideration by everyone, like the tsar of Russia
and the sultan of Turkey. He has, apparently perfectly, the appearance of noble indifference to any small considerations; he has been able, with apparent
ease, to dispense with "the usual aids to success." But Isabel comes to see
that, although Osmond is contemptuous of the rest of the world, of those
who lack his refinement and taste, he actually has them always in view. His
relations to them, though, are in no way a matter of his enabling them to
become more enlightened, to share his refined tastes, to redeem themselves.
His fundamental relation to the world of which he is contemptuous is his
need to extract from it a recognition of his own superiority. It is, on his view,
despicable; but in reality he seeks its favor, fawns on it, takes from it the only
standard he has. There is in reality no one who is less indifferent to what the
world thinks; the certainty of his own superiority is actually entirely hollow.[15]
So far as irony brings to awareness the insecurity that can be seen in such
practical identities, it directly challenges the confident superiority that is essential to their social pretense. (In describing the passage from *The Portrait of
a Lady,* I have tried to make open to view the partial parallel with some parts

of Socrates' dispute with Callicles, a parallel that may have been intended. Callicles is contemptuous of the lowlifes who supposedly form a majority of mankind, contemptuous of the rabble of nondescripts in the state. But Socrates argues that Callicles' desire for political power puts him in the position of having to fawn on the populace. He must at least put himself forward in ways that will please exactly that "rabble" whose favor he needs. He must have them continually in view, just as Osmond has continually in view the base, ignoble world to which he takes himself to be superior. The fawning desire to please those for whom one has contempt reveals the emptiness of the pretense of self-confident superiority.[16]

§5. Conclusions and Further Questions: The Manly Man and *l'homme comme il faut*

I framed my original question in several ways. It turned out to be two questions, to only one of which I have given a definite answer. (1) The answer to the question "Are there practical identities that are unlike those which Lear uses as examples?" is yes. The ironic disruption of the practical identity of the teacher puts forcefully before the person who has taken this to be her identity the question what it is *to be a teacher;* the ironic disruption of the practical identity of *l'homme comme il faut* puts forcefully before the person who has taken this to be his identity the question what it is *to be human,* what it is *to live a human life.* Ironic disruption of this practical identity includes recognition that the ideal to which he takes himself to have been committed is not, as he had thought, that of the perfect appearance of *comme il faut.* He had, as it were, mis-seen what becoming human was, had seen it in a perfection of social appearance. (2) The second question was whether there are practical identities that do not have embedded in them an aspiration that transcends the realm of social pretense. My argument that practical identities of social appearance do not have such an aspiration embedded in them was faulty. But that doesn't settle the question whether there are any other sorts of practical identity that do not have embedded in them an aspiration going beyond social pretense; here I can only note that I haven't answered it.

My argument that the practical identity of *l'homme comme il faut* can be taken to have embedded within it the aspiration to become human allows me to return to the weird idea, mooted in section 2, of taking Socrates to be the only *homme comme il faut* in Athens, despite his apparently being in all sorts of ways *comme il ne faut pas*. (This is not unlike the idea that Socrates, who is—as he himself says, 473e—no politician, is one of the few Athenians who is genuinely a politician; see 521d.) To say of Socrates that he is really *comme il faut*, despite his evident inelegance, would be to take his ironic existence as a form of human excellence. It is to see his philosophical activity as a form of engagement with the aspiration to become human, and to take such an aspiration to be embedded in the practical identity of *comme il faut*. But does that not involve a kind of equivocation on what is meant by *"comme il faut"*, a switch from a Tolstoyan sort of understanding in terms of social grace and polish, and social ease, to an understanding in terms of what it is genuinely necessary to be? That question lies at the heart of an objection raised by James Doyle.[17] A brief account of his objection and of how it might be answered will, I hope, clarify my argument.[18]

Doyle sees my argument as working this way: the category of *l'homme comme il faut* can be subjected to ironic interrogation, which would lead to a genuine raising of the question how to live; but then how (Doyle asks) can this work? If one were to ask, "Of all those who want to be *hommes comme il faut*—all those who take the question how to live and make it a question of superficial matters of style—are there any who are successful in doing this?" that will hardly raise the Socratic question how to live. How, then, he asks, might one try to find a route from the category of the *comme il faut* to the raising of the Socratic question? Reflection on the *expression comme il faut* might lead one to ask what it is really necessary for a person to be like; and, asked in the right way, this could indeed be a raising of the Socratic question. But the problem, Dolye notes, is that this route to the Socratic question proceeds (so it seems) by what Aristotle would call *mere homonymy*: "The expression *comme il faut* as it occurs in the expression *homme comme il faut* means something very different from what it must be made to mean if it is to lead us to a Socratic investigation via some thought along the lines of, 'But, now, *comment est-ce qu'il vraiment faut être, pour être homme?*'" The argument from homonymy here is powerful, and Doyle backs it up by noting that the concept of *comme il faut* "has its home in a world of pure social pretense" and by asking whether even a Tolstoy "could have made ethical progress as well by a creative refinement of his ambition to be an *homme comme il faut*, as by his abandonment of it."

In response to that line of argument, I'd want to focus on the importance of the aspiration to live a truly human life, to be truly superior as a human being, as that aspiration is embedded in the identity of *l'homme comme il faut*. Someone who has adopted that identity has understood what it is to be truly human in terms of pure social appearance; and so the concept does indeed, as Doyle says, have its home in a world of pure social pretense; but it is a more unsettled home for the concept than may appear, since there is in the background of the aspiration understood in social terms that same aspiration, or what can be understood to be that same aspiration, which can be felt to be deeply attractive, though what its content actually comes to remains unclear. The basis of my argument is the possibility of taking the aspiration one had had to be a truly superior human being—the aspiration that had been there in one's aiming to be perfectly *comme il faut*—to be an aspiration that one doesn't know how to deal with, an aspiration leading to one doesn't know what. There are two ways of seeing the practical identity of *comme il faut*, depending on how one sees the aspiration embedded in it. One can see it as did the young Tolstoy; and then one has an understanding of the identity as having essential to it the ease-in-being-human that I have described. Or one can take the practical identity of *comme il faut* to be something other than what one had taken it to be, as one finds oneself with an aspiration that one takes to be *still* the aspiration toward the truly excellent human life, at the same time as one has lost the sense that one knows what this comes to, and that it is to be found in the perfection of social appearance. To take *that*—that unsettling aspiration—to be the aspiration that had been embedded in one's practical identity as *un homme comme il faut* is indeed to resee that practical identity; but it is not necessarily to be under pressure to drop *being comme il faut* as one's practical identity—as opposed to seeing it as a practical identity that one does not any longer take oneself to know how to inhabit. My answer to Doyle's question how the concept *comme il faut* can be taken to be subject to ironic disruption in a way that would raise the Socratic question how to live is that it doesn't work *that way*, in the sort of case I have been trying to describe. He says that, if one were to ask, "Of all those who want to be *hommes comme il faut*—all those who take the question how to live and make it a question of superficial matters of style—are there any who are successful in doing this?," that will hardly raise the Socratic question how to live. But I think the crucial issue is buried in his words *"doing this."* What is essential, as

I see it, in the possible ironic disruption of the identity of the *comme il faut* is that the *"this"* in question comes apart. The attempt to make the question *how to live* into the question *how to have a superb social appearance,* the attempt to yoke those two questions together, has an internal instability, and this is what makes ironic disruption possible. It is not that reflecting on what is necessary to be *comme il faut* (understood in this way or that) can lead one to the Socratic question; it is rather that the whole business of becoming a superior sort of human being may become, for one, deeply questionable, full of uncertainty; the two questions that have been yoked together come apart. For them to come apart is for the question *how to live* no longer to be something one can take to be the question *how to achieve a perfection of social appearance.* If the question *how to live* gets unyoked from the question it had been yoked to, if one is thus confronted by the question with no clue what to do with it, this *is* for one to be confronted by the Socratic question. At this point, I want to return to Lear's point, from which I began, that it is constitutive of the concepts with which we understand ourselves that they are subject to ironic disruption. One way of putting the possibility of such disruption is that these concepts can be thought of as involving a kind of unstable yoking together of two questions, questions that come apart in ironic disruption. The question "What is it really to be *a teacher?*" might be thought of as yoked together (for someone who takes her identity to be that of a teacher) with the question "What is it to live the social existence of a teacher?" The two questions come apart, are seen to be two questions, when one recognizes that one doesn't know what is involved in the aspiration to be a teacher, and takes that aspiration to transcend social pretense. In section 4, I laid out the dissimilarities between these cases and those with which I have been concerned. Here I want to emphasize the similarity: there is in both types of case an unstable yoking together of two questions, one social and the other not. A question that does not anticipate a purely social answer, a question that it is not at all obvious how to answer, may have been taken to be a question that looks to the social realm for an answer. Ironic disruption disrupts that yoking together of the questions. It restores to the open, unsettled, disturbing question its capacity to unsettle and disturb.

In conclusion, I will set out some more questions. I hope at the same time to make clearer how the range of issues I have discussed is connected with the *Gorgias.*

On Lear's account, what makes it possible to ask the ironic question "Among all doctors, is there a doctor?" is the gap between the social pretense of being an doctor and the aspiration embedded in the practical identity of the doctor. Lear draws several of his examples of such ironic questions from the *Gorgias*. The conversation between Socrates and Callicles sets up the possibility of a further example: one might ask whether, among the men of Athens, there is a man. Callicles is (as some have noted) obsessed with manliness.[19] In his long speech (482–486), Callicles says that slaves have to suffer wrongs, but it's not what happens to a real man. One of the ways conventional thought leads us wrong, on Callicles's view, is precisely by treating wrongdoing as worse than suffering wrong, whereas what is conventionally taken to be wrongdoing is by no means incompatible with manliness. A great part of his speech is devoted to the unmanliness of doing philosophy. Philosophy is harmless if engaged in by boys; but engaging in it as a grown man, as Socrates does, is unmanly, and leaves him utterly vulnerable to wrongdoers, and in that regard like a slave, not a man. So Socrates should give up the activity of elenchus.[20] Elenchus, Lear says, is one of the methods Socrates uses to expose a gap between pretense and aspiration, one of the ways in which he engages in ironic disruption of social pretense. We can contrast two views of elenchus, thus understood. According to Callicles, Socrates' practice of elenchus should be given up as unmanly; and indeed it is hardly surprising that it should appear so, since it calls into question *manliness* as Callicles understands it, and leaves one vulnerable to wrongdoing, a vulnerability that is itself unfitting for a man. The alternative view, on the model of Lear's account of ironic disruption of what it is to be a politician or a rhetorician, is that Socrates' philosophical practice opens up a question what it is genuinely to *become a man*.[21] It exposes the gap between pretense as understood by Callicles and aspiration; it thus leaves room for the ironic question whether among the men there is a man. The case is complicated because Callicles himself rejects one form of social pretense, which he identifies with convention. But, as Lear makes plain, there is plenty of room *within* social pretense for the rejection of hypocritical pieties (as Callicles sees them) and their replacement by the ideal of the leonine man, as Callicles puts it forward (in somewhat different ways at different stages of the dialogue). Irony allows doubts to be spoken, allows questioning of what it is really to be a man; it allows itself to speak in a voice of insecurity, uncertainty, about manliness.

Callicles' "real man" is confident in his exercise of power; and Callicles himself, in debate, performs a kind of emphatic certainty and self-confidence. When he asks Socrates if Socrates isn't ashamed of himself asking all these questions about how to live, it's plain that *being perfectly sure of what it is to be a real man* is actually part of the social pretense of the real man, as Callicles sees it. It's at this point that we can see an important resemblance to the social pretense of *l'homme comme il faut* and similar practical identities. The *insecurity* about being human that Lear takes to be expressed in ironic questioning is antithetic to the confident ease that is part of the social pretense of *l'homme comme il faut;* it is in a similar way antithetic to the self-confidence and certainty that belongs to manliness as Callicles conceives it. These two varieties of practical identity have as part of their social pretense a kind of secure confidence in one's superiority, or at any rate the capacity splendidly to perform such apparent confidence. Doyle, writing about the *Gorgias,* mentions the "glamorous allure of political power," which is so strongly felt by Polus and Callicles.[22] A great many practical identities can be taken to have "glamorous allure," including Lear's examples of the teacher, the student, the politician, the doctor, and the Christian. The glamorous allure of the Calliclean manly man-of-political-power and of *l'homme comme il faut* includes the sense that *these* are the truly superior human beings; their confidence and unflappability are part of the social pretense of true superiority. The insecurity that Lear speaks of as constitutive of becoming human is thus in a special relation to such practical identities. Socratic elenchus, in the *Gorgias,* calls into question the equation between *superiority* and various different things in the realm of social pretense, as Callicles, under pressure, shifts his story of what it is to be "better." There is *no* equation of *superiority* with anything in the realm of social pretense that will withstand ironic questioning. If insecurity about being human is constitutive of being human, on one conception of what it is to become human, a profound opposition to irony appears to be part of being human, on other and opposed understandings of what it is to become human, understandings that emphasize the performance within the social realm of greatness or superiority or authenticity or lack of subjection to mere convention.

The questions with which I want to end concern the significance of the acrimonious dispute between Callicles and Socrates. Doyle connects it with the depth of disagreement between those who hold and those who deny that it is worse to do wrong than to suffer it.[23] In the *Gorgias,* that disagreement is connected with a disagreement about what a man should be, a disagreement between a questioning ironic mode of thinking about what a man should be and a mode of thinking that utterly rejects the insecurity of irony as unmanly, and rejects philosophy as an unseemly activity for a man. The first question I want to ask here is what Lear takes to be *opposition to ironic existence* or *resistance* to it. He recommends ironic existence as an understanding of human excellence. How does he think of what is opposed to this understanding? While Lear does describe for us what sort of existence is carried on *undisrupted by irony,* does he think that there are forms of existence which are not just undisrupted by irony but which in a stronger sense reject it? The second question I want to raise is also connected with the idea that there may be forms of practical identity that are antagonistic to ironic existence. The two examples of practical identities that I have been discussing in this section, that of *l'homme comme il faut* and that of the real man, are very different from each other in some ways. But despite these various differences, it is possible to take these practical identities to have embedded in them an aspiration that transcends social pretense. I have suggested that, if we consider these identities so far as they lie within the social realm, we can see in them a profound resistance to ironic disruption (since ironic disruption challenges the confident superiority of the Calliclean man and the ease-in-being-human of *l'homme comme il faut*). If we take these practical identities to have embedded in them an aspiration that transcends social pretense, it will look as if there is a kind of psychological incoherence within them, in their resistance to irony on the one hand (the resistance arising from the character of these identities within the realm of social pretense) and on the other hand the aspiration embedded in them, that goes beyond social pretense. And it will look as if the resistance to ironic disruption is a kind of keeping at bay, or a kind of attempt to keep at bay, the threat of disintegration to which such identities are subject. "It will look as if"; but not from the point of view of Callicles, say. The disagreement about how to live, the disagreement between a questioning ironic mode of thinking and a mode of thinking that rejects the insecurity of irony as unmanly, is also a disagreement about whether ironic questioning, ironic experience of any kind, does reveal a gap between pretense and a genuinely owned aspiration that transcends the social realm. In the *Gorgias,* Socrates says that the question how to live is the question whether to live the Calliclean life or the life of philosophy; and Lear would (I think) have us understand the latter alternative as being what he calls *ironic existence.* Ironic activity exposes the gap between pretense and aspiration; but the very understanding of ironic existence as the answer to the question how one should live depends upon *owning* that gap, taking oneself to be aware of an aspiration that is genuinely *one's own,* revealed in ironic activity, an aspiration utterly distinct from social pretense. This second question of mine is really a development of the first question, about how to understand resistance to ironic existence. Is there, as Lear understands the situation, a kind of *disowning* of ironic experience, so far as it purports to open up a gap between one's aspirations and social pretense? Lear says that the experience of irony is essentially first-personal. Is there also therefore a way of responding to what might otherwise be ironic experience, which consists in refusal to own such a gap, refusal to recognize any aspiration as one's own, going beyond the social realm? Here it seems I have to rethink one of my two original questions: the question whether there are any practical identities that do not have embedded in them an aspiration that transcends social pretense. If we follow what Lear suggests about the importance of the fact that ironic experience is essentially first-personal, it looks as if my question "Are there practical identities that do not have an embedded aspiration that goes beyond social pretense?" is misleadingly phrased, through abstracting from the fact that such an aspiration is essentially one that is *owned* and that can be *disowned.* There can be no impersonal answer to the question whether such-and-such sort of practical identity has an aspiration going beyond social pretense embedded in it. I began my comments with a quotation from Lear: "It is constitutive of our life with the concepts through which we understand ourselves that they are subject to ironic disruption." So far as *thinking of our lives as subject to ironic disruption* involves willingness to own aspirations going beyond social pretense, does this mean also that what is or isn't "constitutive of our life with the concepts through which we understand ourselves" is a first-personal matter, a matter of what we can *own,* and cannot be given a general impersonal answer? Is it a question that, by its nature, is liable to lead to just the kind of breakdown in communication that we see in the conversation between Callicles and Socrates?[24] I have, throughout my comments, taken the questions raised by Lear to be capable of impersonal philosophical discussion. But that approach, followed through, seems to lead to the conclusion that the questions cannot be asked in that way, and are essentially first-personal. But I do not think this conclusion should be un-welcome to Lear. My last question is whether this is right.[25]

Appendix

I have stumbled back and forth between speaking of what it is to become *hu-man* and speaking of what it is to be a *man*. I have spoken of the aspiration embedded in practical identities of social appearance as the aspiration to be-come human, but I have written about the gap between pretense and aspira-tion in the *Gorgias* as it might be reflected in the question "Among the men of Athens, is there a man?" My formulation pushes the two cases apart in a way that I think is misleading. But it would be equally misleading to phrase the question, as it is implicit in the *Gorgias,* in any other terms. "Man" in English is rarely used any more in the way it was in "the rights of man," to cover men and women. We now try to avoid the usage for good reasons: the word wasn't as gender-neutral as the official story had it. But this leaves us without a word that in some contexts means *male* and in others *human.* Callicles, when he speaks of what is manly or unmanly, means what is suitable for or character-istic of a real man. He does not mean *human.* It is possible to pick up the lan-guage of manliness that he uses, and to shift or open up what will count as manly or genuinely manly, as Socrates does.[26] Socrates, then, in replying to Callicles, is using his language and doing with it something different from what Callicles would take to be appropriate, but it is important not to depart from the language of masculinity in giving the dispute or setting out the ironic question that can be taken to be implicit in the dispute.

8

Flight from Irony

A Response to Cora Diamond

Cora Diamond's illuminating comments are an evolving meditation. She quotes my statement that "it is constitutive of our life with the concepts with which we understand ourselves that they are subject to ironic disruption"; and she asks: "Are there no concepts with which we understand ourselves that are not subject to disruption in the way Lear describes?" Well, there are certainly concepts with which we understand *each other* that are not easily subject to such disruption. If one asks, for example,

Among all the bores in the world, is there a single bore?

or

Among all the hypocritical, pompous asses in the world, is there to be found a single hypocritical, pompous ass?

one can see immediately that, if there is any humor here at all, it arises because the possibility for irony seems to be foreclosed. It is not simply that those who seem to be pompous asses are overwhelming likely to be such. Rather, the categories of being a *bore, hypocrite,* or *pompous ass* are categories we associate with being somehow bad rather than somehow good. As such, we do not think of people as willingly and self-consciously taking on such an identity; and though the pompous tend to get more pompous over time, it is only with sarcasm that we say that they are getting *better* at it. This tells us something important about irony and something important about ourselves. If we consider categories that we apply to ourselves—in the sense of identifying with them, taking them on as a self-characterization to which we are in some way committed—in general there will be something about them that we ourselves sense as somehow good. This goodness may or may not be something we can explicitly articulate in any detail. But the possibility of irony, as I have been trying to capture it, arises from an outbreak of anxiety as to what this goodness amounts to. It is this anxiety that can put me at a distance from the practices of social pretense.

That is why I want to say that "it is constitutive of our life with the concepts with which we understand ourselves that they are subject to ironic disruption." It is characteristic of our own self-understanding that we try to understand ourselves as up to something good—and this makes us vulnerable to ironic disruption. I take this to be characteristic of human being. And that is why I want to place the emphasis on *constitutive:* this vulnerability is an intrinsic aspect of our life with the concepts with which we understand ourselves.

But I do not thereby mean to deny the astonishing variety of human life. (I have spent my life in the company of unusual instances.) As an unconscious strategy, the motivated attempt to become boring is not all that uncommon. It spares one the strain of sociality. And though it would be unusual, I think it possible for a person self-consciously and willingly to strive to become a bore. Someone might genuinely try to get better at it. But for any such person we would want to know more about what is going on. We recognize such a case not only as unusual but as somehow perverse: we seek to understand not just how such an unusual case could arise, but how this particular instance of human striving goes against the human current. Our first attempt would be to see if we could discover how this person thought there was something good about being a bore. (Perhaps it protects one from having to engage in conversation.) It is only when such efforts failed that we might feel we have to look in a more malign direction: the thought that there is something in this person *aiming* toward the bad as bad. This is a difficult phenomenon to comprehend, though psychoanalysts influenced by Melanie Klein have tried to characterize it under the concept of *envy*.[1]

*   *   *

Diamond wants to know whether any of the concepts with which we understand ourselves are "social pretense through and through." There are certainly concepts whose general cultural deployments are such that they can be seen as *attempts* to be social pretense through and through. Indeed, the concept of *irony* is a paradigm. The culture tends to view *being ironic* as a form of social pretense through and through. And those in popular culture who take up an ironic stance consider it *comme il faut* to do so. Obviously, I think this is a shallow image of irony's possibilities, but there is no doubt that irony is widely seen as a kind of social performance—in a broad family of categories like being cool, fashionable, or *comme il faut*.

Let me take up Diamond's example of the case of the young Tolstoy wanting to be *comme il faut*. Obviously, in the first instance the *attempt* to be *comme il faut* is an attempt to manifest a special social appearance; and its obvious aspiration is about manners of appearing. But it is a much stronger claim to say that *"whatever* aspiration is embedded [in the category], it is an aspiration that remains within the realm of social pretense" (my emphasis). I do not think this stronger claim is true. Indeed, though the young Tolstoy may have been obsessed with the appearances required to be *comme il faut*, the aspiration embedded in his striving seems pretty clearly to be that of transcending the realm of social pretense. Tolstoy's attempt to be *comme il faut* is, I think, an expression of anxiety about inhabiting any social pretense. Though it is not itself an instance of ironic anxiety, it does bear some similarity to it. So, to the question "Is the desire to be *comme il faut* impervious to anxious disruption?" I want to claim that in this particular case, the desire to be *comme il faut* already contains a moment of anxious distance from the social world.

Here are some reasons for thinking so. If we consider the social and historical context in which the young Tolstoy grows up—especially as depicted in his autobiography—we see ample signs of a culture that is anxious about its own social pretenses.[2] And, of course, with hindsight we know that these are the last days of—shall I put it in French?—*l'ancien régime*. The high culture into which Tolstoy was born is about to be swept away. And why is the Russian aristocracy speaking French? There is, of course, the obvious point about the way in which one social class can put on display its superiority over another. But the fact that the aristocracy turns to French betrays unease about its own previous ways of going on. It is as though all the social pretenses that can be expressed only in vernacular Russian are thereby shown to be inadequate. The very use of French in the household is at once an attempted man-ifestation of cultural superiority *and* a manifestation of anxiety about available social roles.

In his autobiography, Tolstoy repeatedly shows us the special ways in which French is deployed. It is regularly used by a figure of authority when he or she wants to break through to reality. To take one example, Tolstoy gives an account of his grandmother and her cousin, a prince, in conversa-tion. She is criticizing one of his friends for being a cad, and the prince re-sponds: "Eh, ma bonne amie," said the prince reprovingly, "I can see you've not grown any wiser—always grieving and lamenting over some imaginary sorrow. Shame on you. I've known *him* a very long time and I know him for a kind attentive and excellent husband and, most important—for a gentleman, *un parfait honnête homme.*"[3] The initial address *"Eh, ma bonne amie"* is a way of saying we *really are* friends; and then *"un parfait honnête homme"* is meant to get to the real essence of this man, in spite of his social appearance. So the use of French is not just a sign of refinement; it is a socially acceptable way of signaling that one is breaking through appearances to a deeper reality.[4] The need to break through social pretense is present in this use of language. Tol-stoy imagines a case of *un homme comme il faut* who dies and goes to heaven. "Asked in the next world who he was and what he had done down below, this man replies, *'Je fus un homme très comme il faut.'* It is important to the story," Diamond tells us, "that even when he is dead the man speaks French." For Diamond, Tolstoy's point is that part of being *comme il faut* is to be able to keep it up in the next world. But as I read it, French is the language it would be appropriate to speak in a world transcending social pretense. This is young Tolstoy's fantasy.

So when Diamond says at a certain point in her reflections

> So, if Tolstoy asks in French, "Of those who are *comme il faut,* is anyone *comme il faut?,*" the very asking of the question in French marks it as a question that attends to social pretense and does not disrupt it.

—I do not agree. Obviously, the question may be a dud on any particular occa-sion it is asked. That is true of any ironic question. But there is nothing about this particular question that insulates it from hitting a target, occasioning an outburst of ironic anxiety. It seems to me that we need to understand the category of *comme il faut* as itself anxious, ambiguous, and unstable.

One way to do this is to recognize that the desire to be *comme il faut* (at least, in one ordinary understanding of that phrase) is pervasive among rising members of a society's upper class. If one considers a contemporary graduating class of any elite undergraduate college one would expect to find a large swath of students wanting to be *comme il faut*—but with this caveat: they want to be *comme il faut as* a doctor, as a lawyer, as an investment banker, as a business executive, as an academic, and so on. Hence, in part, the preoccupation with getting into "the best" graduate and professional programs, gaining entry into the most prestigious firms, and so on. So described, this is not at all an uncommon phenomenon. What makes Tolstoy's version such a rare orchid is that he tries to do away with the *as.* Young Tolstoy wants to be *comme il faut*—period. It is as though one retained some last vulgar traces if one was satisfied with being *comme il faut as* . . . The mature Tolstoy, the author of the autobiography, tells us:

> The main evil [of being *comme il faut*] consisted in a conviction that *comme il faut* was a self-sufficient position in society, that a man did not need to try to be a civil servant or a coachmaker or a soldier or a scholar if he was *comme il faut;* that having reached this position he was thereby fulfilling his vocation and even became higher than the majority of people.[5]

Leaving aside Tolstoy's moral condemnation, we can see here an uncomfortable longing for transcendence. It is as though every social role—every socially available pretense (as ordinarily understood)—is inadequate when it comes to living a truly meaningful, worthwhile life—that of *l'homme comme il faut.* Of course, the role of *l'homme comme il faut* is a socially available role too; but it is one that is calling into question the worthiness of social roles (as normally understood) to be the sort of thing that could give one's life value. This stance of *comme il faut* injects a certain discomfort with respect to the adequacy of our lives in ordinary social roles. One can see it thus as an attempt both to transcend society and to remain within it (aloof but there); and, so understood, it betrays anxiety and ambivalence about social life. Certainly, Tolstoy's own attempt to maintain himself as *un homme comme il faut* was unstable: his own development depended upon its coming undone.

Diamond considers the difference with respect to ironic disruption between what she calls identities of social appearance—such as being *comme il faut*—and identities understood in terms of social roles, like that of doctor, parent, teacher, friend. At an early stage of her reflection she characterizes the difference in this way:

> In the case of the teacher, the ironic disruption of practical identity as a teacher leaves the person utterly without any kind of idea what it is *to be a teacher;* whereas the ironic disruption of Tolstoy's understanding of human excellence as being perfectly *comme il faut* might be, not a sense that one had no idea what it really was to be *comme il faut,* but rather a sense that truly realizing being human could not be understood as being *comme il faut and* one had no idea what it was instead.

This characterization can be misleading in two ways. First, while it is true that in a moment of ironic disruption one is called to a bewildering halt about what it is to be a teacher—and in that practical sense one is "without any kind of idea about what it is to be a teacher"—it is nevertheless true that even in that moment the category of teacher remains located in a network of associated signifiers. So, to be a teacher is to have a *student* or students; it is to have some *knowledge* and to have some *method* of transmitting the knowledge from teacher to student. The problem in the moment of ironic disruption is not that this network is disrupted, but that each signifier becomes as problematic as the next. If I am at a loss about what it is to be a teacher, I am equally at a loss about what it is to have a student, what it is to have knowledge, what it would be to pass it along. In *that* sense, I am without any idea of what it is to be a teacher; but I also know that being a teacher essentially involves having a student. In *that* sense, I do have some idea. Second, the crucial issue is not whether the experience of ironic disruption around *comme il faut* "might be" as Diamond describes, but whether it must be such. I don't think it must be as she describes because, as she tells tells us, being *comme il faut* was, for Tolstoy, similarly embedded in a family of signifiers. Being *comme il faut* was essentially a means of *being superior* to the mass of humankind, of *holding oneself at a distance* from ordinary social ways of going on, and, in that way, of *being extraordinary*. It was also taken to be a form of *human excellence* and, in that sense, a way of *getting at the truth* of human life. This network can continue to hang together even as, in a moment of ironic disruption, one loses a sense of what any of them amounts to.

But if there is this similarity between the ironic disruption of being a teacher and the ironic disruption of being *comme il faut,* then I suspect that Diamond cannot make the distinction between them she wants to make. I completely agree with her emerging sense that with "the practical identities of social appearance, there may well be an embedded aspiration that transcends the realm of social pretense." But then she concludes, "but, if so, the aspiration is nothing but the aspiration to *become human*." I do not see why this must be so. If we look at the case of Tolstoy, and allow our imagination some rein, I do not see why the category of being *comme il faut* might not have developed, through ironic disruption, into the practical identity of being an author. In both, one holds oneself at a certain distance from the ordinary social roles of the social world; in both there is the assumption of a position of superiority: in the case of the author one takes upon oneself the role of someone who can so perceptively observe the social world as to be able to comment on it in enlightening ways, and so on. In short, in this imagined example, Tolstoy comes to recognize through ironic disruption that the way to be *comme il faut* is to become an author. In this way, he can transform an immaturity (which could well develop into a vice) into a mature, creative, and ethically virtuous activity—*while all along maintaining a certain constancy in his commitments and values*. It is not that he ceases wanting to be superior; he finds a better way of doing it. To be sure, this is one way of becoming excellent *as a human;* but so is becoming a teacher. Diamond's point is that, in the case of identities of social appearance, there is no way to get to human excellence other than through the category of *being human;* whereas I am suggesting that Tolstoy *might* have reached human excellence by ironic disruption of, but also through, the category of being *comme il faut*. It is not just that the ironic instability might break out over *falloir* (which it well might), but that *comme il faut* is located in its own nexus of signifiers, any of which could serve as a trigger for ironic anxiety. While there may be *other* differences, in this way at least there need not be an asymmetry between ironic disruption of a social role—like being a teacher—and ironic disruption of a identity of social appearance like *comme il faut.*[6]

Identities of appearance—like being *comme il faut,* cool, or fashionable—have it in common that they purport to offer those who pursue (or effortlessly inhabit) them avenues of human excellence. Though it may ultimately be bad judgment to take these routes to excellence seriously, as purported routes, they each strenuously insist on the distinction between appearance and reality. There is nothing so uncool as *trying* to be cool. The Cool Police are ever vigilent for any appearance of cool that is not really cool. It is this striving for purported excellence, the concern with the distinction between appearance and reality as well as vigilent policing of the boundaries that makes *being cool* ripe for irony. Indeed, it seems to me that both the really cool and the wannabes are especially vulnerable to anxious disruption by the question "Among the cool, is anyone *really* cool?" Indeed, it is just such an ironic disruption that might help a wannabe make that mysterious transition to the genuinely cool. Notice how different this question is from the question with which we began: "Among the boring, is anyone really boring?"

At the end of her meditation, Diamond states a profound conflict:

> There is *no* equation of *superiority* with anything in the realm of social pretense that will withstand ironic questioning. If insecurity about being human is constitutive of being human, on one conception of what it is to become human, a profound opposition to irony appears to be part of being human, on other and opposed understandings of what it is to be human, understandings that emphasize the performance within the social realm of greatness or superiority or authenticity or lack of subjection to mere convention.

She asks me, first, what I think of *opposition to ironic existence* or *resistance* to it; second, whether there might be forms of practical identity that are antagonistic to ironic existence.

To move to the realm of individual human life, I believe I see instances of this opposition almost every day in my psychoanalytic practice. But the important point in the individual case is that these opposing principles tend to be dynamically related: a heightened sense of the importance of performing well in some aspect of the social realm often covers over a deeper anxiety about what performing well in life might be. One of Freud's deepest insights—which philosophers have tended to ignore—is that transference as it arises in the psychoanalytic situation tends to function as a resistance.[7] At first, the idea that transference is a resistence might seem counterintuitive. After all, if someone came in and immediately started treating me like his mother (a strong maternal transference), might we not be able to gain insight into his formative life with his mother? But things do not work that simply. Suppose an adolescent like the young Tolstoy came to analysis, a man obsessed with being *comme il faut*. It is not impossible that this should occur: there was a short window in American urban history when, for a certain class of people, going to a psychoanalyst was *comme il faut*. One of this analysand's first acts would be to decide whether or not I was *comme il faut*. If I were *comme il faut*, then perhaps we could work together. I would at least be one of that superior bunch with whom he could relate; perhaps he could learn something from me. If I were not *comme il faut*, then the analysis would be hopeless (at least, from the analysand's point of view). I would be one of those dolts who have no understanding of what life is about. Even worse, I might be one of those pathetic creatures who was *trying* to be *comme il faut*, perhaps to win his confidence. But suppose he could not immediately decide whether or not I actually was *comme il faut:* then he would have to keep an eagle eye out for clues, perhaps set tests for me to pass or fail. The important point is: *whichever* of these choices he makes, it will function as a resistance to the analytic task of letting one's mind wander and saying whatever it is that comes to mind. Even in what looks like the best-case scenario—his deciding that I am *comme il faut* and thus someone he wants to confide in—his efforts will be directed toward *participating* in being *comme il faut with* me rather than analyzing what it means for him to be *comme il faut*. Freud's point is, *that* is why this positive transference fantasy is in place: to keep us talking about what is *comme il faut* as a way of avoiding analyzing what it means for this young man to be so preoccupied with striving to be *comme il faut*. Freud's eventual strategy for dealing with this problem was to embrace it. Rather than try to circumvent the resistance, one focuses on it, trusting that the resisted material is somehow showing up in the resistance. As Freud famously put it, "transference, which seems ordained to be the greatest obstacle to psychoanalysis, becomes its most powerful ally."[8]

One way to read Tolstoy's autobiography is as a report of and continuation of a sort of self-analysis: an analysis that helped him make the move from an adolescent obsessed with being *comme il faut* to a great writer who could look back on this stage of his life with both sympathy and scorn. Obviously, the point here is not to get to the truth about Tolstoy but to envisage a dynamism that might have been true. One way to look at this is to think that there were two opposing principles in him—one obsessed with society, which got expressed in adolescence, the other expressed later in life, which was utterly indifferent to the demands of social life. But another way to look at it is that these are both strivings for excellence. The young man's attempt, from the perspective of maturity, may appear both foolish and cruel, but one can see how it can function to contain anxiety about what human excellence consists in. The certainty that one *knows* what is *comme il faut*—and the energy and attention one directs toward achieving such status—this very activity keeps at bay the anxious recognition that this project cannot deliver what it promises. This would be a way of seeing the concern with being *comme il faut* not just as an opposed principle to some pretense-transcending identity, but as a resistance to it. As such, one can begin to see the anxiety right there in the certainty, in the insistence that being *comme il faut* will supply that missing *it* that will secure human excellence. For some people the threat of the anxiety is so overwhelming that they spend their lives obsessed with being *comme il faut*. That provides them with a sufficiently contained image of what human excellence consists in—and it gives them enough to be anxious about. For Tolstoy, perhaps through his own self-analysis, perhaps through an ironic disruption over what it is *really* to be *comme il faut,* he allowed his lifelong concern for human excellence to take more excellent shapes.

If something like this picture is correct, then the issue is not about choosing between two opposing principles but about learning to live well with them both. Resistance to irony is as constitutive of human life as is the ironic impulse. I take it that ironic existence—considered as a human excellence—does not single-mindedly take up the cause of irony, but finds healthy and life-affirming ways of embracing the inevitable resistance to it.

9

On the Observing Ego and the Experiencing Ego

Robert A. Paul

What sort of psychic unity is available to us? Early in his second lecture, Lear states that "getting the proper psychology in view will require us to rethink what it is to be a unified self. The unity that is genuinely available to us is, I think, marked by disruption and division," and that the aim of unity, such as might be expected to emerge after a successful psychoanalysis, "should not be to overcome . . . disruptions, but to find ways to live well with them." I agree and want to refine this idea, since perhaps unlike philosophers, who he claims "have tended to rely on an idealized conception of unity that does not really fit the human soul," psychoanalysts have never entertained any such ideas about the unity of the self. Everyone knows, of course, about Freud's divisions of the mind first into the regions of the Unconscious, the Pre-Conscious, and the Conscious and later the Id, Ego, and Superego. But a more relevant (and I think less familiar) formulation comes very late in Freud's career, in the *New Introductory Lectures in Psycho-analysis*, written in 1933, when Freud was seventy-seven:

> We wish to make the ego the matter of our inquiry, our very own ego. But is that possible? After all, the ego is in its very essence a subject; how can it be made into an object? Well, there is no doubt

that it can be. The ego can take itself as an object, can treat itself like other objects, can observe itself, criticize itself, and do Heaven knows what with itself. In this, one part of the ego is setting itself over against the rest. So the ego can be split; it splits itself during a number of its functions—temporarily at least. Its parts can come together again afterwards.[1]

One of the most important such divisions in the ego is that between what Richard Sterba called the observing ego and the experiencing ego.[2] The latter is the subject of our experiences and actions, while the former is that agency that is aware of our experiences and actions and accompanies them with an ongoing inner linguistic narrative, like Homer running alongside Ulysses and singing his exploits, or—to allude to a different tradition—like a simultaneous Rashi commentary on the self and its acts and experiences. This seems self-evident not only from doing philosophy but from just being reflective. Doing analysis, in particular, depends on the analysand's being able to carry out the task of the observing ego and doing so aloud in the presence of, and at least sometimes, in real communication with the analyst. I now want to follow out Sterba's formulation a bit further, basing my comment on a recent clinical experience.

As I was immersed in reading and thinking about Lear's second lecture, I myself conducted a session of psychoanalytic psychotherapy with a patient whose previous appointment I had had to cancel. After a few preliminary comments, she said "Well, I'm angry at you," and went on to add, "your canceling the last session was just another abandonment," alluding to the theme that was pervasive in her sessions. When I asked her whether she was angry at the actual time of the missed session, she said no, that what she had experienced instead was an exacerbation of her symptoms. Only later did she realize she was angry at me, and was now able to say it to me. Thinking about Lear's lecture, I wondered whether she was really experiencing her anger when she told me she was angry with me, or was she using this third-person observation as an intellectualizing defense? Probably both. In any event, in the course of this discussion she uttered the following seemingly unremarkable sentences, and it is these that I want to examine more closely: "At the time, I was angry at you, but I didn't know it. Only later did I realize that I must have been angry."

Who is the "I" who was angry at the time of the missed session? It cannot have been the same "I" who later came to realize it, because at the time this "I" did not know anything about her anger; all she consciously observed was that her symptoms got worse, and had she had an interlocutor, that's what she would have told him, not that she was angry. But someone also called "I" was, nonetheless, actually angry. And later, the "I" who previously didn't know it was angry at me realized that that "I" that it didn't know was angry was angry after all.

From reflections such as these, I cannot escape the conclusion that we regularly use the word "I" in two radically different ways, to refer to two very different aspects of our experience of ourselves. One is the "I" who is the subject of the statement "I didn't know it" (namely, that I was angry) and also of the statement "only later did I realize it". The other "I" is the subject of the statements "I was angry at you" and "I must have been angry." The first "I" is the observing ego as subject of conscious awareness, the one who under-stands the inner monologue as it explains and puts into potential speech what consciousness presents to awareness. The second, the experiencing ego, is the subject of action and reaction of our being as a lived body, an organism. This latter form of subjectivity we share with organisms from one-celled animals on up the evolutionary scale: they all are able to act to avoid threats and seize opportunities to fulfill their developmental agendas as living beings. (In hu-mans that agenda is set by a combination of genetics and social and cultural learning and experience.) The former kind of subjectivity is unique to hu-mans, since it depends on internalized language as its medium. It is the sub-ject we mean in this sentence when we say "we"—those of us who know things together (as in the literal meaning of the etymology of the word "con-scious") and can communicate with each other about ourselves and our expe-rience in a shared social arena.

Psychoanalytic experience as well as ordinary self-reflection shows that the observing ego, the "knower," as the subject of conscious awareness, doesn't actually know very much about what is going on with that other "I," the organismic subject or "agent." If I ask you whether you know how to metabolize sugar or to circulate your blood, your answer will be no or yes depending on whether you take me to be addressing you as a knower, or you as the subjective organismic agent. The former does not know how to do these things (unless it is a student of physiology); the latter just as certainly does. Likewise, if I ask you if you know how to form a grammatical sentence, or solve a math problem, or mobilize a defense mechanism, or get angry, your answer will depend on whether you are answering for yourself as a total organism who does of course know how to do these things, since it does them, or for yourself as an observing knower or subject of conscious knowledge, who generally has little or no clue as to how it actually manages to perform those various feats, even though it may well be aware that it is able to do so.

I believe that one key role of the observing subject of conscious awareness, the "I" we normally think of as our own identity, is to take responsibility in the social arena for the actions of the experiencing, agentic organism with which it is associated, which means it could give a verbal accounting of them if asked, and in many cases feels as if it can claim that it was the author of them. I myself do not believe that this entity or whatever it is could actually be the author of action, but rather that what it does is to give its imprimatur to the actions that originate from the organismic subject, including mental processes that are in their essential form not conscious. I posit, further, that this effect of having an existence as a self who is a subject of conscious awareness is a product of the unique human embeddedness in a social milieu saturated with language, and that we learn to construct this internal entity through interaction with significant speaking others in the course of primary socialization. This observing self originates in the internalized observing other with whom we interact as we develop under the care of one or more caregivers. This view, typical of object relations analysts of all kinds, has a wider genealogy that includes such thinkers as William James, G. H. Mead, Lev Vygotsky, and Alfred Schutz, along with analysts as disparate as Henry Stack Sullivan, Ronald Fairbairn, D. W. Winnicott, Jacques Lacan, and many others.

As Lear shows, an important corollary idea was contributed by Wittgenstein: that the child learns to replace the response of the subjective organism to some situation—let us say its screams of hunger and thirst—with verbal expressions that are not merely expressive of the state of the organism but have "truth value" in the sense—as I take it—that they communicate useful information to another about the actual state of affairs of one's organism. After all, one does not say "I am hungry" or "It hurts" except to another person, another occupant of the conscious social arena, who (we hope) is in a position to do something about it. In solitude, one would simply make oneself a sandwich, or yell "ouch!" (though as we are constituted, it should be observed, even when we are physically alone we generally remain accompanied by our internalized observers).

Freud, in his *Project for a Scientific Psychology* (1895), assumed that the baby's hungry screams are simply the release of unorganized mental energy, excess stimuli stemming from the body's need for food, but which, thanks to the cunning of evolution, the mother knows to recognize as a call for her to help by feeding her child. Wilfrid Bion, in his influential book *Learning from Experience* (1963), refined this idea by proposing that the infant's mind is filled with disorganized entities called beta elements, at least when stirred up by strong emotion or discomfort, and that in fantasy the baby projects these into the mother, who picks the baby up, comforts it, and feeds it. The key innovative idea for Bion is that in her state of reverie as she soothes and nurses her baby, the mother in effect metabolizes the baby's beta elements and, being a mature adult, organizes them into alpha elements and returns them in the form of verbal symbols, which are the building blocks of both thinking and dreaming. She thus reflects back to the infant its previously chaotic experience in newly manageable form as soothing sounds and speech: "There there, I know you're hungry, but mommy is right here," and so on. This provides the basis on which the baby can "mentalize," that is, learn to recognize and symbolize its own experiences as well as internalize the intentions of another and see its own actions through the eyes of the other.

From the beginning of his theorizing, Freud recognized language as a system of tokens that can be internalized and used for the process of thinking, that is, for carrying out a proposed action on a trial basis, to see if it leads to danger or to satisfaction. In this way the social origin and function of speech also serve the interests of the individual organism in providing it with a neutral, consequence-free area of inner space in which to conduct mental experiments. Much later, in 1933, Freud characterized the function of what we are calling the observing ego, using inner speech, "in the same way as a general shifts small figures about on a map before setting his large bodies of troops in motion."[3]

So now let's think about fury. I do not believe that a person, no matter how furious, who says "I am furious at you" is in the realm of pure agentic expression. A person really in the grip of fury would yell obscenities or, if behind the wheel, make an obscene gesture and lean on the horn, or, if less inhibited, might punch you in the nose or worse. When someone is able to say "I am furious" while furious this indicates, I believe, that they are already beginning the process of turning the pure expression of the organismic subject into a third-person observing commentary. We must not be fooled by the use of the word "I": the sentence "I am angry" still has the form of a third-person state-ment, and by creating this distance between the experiencing ego and the ob-serving ego the furious person is already beginning to get a grip on herself.

The organized unconscious fantasies to which Lear rightly refers have been constituted in order to deal with otherwise insoluble problems that stem from the ego's fear of its own impulses—"its own" in the sense that they originate from the experiencing and acting body of which the knowing sub-ject finds itself to be the custodian and representative in the social world around it. In Freud's late thinking, the reason the unconscious dimensions of the ego mobilize defense mechanisms is out of fear of an anticipated danger that will eventuate if the impulse is allowed to be carried into action. The prototype of this danger is feared abandonment by the caretaking other. Thus, another of my patients is not able to know at the time she feels aban-doned by me that she is angry because, paradoxically, she believes it is her anger that leads to her being consistently abandoned, as a punishment for her hostile badness. She therefore cannot put into inner speech the thought "I am angry" because this arouses the threat of the much-dreaded danger of aban-donment by me, instantiated by my actually having not met with her when she had a right to expect that I would.

It is this wishful nature of fantasies stemming from the unmodified im-pulses of the organism which leads to their formation, and puts them into conflict with other wishes, generally at the more "socialized" level. This con-flictual dimension, and the elements of dread and danger, are what make analysis such a difficult process, as the conflicts start getting enacted in the transference, and patients fear that the analyst is trying to take away from them the one thing that keeps them from the punishment or dire danger they think they would otherwise face, namely the premises of their unconscious fantasies. The analyst, once seen as an ally, becomes a dangerous provocateur and even enemy to be warded off with all the defensive means at the patient's disposal; hence the element of painful struggle that characterizes many good analyses.

The ability to manage one's wishful fantasies in a viable way depends on the ability to distinguish between an impulse, a thought, a speech-act, and a physical action. If I am angry, and would like to physically attack and hurt you, I may defensively keep this impulse entirely away from conscious awareness, and instead give myself a somatic ailment, because of my fear that if I become conscious of the impulse I might then go on to actually hit you and then you would hit me back. I (consciously) skip the intermediate steps and just give myself the expected pain as if I had been hit. The neurotic cannot fully believe that it would be possible to have the thought "I'd like to punch you" without either going ahead and doing it, or suffering unconscious repercussions from the superego for even having had the thought. And indeed even just saying such a thing in most social situations, with true feeling behind it, would very likely lead to unpleasant social consequences. In analysis, the patient gradually figures out that one can put such thoughts into words in the very special and peculiar social arena of the consulting room, without any awful consequences. As a result, patients gradually learn to allow conflictual or danger-laden thoughts and impulses into conscious awareness in the form of inner speech, and to articulate them to the analyst, who will not respond in the feared way. As Winnicott said, the analyst helps by simply surviving to be present at the next session after the analysand has given voice to thoughts previously inhibited out of deeply rooted anxiety.

Thus analysis at its best is a *via negativa* in that it does not propose anything, but simply removes the defensive obstacles the patient has erected to keep the "I" as the knowing, observing subject from consciously entertaining certain topics cropping up in that other "I," to keep it from following the exploration of chains of association down certain paths long defensively marked "danger—do not enter." The unity of soul that we can achieve is that of the one "I" knowing what the other "I" wants, intends, or fears, and the vehicle for this is language, the medium of the knowing "I," which enables us to constantly shift subject positions from "first person" to "third person," from experiencing to observing ego and back again. That is why there can be such a thing as a "talking cure" in the first place.

10

Observing Ego and Social Voice

A Response to Robert A. Paul

Robert Paul reminds us of an important reason that psychic unity matters to us: the alternative is painful. Professor Paul is a distinguished psychoanalyst and anthropologist; and I want to thank him for being willing to join in a discussion with philosophers. Of any legitimate psychoanalytic theorizing, we ought to be able to see how it arises out of life experience. Obviously, we know very little of Paul's patient. But we can use our imaginations to expand the case. So, imagine that *you* are Robert Paul's patient. You have come to your regular Tuesday morning session, and Paul tells you he will not be able to make your regularly scheduled Thursday hour. He does not explain why. You have already had some experience in psychotherapy, and, in any case, you are a reflective person, so you ask yourself: How do I feel about this? In the language of the philosophers, you use the occasion of Paul's comment to step back, get some reflective distance, and ask yourself what you think about Paul's doing this, and how you feel about it generally. In reflective self-consciousness, you are trying to take your emotional life into account. To use Paul's more psychoanalytic vocabulary, your "observing ego" is trying to make an assessment of how you are experiencing things.

Suppose you decide you are not particularly bothered. You are curious about Paul: has some crisis come up in his family life? Or is it just that he is going off to give a lecture somewhere? But if that, why hasn't he given you more notice? However, you know he is not going to answer your questions, and, in any case, you are not *that* curious. You realize that his canceling means that you get some extra time freed up on Thursday: you can use it to finish that paper, even go for a swim. It's a minibreak. And you don't have to pay for the missed session: you can use that extra money to go out to dinner. Not only that, but he is the one responsible for the break, so you do not have to feel guilty. *Pas mal!*

Now it is Thursday morning. You feel fine. After breakfast, you go to the toilet as you usually do, for a regular bowel movement. Perhaps you take the newspaper with you. It is only as you are about to flush the toilet that you get a strange glimpse: the water in the toilet bowl is red. You realize it's red with your blood. What is *that* doing there? And you have an uncanny sense that this is not entirely unfamiliar: it has happened to you before, though not often. A few years ago you went to a gastroenterologist who diagnosed a mild case of colitis and asked you whether you were under any particular stress. In fact, you had just finished taking final exams. You have a vague sense that maybe there have been other times too: for instance, when you went off to summer camp, so long ago.

So, now, as a reflective agent you have a puzzle. It *seems* as though that initial comment by Paul—that he is canceling the next session—has triggered two different sorts of reactions in you. On the one hand, it was an occasion for you to step back and reflectively take stock; on the other hand, it seems to have also been the trigger for stressful psychic activity of which you were unaware (until you glimpsed the bloody toilet water). It seems to you now as though there is this other psychical site—that somehow also is *you*—that doesn't seem to be taking Paul's cancelation with the equanimity that you are. You take it to be a sign (and, for the sake of the argument, let us just assume that your assumption is correct) that *you are* upset—in spite of initial appearances. And, now that you think about it, you remember an anxious dream from last night, about trying to hold everything together and not let anything get out. As if from nowhere, a memory of waiting for your mother to pick you up from school pops into your mind. And so on.

I wanted to draw out this picture a bit in order to make clear the kind of experience Paul is talking about when he says that his patient did not feel anger at the time, but did experience an exacerbation in her symptoms. This is disturbing not merely because of any pain associated with the symptoms, but also because of the anxiety in recognizing that you do not really understand what is going on in your own emotional life, you don't know how things are going to continue to unfold, and the standard modes of achieving self-conscious understanding do not seem up to the task.

When Paul's actual patient comes to the next session, she says, "Well, I'm angry at you . . . your canceling the last session was just another abandon-ment," and later, "At the time, I was angry with you, but I didn't know it. Only later did I realize that I must have been angry." Paul asks whether she was actually experiencing her anger or whether she was using these expres-sions as an intellectualizing defense, and answers: probably both. That seems right. I would like to add something about each option. Obviously, she is not my patient, and I know almost nothing about her. So I am not trying to say more *about her,* but to open up imaginative possibilities that a patient might occupy. As intellectual defense, it is possible that anger is a red herring. She is not angry *at all.* She is not expressing newly won emotional insight, but seek-ing relief from the anxiety of experiencing herself as disunified; the anxiety of knowing that she does not know what is going on with her. She is anx-iously motivated to restore her capacity for self-conscious understanding, and she seeks the analyst's collaboration in constructing a plausible emotional narrative. What matters to her is to construct a narrative that fits the avail-able evidence and is one that her analyst will endorse. For she seeks the relief of having some plausible story about her emotional life. To that end, she may *also* "experience" her anger in the sense of a sincerely mimed performance. The "experience" might be, as it were, a dress rehearsal, a tentative trying out of what it might be like to express anger. In such a case, one and the same sincere utterance might be *both* a transparent avowal of one's emotional life *and* the taking up of an empirical stance toward one's emotional life ("I see that I'm angry at you"), and both might be used in the service of *staying away* from the deeper current of one's emotional life.

And yet, even this situation *might* be the occasion for an experience of irony. Paul's cancelation is a minor rupture in the day-to-day workings of the analytic relationship. At least, that's how it looked to the patient at the time. But tell that to the Unconscious! Obviously, I am speaking metaphorically here, but in a weird way it is the Unconscious that is questioning the deeper meaning of the purportedly quotidian act. What does it mean for the relationship? What is it for there *to be* an analytic relationship? Is my analyst an *analyst*? If so, why is he canceling sessions? The Unconscious does not self-consciously ask these questions; but it provokes the anxious disruptions from which such questions can genuinely arise.

I am not persuaded by Paul's claim that "I" is used in two radically different ways. When I say, "At the time I was angry with you but I didn't know it. Only later did I realize that I must have been angry," I am all along referring to myself. The claim is instantly understandable because we do not take ourselves to be transparent to our self-conscious understanding. But the *I* who was angry and the *I* who didn't know it is me: *that's* what makes the claim interesting. I am also not persuaded by the way in which Paul carves up the distinction between the observing and experiencing egos. I think he reifies this distinction too much; and I do not think one can ultimately succeed in dividing things up in the ways he is trying to do. But I don't want to get bogged down in these disagreements. The important point that Paul is making here concerns the irreducibly social dimension of the individual human psyche. It does not surprise me that an anthropologist should bring this to our attention.

One conundrum we face is, as Paul tells us, that "the observing subject of conscious awareness . . . [must] take responsibility in the social arena" for a subject about which it has limited understanding. We see this problem illustrated even in the microcosm of Professor Paul's patient's trying to explain to him what was going on with her during his absence. In ascribing the anger to herself—even though she did not self-consciously feel it at the time—she is taking some responsibility for it, in the social sphere of the analytic situation.

According to Paul, the only reason we can give an accounting of ourselves in the social arena is that society has already colonized our inner world, instilling the capacity to give just such an accounting. As he says, "this effect of having an existence as a self who is a subject of conscious awareness is a product of the unique human embeddedness in a social milieu saturated with language, and . . . we learn to construct this internal entity through interaction with significant speaking others in the course of primary socialization." Paul concentrates on the benign and nuturing aspects of this process: paradigmatically the mother who is able to contain and transform the infant's chaotic experience and give it back to him in emotionally soothing and mentally organized speech. "This," Paul says, "provides the basis on which the baby can 'mentalize,' that is, learn to recognize and symbolize its own experiences as well as internalize the intentions of another and see its own actions through the eyes of another." It is this process which is taken up again—resumed at a different level—in the analytic situation.

It is precisely because of this social influence in psychic life that I want to take issue with what Paul says about a person who is "really" in the grip of fury. Certainly, there are more primitive ways of expressing one's fury than a furious use of the verbal utterance, "I am *furious* at you!" But I do not think that those more primitive uses are therefore more real. It is true that the ability to express one's emotions in language is a developmental achievement—and one can certainly experience and express fury before one could put it into words. It is also true that when one is in the grip of fury, the mere verbal expression can seem pale. Nevertheless, fury, too, is a developmental achievement. As Aristotle pointed out about anger in general, fury in its core claims to be right: it takes the object of the fury to be deserving of a furious response.[1] One can express hostility without language, but it is difficult to express the claim to just desert without the linguistic expression of fury.

This social dimension of psychic life also comes with characteristic vicissitudes. If the very constitution of observing self-consciousness is dependent on the internalization of social voices, this situation raises two dangers—one of which Freud warned us, the other of which is associated with Jacques Lacan. Freud's warning, of course, was that the observing ego can be used for punitive purposes: functioning as a superego, it keeps us guiltily bound up with society's demands. Lacan's warning is that these social voices form a hopeless cacophony: there is no way of keeping up with all the disparate demands to which we experience ourselves as subject.

The significance of this insight for moral psychology has not yet been adequately explored. In various places in these lectures and comments I have tried to distinguish the experience of irony from a standard superego phenomenon of falling short. This distinction is crucial to my interpretation. In the superego experience, I experience myself as falling short—perhaps pitifully short—in relation to an ideal that has been installed in me—and perhaps worked over and made more aggressive in fantasy. In the experience of irony, by contrast, the experience of falling short—insofar as the experience of irony can be described that way—is the experience of the socially implanted ideal's itself coming undone as an internal source of authority. Rather than enforcing the demands of social pretense, those very demands are coming in for anxious disruption.

However, much more needs to be said than I have been able to say in these lectures about the nature of the instability of the signifier in me that facilitates the experience of irony. One avenue for future research is whether the disparate social voices, which place us under impossibly conflicting demands, also provides the right sort of instability for ironic experience.

I shall close on a note of wholehearted agreement with Robert Paul. Citing D. W. Winnicott, he says that the analyst helps by simply surviving to be present at the next session, after the analysand has given voice to previously inhibited thoughts. Simply enduring in the company of the analysand as he or she speaks her mind is, I think, a significant part of the psychoanalytic cure. Perhaps in that context I can say that, as it seems to me, I have now survived all of my commentators' comments. I thank you all.

NOTES

COMMENTATORS

INDEX

Notes

Preface

1. See, for example, Gregory Vlastos, *Socrates: Socrates, Ironist and Moral Philosopher* (Cambridge: Cambridge University Press, 1991); Melissa Lane, "Reconsidering Socratic Irony," in *The Cambridge Companion to Socrates,* ed. Donald Morison (New York: Cambridge University Press, 2010); Allan Bloom, "Interpretive Essay," *The Republic of Plato* (New York: Basic Books, 1968); Alexander Nehamas, *The Art of Living: Socratic Reflections from Plato to Foucault* (Berkeley: University of California Press, 1998); Donald Morrison, "On Professor Vlastos' Xenophon," *Ancient Philosophy* 7 (1987: 99–22).

2. In his love song to Socrates, Alcibiades describes him as making divine melodies that have the power to transport us, to completely possess us. And yet he uses no musical intrument, only words. Plato, *Symposium* 215b–d (many editions).

1. To Become Human Does Not Come That Easily

1. *Søren Kierkegaard's Journals and Papers,* vol. 2: *F–K,* ed. H. V. Hong and E. H. Hong (Bloomington: Indiana University Press, 1970), p. 278.

2. See Michael Thompson, *Life and Action: Elementary Structures of Practice and Practical Thought* (Cambridge, Mass.: Harvard University Press, 2008).

3. Plato, *Platonis Rempublicam,* ed. S. R. Slings (Oxford: Clarendon Press, 2003); Plato, *Republic* (many translations; but my two favorites are those by C. D. C. Reeve [Indianapolis: Hackett, 2004]; and by Paul Shorey [Cambridge, Mass.: Harvard

University Press, 1987]). In general, I use the Reeve translation; though on occasion when I think there is something in the Greek that needs to be highlighted, I make my own translation. Christine M. Korsgaard, *Self-Constitution: Agency, Identity, and Integrity* (Oxford: Oxford University Press, 2009); and Korsgaard, *The Sources of Normativity* (Cambridge: Cambridge University Press, 1996).

4. See, e.g., Korsgaard, *Sources of Normativity*, pp. 90–130; Korsgaard, *Self-Constitution*, pp. 72, 104–105, 109, 119–120, 125–126. See also Thomas Nagel, "Universality and the Reflective Self," in Korsgaard, *Sources of Normativity*, pp. 200–209. In these lectures, when I talk about a *standard* form or model of reflective self-consciousness, I use that as shorthand expression for the form of reflection described in these passages.

5. Korsgaard, *Sources of Normativity*, p. 100.

6. Ibid., p. 101.

7. *Søren Kierkegaard's Journals*, p. 278.

8. Ibid., p. 277.

9. This would include what Charles Taylor has called the social imaginary of Christianity: shared images, fantasies, and myths that are embedded in and elaborate those rituals and customs. See *Modern Social Imaginaries* (Durham: Duke University Press, 2004).

10. The claim, then, is not that it is absolutely impossible to use reflection to break out of, say, Christendom, but that there are practices and institutions that contain and metabolize reflections upon them; so the thought that, in reflection, one is thereby stepping back from the practice itself may itself be illusion.

11. Søren Kierkegaard, *The Point of View on My Work as an Author,* ed. H. V. Hong and E. H. Hong (Princeton: Princeton University Press, 1998), pp. 41–44. He also calls it an enormous illusion, a delusion: see pp. 48–49.

12. A reader might wonder: why start an inquiry into irony with a single journal entry rather than a historical or critical survey of all the various interpretations? I do not think the latter strategy works, for it tends to flatten an understanding of irony's possibilities. And by now "irony" has been used for pretty much everything. To take one example, the distinguished literary critic Cleanth Brooks said that irony is "the most general term we have for the kind of qualification which the various elements in a context receive from the context" (*The Well Wrought Urn* [New York: Harcourt, Brace, 1947], p. 191). And in "Irony as a Principle of Structure" he says, "the *obvious* warping of a statement by the context we characterize as 'ironical'" (online: http://74.125.155.132/scholar?q=cache:xfe7l8hSgoJ:scholar.google.com/+Irony+as+a+principle+of+structure&hl=en). One would be better off never to have read these sentences; but, if one does, they should be in a footnote surrounded with warnings and lamentations. For those who do want a survey, among the best are D. C. Muecke, *The Compass of Irony* (London: Methuen, 1969); Nor-

man Knox, *The Word Irony and Its Context, 1500–1755* (Durham, N.C.: Duke University Press, 1961); Wayne C. Booth, *A Rhetoric of Irony* (Chicago: University of Chicago Press, 1974); Northrop Frye, *Anatomy of Criticism* (Princeton: Princeton University Press, 1957). For those who would like an introduction to certain historically important moments regarding the concept of irony, see Friedrich Schlegel, *Philosophical Fragments*, trans. Peter Firchow (Minneapolis: University of Minnesota Press, 1991); Gérard Vallée, ed., *The Spinoza Conversations between Lessing and Jacobi: Text with Excerpts from the Ensuing Controversy*, trans. G. Vallé, J. B. Lawson and C. G. Chapple. Vallée (Lanham, Md.: University Press of America, 1998); G. W. F. Hegel, *Lectures on the History of Philosophy*, trans. E. S. Haldane and F. H. Simson, vol. 1 (London: Routledge, 1982), pp. 384–448; Paul de Man, "The Concept of Irony," in *Aesthetic Ideology* (Minneapolis: University of Minnesota Press, 1996), pp. 163–184. For an introduction to the secondary literature on Kierkegaard's treatment of irony, see John Lippitt, *Humour and Irony in Kierkegaard's Thought* (London: Macmillan, 2000); Michael Strawser, *Both/And: Reading Kierkegaard from Irony to Edification* (New York: Fordham University Press, 1997); Michelle Stott, *Behind the Mask: Kierkegaard's Pseudonymic Treatment of Lessing in the Concluding Unscientific Postscript* (Lewisburg, PA.: Bucknell University Press, 1993); John D. Caputo, "Either/Or, Undecidability, and Two Concepts of Irony: Kierkegaard and Derrida," in *The New Kierkegaard*, ed. Elsebet Jegstrup (Bloomington: Indiana University Press, 2004), pp. 14–41; Jamie Lorentzen, *Kierkegaard's Metaphors* (Macon, GA.: Mercer University Press, 2001); M. Holmes Hartshorne, *Kierkegaard, Godly Deceiver: The Nature and Meaning of His Pseudonymous Writings* (New York: Columbia University Press, 1990); Ronald M. Green, *Kierkegaard and Kant: The Hidden Debt* (Albany: State University of New York Press, 1992). See also Claire Colebrook, *Irony in the Work of Philosophy* (Lincoln: University of Nebraska Press, 2002); Samuel Scolnicov, "Plato's Ethics of Irony," in *Plato Ethicus: Philosophy Is Life*, ed. Maurizio Migliori and Linda M. Napolitano Valditara (Sankt Augustin, Germany: Academia Verlag, 2004), pp. 289–300; Ronna Berger, "Socratic *Eirōneia*," *Interpretation: A Journal of Political Philosophy* 13 (1985): 143–149.

13. One caveat about terminology: Kierkegaard's pseudonymous author Johannes Climacus distinguishes irony from humor, and, if one wants to make clear the distinction between ethical and religious spheres of existence, the distinction is important. (See, e.g., Johannes Climacus [Søren Kierkegaard], *Concluding Unscientific Postscript*, trans. Alastair Hannay [Cambridge: Cambridge University Press, 2009], pp. 227–230, 243–245, 420–439, 462–464, 501–504, 520–521. The footnote at p. 462 is especially helpful.) However, on occasion he and Kierkegaard use *irony* as a general term to cover both irony and humor. (This is similar to Aristotle's use of *energeia*, which is often distinguished from *kinēsis*, but on occasion is used as a general term to cover both *energeia* and *kinēsis*.) As Climacus himself says, "humor

does not differ essentially from irony" (Hannay, p. 228). I am going to follow that broad use of *irony* as a general term to cover both irony and humor, as Johannes Climacus understood those categories.

14. *Oxford English Dictionary* online. The Danish is "udgive sig . . . for," literally, "give themselves out to be." On its own *udgive* is "publish," "put something out there." With *for* the meaning is "present themselves as." Thus "udgive sig for" is not normally predicated of animals. My thanks to David Possen for help with the Danish.

15. Elizabeth Anscombe, *Intention,* 2d ed. (Cambridge, Mass.: Harvard University Press, 2000), esp. pp. 8–9.

16. See Robert Brandom, *Making It Explicit: Reasoning, Representing, and Discursive Commitment* (Cambridge, Mass.: Harvard University Press, 1994).

17. To be sure, one can imagine circumstances in which this form of question does make sense in nonhuman animal life. For instance, if all the remaining tigers in the world existed in captivity one might ask,

> (**) Among all tigers, is there a tiger?

One would be asking whether the actually existing tigers were able to live a life appropriate to their species. In this case there would be no pretense, but captivity would impose conditions about which it would make sense to ask whether it was any longer possible to live a tiger's life. A gap would have opened between mere biological life and the possibility of flourishing as a tiger. But the extraordinary conditions needed for this question to make sense shows that in general it doesn't make sense to think of nonhuman animals as falling short in their own lives. This is because the identity of other species doesn't depend on their making claims about their identity; it doesn't depend on their making any claims at all. (I am indebted to Professor Marian David of Notre Dame for asking me the question to which this is my response.)

18. Sigmund Freud, "The 'Uncanny,'" in *The Standard Edition of the Complete Psychological Works of Sigmund Freud,* ed. and trans. James E. Strachey (London: Hogarth Press, 1981), 17: 219–252; Ernst Jentsch, "Zur Psychologie des Unheimlichen," *Psychiatrisch-Neurologische Wochenschrift* 8 (1906): 195–198 and 203–205. Translated by Roy Sellars as "On the Psychology of the Uncanny," online: www.cpmg.org.br/artigos/on_the_psychology_of_the_uncanny.pdf. For an insightful account of Heidegger's treatment of uncanniness see Katharine Withy, "Heidegger on Being Uncanny" (Ph.D. diss., University of Chicago, 2009).

19. It is worth comparing this experience to the illusions that Wittgenstein diagnosed, especially as that issue has been taken up in contemporary philosophical literature. See Cora Diamond, "Throwing Away the Ladder: How to Read the *Tractatus,*" in *The Realistic Spirit: Wittgenstein, Philosophy, and the Mind* (Cambridge, Mass.:

MIT Press, 1995), pp. 179–204, esp. pp. 184–185; and John McDowell, "Non-Cognitivism and Rule-Following," in *Mind, Value, and Reality* (Cambridge, Mass.: Harvard University Press, 1998), pp. 198–218; Alice Crary, "Introduction," in *Wittgenstein and the Moral Life: Essays in Honor of Cora Diamond* (Cambridge, Mass.: MIT Press, 2007), pp. 1–26; James Conant, "Mild Mono-Wittgensteinianism," ibid., pp. 31–142. As Crary sums up Diamond's interpretation: "Her point in speaking of illusion here is that Wittgenstein should be understood as saying that, when we envision ourselves occupying a transcendent perspective on language, we do not wind up saying anything coherent about the way things stand . . . Rather, he wishes us to see that we do not succeed in articulating any thoughts and that the idea of a perspective is properly characterized as creating the illusion of understanding words we want to utter in philosophy" (p. 5). That is, the illusion is an illusion of understanding derived from an implicit, unexamined fantasy of being able to adopt a transcendent perspective on language, logic, or life. By contrast, the moment of ironic experience could function as a moment of disruption of such an illusion. The version "what does any of this have to do with *teaching?*" that is genuinely uncanny and ironic is not the adoption of any perspective—certainly not the fantasy of adopting a transcendent perspective on the Platonic form of teaching; rather, it is the experience of breakdown in the perspective one has hitherto taken oneself to have. Now the moment of ironic disruption might be followed by anything at all—including the creation of an illusion of a transcendent perspective, say, on teaching. This would be a paradigmatic instance of an intellectual defense. It should not be conflated with the experience of irony itself.

20. Johannes Climacus [Søren Kierkegaard], *Concluding Unscientific Postscript to Philosophical Fragments*, trans. H. V. Hong and E. H. Hong (Princeton: Princeton University Press, 1992), p. 277n. I prefer this to the Hannay translation (p. 232n): "But it doesn't follow from irony being present that earnest is excluded. That is something only *privat-docents* assume."

21. I rely here on the translation of C. J. Rowe, *Plato, Phaedrus* (Warminster, England: Aris & Phillips, 2000).

22. See, for example, Socrates' account of how the prisoners in the Cave break their bonds (*Republic* VII.515c–d). The prisoner is *suddenly* (*exaiphnês* ἐξαίφνης) compelled to stand up (515c6), and is and is pained and puzzled (*aporeîn* ; d6) to turn around. And see Alcibiades' description of Socrates' disruptive effect upon him in *Symposium* 215d–216d.

23. See Hugh Brody, *The Other Side of Eden: Hunters, Farmers and the Shaping of the World* (London: Faber and Faber, 2002).

24. Thomas Nagel, "The Absurd," in *Mortal Questions* (Cambridge: Cambridge University Press, 1979), pp. 11–23.

25. Ibid., p. 15.

26. For an excellent article on Socrates as shepherd, see Rachel Barney, "Socrates' Refutation of Thrasymachus," in *The Blackwell Guide to Plato's Republic*, ed. Gerasimos Santas (Oxford: Blackwell, 2006), pp. 44–62.

27. See Gregory Vlastos, *Socrates, Ironist and Moral Philosopher* (Cambridge: Cambridge University Press, 1991), esp. pp. 46–80.

28. I discuss this further in "Socratic Method and Psychoanalysis," in *A Companion to Socrates*, ed. Sara Ahbel-Rappe and Rachana Kamtekar (Oxford: Blackwell, 2006), pp. 442–462.

29. Of course, in some sense that is always true: in a moment of philosophical reflection one can always imagine a weird case in which someone systematically misinterprets conditions. The point here, by contrast, is that normal participants in an established form of life laying down conditions in a way that they take to be an instance of standard reflection will thereby miss the distinction they are purportedly attempting to capture.

30. Sebastian Rödl, *Self-Consciousness* (Cambridge, Mass.: Harvard University Press, 2007), esp. pp. 34–42, 81–83, 173–175.

31. Korsgaard, *Sources of Normativity*, p. 105.

32. Ibid.

33. Ibid., p. 106.

34. That is, *genuine* irony; not the tame, left-hand version that Christendom contains.

35. See Climacus [Kierkegaard], *Concluding Unscientific Postscript* (Hannay), pp. 501–504. And see Plato, *Apology* 21e, 23b, 30a–b, 38a, 41a–c.

36. Søren Kierkegaard, *The Concept of Irony with Continual Reference to Socrates*, trans. H. V. Hong and E. H. Hong (Princeton: Princeton University Press, 1989), e.g., p. 279.

37. Vlastos, *Socrates*, p. 43, fn. 81.

38. Even Alexander Nehamas, who argues forcefully against Vlastos' interpretation of Socrates, follows Vlastos in his interpretation of Kierkegaard: "Vlastos cannot possibly accept Kierkegaard's position, and in this strong version, neither can I. Truth is much more important to Socrates than Kierkegaard allows, both as a means and as a goal" (*The Art of Living: Socratic Reflections from Plato to Foucault* [Berkeley: University of California Press: 1998], p. 52; cf. p. 71). But this view looks plausible only if, following Vlastos, one regards *The Concept of Irony* as providing Kierkegaard's settled view of irony. In fact, one needs to look at the entire pseudonymous authorship; but, in particular, to Johannes Climacus' hilarious critique of *The Concept of Irony*. (See e.g. Climacus [Kierkegaard], *Concluding Unscientific Postscript* (Howard V. Hong and Edna H.Hong), pp. 500-504; p. 90n). Nehamas valuably distinguishes Platonic irony from Socratic irony, and he makes apt criticisms of Vlastos' interpretation. However, in following Vlastos in this misplaced criticism of Kierkegaard, Nehamas misses what, from a Kierkegaardian perspective, makes irony such a philosophically and ethically powerful phenomenon.

39. Climacus [Kierkegaard], *Concluding Unscientific Postscript* (Howard V. Hong and Edna H.Hong), p. 503

40. Ibid. p. 90n.

41. I here use the translation of Alexander Nehamas and Paul Woodruff in *Plato: Complete Works*, ed. J. M. Cooper (Indianapolis: Hackett, 1997).

42. It is this balance which is lost on his ersatz followers, for example Apollodorus (*Symposium* 172–174)—as though what it is to follow Socrates is literally to follow him around.

43. I here use the translation of Rosamond Kent Sprague in *Plato: Complete Works* op. cit.

44. I use the translation of G. M. A. Grube in in *Plato: Complete Works* op. cit.

45. Vlastos, *Socrates*, p. 234. Johannes Climacus uses the phrase "movement of infinity" to characterize ironic activity—a phrase that has shed any particular emphasis on negativity—and he says that the ironist inhabits a border area between aesthetic and ethical forms of existence. This intermediate zone is a play-space with an ethical dimension. The aesthetic—taken from the Greek word for perception, *aisthēsis*—is a life organized around appearances: how things appear, seem, are given to one. It is the world of social pretense, the world of practical identity understood in terms of social role. And because social pretense is as rich and variegated as we have seen, one does not leave it simply by reflecting on its terms. Thus aesthetic existence can include attempts to ground the ethical in terms of such practical identities. The issue would depend on the basis on which reflective judgment is made: e.g., if one *finds* one's identity meaningful and thus sticks with its requirements one has a reflective judgment that, in Kierkegaard's terms, would remain within the aesthetic. The problem with the aesthetic is that when one is living that form of life, it feels like a world that itself encompasses the distinction between aesthetic and ethical. The ironic "movement of infinity" is the disruption of that world—a disruption of the sense that we have grasped the ethical. We cannot tell, Climacus tells us, whether the ironist is actually living an ethical life; but he does open up the possibility of ethical life by disrupting the ersatz totalities of social pretense. See, e.g., Climacus [Kierkegaard], *Concluding Unscientific Postscript* (Hong and Hong), pp. 500–502.

46. Kierkegaard, *The Concept of Irony*, p. 326. See also Thesis XV: "Just as philosophy begins with doubt, so also a life that may be called human begins with irony" (p. 6).

47. Richard Rorty, "Private Irony and Liberal Hope," in *Contingency, Irony and Solidarity* (Cambridge: Cambridge University Press, 1989), p. 73.

48. It is beyond the scope of this essay to discuss this in detail, but Kierkegaard would treat this as ultimately an aesthetic phenomenon. Rorty's ironist is living according to what "strikes" him as interesting, "strikes" him as an occasion for doubt, etc. These are for Kierkegaard aesthetic phenomena: and Kierkegaard considered a life organized by such phenomena an aesthetic form of existence.

49. As Judge William writes to A, "There is something treacherous in wishing to be merely an observer." See Victor Eremita ed. [Søren Kierkegaard] *Either/Or*, trans. Walter Lowrie, vol. 2 (Princeton: Princeton University Press, 1949), p. 7; and see Judge William's advice to A to choose despair, esp. pp. 175–181.

50. To put it in a nutshell: Socrates' accusers charge him with deception, but they do so because they are deaf to the right-hand meanings with which he is speaking.

51. There are many strands to the story of how the resonance of the right-hand column got lost. But one strand flows from the historical use to which concepts of identity have been put over the past few centuries. Our contemporary paradigms of identity have arisen out of histories of discrimination, oppression, and victimization. In the waves of immigration to the United States in the nineteenth and twentieth centuries, people were labeled *Italian, Irish, Jew* in part to tag them and keep them separate from dominant culture. There would then be little social room for an ironic question whether anyone fitted the category. The point of the tag was to keep people inside the category and not let them out. Another route has traced identity as having been formed in conscious response to a history of oppression. Prime examples are *black* and *African-American*—formed in response to pejorative terms that had previously been used. Another would be *gay*, a term self-consciously dignified by homosexuals themselves, as in "gay pride." These formulations are self-consciously part of a process aimed at encouraging self-esteem in a group that historically has been demeaned by the dominant culture. It would run counter to one of the aims of such formulations if, in the conceptualization, it left open the possibility that almost no one in the hitherto oppressed group lived up to the demands of the category. Of course, it is possible to formulate an ironic question in any of these cases. And there have certainly been debates within each of these groups as to what their central ideals should be and how they should be understood. However, given the various histories of discrimination and oppression, the focus has been on how the social pretense should be understood. And this has provided a paradigm for our contemporary conception of identity.

52. See, as a paradigm, James Conant, "Putting Two and Two Together: Kierkegaard, Wittgenstein, and the Point of View of Their Work as Authors," in *The Grammar of Religious Belief*, ed. D. Z. Phillips (New York: St. Martin's Press, 1996).

53. Ibid., p. 258.

54. Kierkegaard, *The Point of View of My Work as an Author*, p. 31; my emphasis.

55. Conant, "Mild Mono-Wittgensteinianism," p. 262.

56. Ibid., pp. 249, 274–275.

57. Climacus [Kierkegaard], *Concluding Unscientific Postscript*, (Hong and Hong) pp. 502, 505–507.

58. Ibid., pp. 505–506 (my emphasis).

59. The issue of what Climacus' humor consists in is itself a difficult interpretive problem. Climacus describes the humorist as bringing out the contradiction between God and anything else. That a humorist brings out a contradiction does not, of course, imply that he is involved in his own performative contradiction. It is conceivable that Climacus *stages* a performative contradiction, but in such a case we would not have a performative contraction but a humorous, mimetic enactment of one. All this, of course, needs further elaboration.

60. Conant, "Mild Mono-Wittgensteinianism," p. 275.

61. Ibid., p. 281.

2. Ironic Soul

1. Plato, *Phaedrus* 244a–253a and *Symposium* 206d-e, both in *Platonis Opera*, v.2 ed. Ioannes Burnet (Oxford: Clarendon Press, 1976); *Republic* VII.524, VIII.548c–554e, in *Platonis Rempublicam*, ed. S. R. Slings (Oxford: Clarendon Press, 2003). Subsequent citations of Platonic sources are drawn from these editions.

2. Christine M. Korsgaard, *The Sources of Normativity* (Cambridge: Cambridge University Press, 1996), pp. 37–40; Bernard Williams, *Shame and Necessity* (Berkeley: University of California Press, 1993), pp. 42–46.

3. Plato, *Republic* IX.580d10–e1.

4. Sigmund Freud, *Civilization and Its Discontents*, in *The Standard Edition of the Complete Psychological Works of Sigmund Freud*, ed. and trans. James E. Strachey (London: Hogarth Press, 1981; cited hereafter as *SE*), 21: 64–145.

5. Freud, "The 'Uncanny'," in *SE* 17: 245.

6. I have argued for the world-structuring nature of unconscious fantasy in *Freud* (New York: Routledge, 2005), pp. 117–143; in "Transference as Worldliness," in *Therapeutic Action: An Earnest Plea for Irony* (New York: Other Press, 2003), pp. 181–211; and in "An Interpretation of Transference," in *Open Minded: Working Out the Logic of the Soul* (Cambridge, Mass.: Harvard University Press, 1998), pp. 56–79.

7. After the seminar associated with the Tanner Lectures was over, a woman came up to me and in a private moment told me that she could see herself in Ms. A., And although it would be an exaggeration to say that this has happened every time, it is uncanny how often it has happened when I subsequently delivered versions of this lecture.

8. David Finkelstein, *Expression and the Inner* (Cambridge, Mass.: Harvard University Press, 2003). I also learned from his seminar on first-person authority.

9. Finkelstein is adapting Wittgenstein's account of how we acquire the ability to express our pain in language. Wittgenstein's suggestion in *Philosophical Investigations* §244 is that "words are connected with the primitive, natural expressions of the sensation and used in their place. A child has hurt himself and he cries;

and then adults talk to him and teach him exclamations and, later, sentences." Ludwig Wittgenstein, *Philosophical Investigations,* G.E.M. Anscombe trans. (Oxford: Blackwell, 1978), p. 89. In this way, "the verbal expression of pain *replaces* crying" (Ibid. my emphasis). The point about replacement does not imply that a verbal expression can have no more semantic meaning than crying, nor that it must lack a truth-value because it is an expression of pain. "That hurts!" can both be true *and* express the pain. The point is, rather, that because the child can learn verbal expressions—say, "Ouch!" (which, like crying, can express pain *and* lacks a truth-value), and "That hurts!" (which, like crying can express pain, but unlike crying does have a truth-value)—these verbal expressions can *replace* crying as they become alternative vehicles for expressing the very pain that crying would have expressed.

10. For an account of how this might be possible without invoking any objectionable theory of homunculi or being an instance of the bad faith Sartre criticized, see my *Freud* and Sebastian Gardner, *Irrationality and the Philosophy of Psychoanalysis* (Cambridge: Cambridge University Press, 1993).

11. Freud, *Fragment of an Analysis of a Case of Hysteria, SE* 7: 77–78.

12. Richard Moran, *Authority and Estrangement: An Essay on Self-Knowledge* (Princeton: Princeton University Press, 2001); see esp. pp. 84–90, 101–107.

13. Moran: "The notion of avowal here has been developed in relation to the . . . idea of transparency. A statement of one's belief about X is said to obey the Transparency Condition when the statement is made by consideration of the facts about X itself, and not by either an 'inward glance' or by observation of one's own behavior. An avowal is a statement of one's belief which obeys the Transparency Condition." Ibid., p. 101.

14. Ibid., p. 85 (my emphasis).

15. For example, a much-discussed case in the psychoanalytic world is of a Mr. A. who, while in the midst of thanking his analyst for all the gains he has made, falls into an extended coughing fit, which then turns into an f-*cough*: *"Do I want to tell you to fuck off!"* Lawrence Levenson, "Superego Defense Analysis in the Termination Phase," *Journal of the American Psychoanalytic Association* 46 (1998): 847–866. I discuss this case at length in "Technique and Final Cause in Psychoanalysis," *International Journal of Psychoanalysis* 90 (2009), pp. 1299-1317. (2010). I also discuss it in *Therapeutic Action,* pp. 122–133. The idea of a movement from cough to f-cough to "fuck off!" was made by Dr. Nancy Olson in an online discussion of this case: L. Levenson, S. H. Phillips. C Paniagua, S. Sonnenberg, and R. White, "Paul Gray's Narrowing Scope: A Developmental Lag in His Theory and Technique", online: http://www.psychoanalysis.net/JPN-Archive.

16. Such voices of boyishness are used on American television both in humor and in advertising. For humor, think of the *Saturday Night Live* sketch "Da Bears, Da Bulls" (e.g., "Da Super Fans Talk—Da Bulls," http://www.evtv1.com/player

.aspx?itemnum=6203. For a history of this sketch see the Wikipedia entry under "Bill Swerski's Superfans"). Almost all the humor circulated around imitations of "guy talk." For an example of an advertisement that relies on the idea that black masculinity must be present in the speech, not just as content but as animating principle of the speech, see the Budweiser ad "Wassup" at http://www.adbrands .net/us/budweiser_us.htm.

17. See my "Technique and Final Cause in Psychoanalysis."

18. Freud, "Remembering, Repeating and Working-Through," in *SE* 12: 154.

19. Readers interested in the psychoanalytic use of intermediate spaces might want to consult D. W. Winnicott, "Transitional Objects and Transitional Phenomena," in *Playing and Reality* (London: Tavistock, 1971), pp. 1–25; and Hans Loewald, "On the Therapeutic Action of Psychoanalysis," in *The Essential Loewald: Collected Papers and Monographs* (Hagerstown, MD.: University Publishing Group, 2000), pp. 221–256.

20. See, for example, Plato's use of *andreīa*—literally, *manliness, manhood, manly spirit*—in his investigation of courage in the *Laches.*

21. Ms. A., for example, may have had training in how to face circumstances courageously as a woman; and she had training in how to face them courageously as a boy; but what she faces in analysis is a disruption, or even a breakdown, of the idiosyncratic, individual form of life in which those images had application. The ironic question becomes: How does one face courageously the disruption or breakdown of courage as one has inherited and internalized it? That is, what does courage have to do with courage? This may occur against a background in which available social pretenses are robust and fairly stable, or it may occur when available social images are themselves undergoing transformation and disruption. Either way, there is room for ironic questioning of the virtues. A dramatic inverse case is when the social understandings of the virtues themselves break down (regardless of what is happening to the individual). This is a central topic in my *Radical Hope: Ethics in the Face of Cultural Devastation* (Cambridge, Mass.: Harvard University Press, 2006).

22. Plato, *Phaedrus* 229e–230a, translated by Alexander Nehamas and Paul Woodruff in *Plato: Complete Works,* ed. J. M. Cooper (Indianapolis: Hackett, 1997). For a description of the horrific nature of Typhon see Hesiod, *Theogony* ll. 820–880. From a psychoanalytic perspective, it is interesting that the Sphinx, whose riddle Oedipus solved, was an offspring of Typhon. And, according to legend, Typhon, in revenge for Oedipus' killing the Sphinx, sent a human servant to reveal who Oedipus was.

23. Christine M. Korsgaard, *Self-Constitution: Agency, Identity, and Integrity* (Oxford: Oxford University Press, 2009), p. 7.

24. In logic, a theory T2 is a conservative extension of theory T1 if every theorem in T2 that uses only the symbols of T1 is already a theorem of T1. Obviously, the idea

of a nonconservative extension in the current context can be only analogical and suggestive.

25. Moran, *Authority and Estrangement*, p. 85 (my emphasis).

26. Freud, "The Dynamics of Transference," in *SE* 12: 108; my emphases. Similar points are made elsewhere in Freud's writings. See, e.g., "Remembering, Repeating and Working Through," in *SE* 12: 152.

27. The psychoanalyst Hans Loewald describes it as a process of turning ghosts into ancestors: "The transference neurosis, in the technical sense of the establishment and resolution of it in the analytic process, is due to *the blood of recognition,* which the patient's unconscious is given to taste so that the old ghosts reawaken to life. Those who know ghosts tell us that they long to be released from their ghost life and led to rest as ancestors. As ancestors they live forth in the present generation, while as ghosts they are compelled to haunt the present generation with their shadow life. Transference is pathological insofar as the unconscious is a crowd of ghosts, and this is the beginning of the transference neurosis in analysis: ghosts of the unconscious, imprisoned by defenses but haunting the patient in the dark of his defenses and symptoms, *are allowed to taste blood, and are let loose.* In the daylight of analysis the ghosts of the unconscious are laid and led to rest as ancestors whose power is taken over and transformed into the newer intensity of present life . . ." Loewald, "On the Therapeutic Action of Psychoanalysis," pp. 248–249 (my emphases).

28. Moran, *Authority and Estrangement*, pp. 89–90 (my emphasis).

29. Ibid., p. 90.

3. Self-Constitution and Irony

1. Christine M. Korsgaard, *The Sources of Normativity* (Cambridge: Cambridge University Press, 1996), §3.3.1, pp. 100–102.

2. Christine M. Korsgaard, *Self-Constitution: Agency, Identity, and Integrity* (Oxford: Oxford University Press, 2009), §1.4, pp. 18–26.

3. This is the general argument of *Self-Constitution,* but see especially §§4.4–4.5, pp. 72–80; and chap. 9, pp. 177–206.

4. One response to this that I have mentioned, but not discussed much, is to redesign the role: find a new way of carrying it out that is compatible with other demands, or with other features of the situation more generally. See *Self-Constitution,* §1.4.4, p. 21. I mention this here because I think it might be a particularly apt response to ironic experience in Lear's sense, and it is one way to understand Lear's account of what Ms. A., whom I will be discussing later, does. In Alfred Hitchcock's movie *Stage Fright,* Commodore Gill (wonderfully played by Alasdair Sim), the father of the heroine Eve, is scolded by a police detective for helping his daughter to involve herself in a dangerous situation in order to save the man she thinks she loves.

"What kind of a father are you?" demands the detective. "Unique," replies Gill. That of course is Alcibiades' word for Socrates: unique.

5. *Republic* 588c–d, in *Plato: Complete Works,* ed. J. M. Cooper (Indianapolis: Hackett, 1997), pp. 1196.

6. Cf. also Lear's remark in the first lecture, after quoting Kierkegaard, that "The suggestion here is *not* that if only we would reflect on what our practical identity already commits us to then we would be taking on the difficult task of becoming human." That is not my suggestion either. As I am about to argue, we are always actively re endorsing, and potentially reconsidering, our identities, not just living up to established commitments.

7. Except in "Conjectures on the Beginning of Human History" (in *Kant: Political Writings,* 2d ed., ed. Hans Reiss, trans. H. B. Nisbet [Cambridge: Cambridge University Press, 1991]), where Kant does envision the participation of reason, and therefore the agent's thinking, as contributing to the formation of uniquely human desires. See my account of this in *Self-Constitution,* §6.2.1, pp. 117–118.

8. Immanuel Kant, *Groundwork of the Metaphysics of Morals,* trans. Mary Gregor (Cambridge: Cambridge University Press: 1997), pp. 37 (4:428) and 62 (4:458), respectively. But in *Religion within the Boundaries of Mere Reason* (trans. George di Giovanni [Cambridge: Cambridge University Press, 1998]) he takes it back. "Considered in themselves, natural inclinations are good, i.e., not reprehensible, and to want to extirpate them would not only be futile, but harmful and blameworthy as well; we must rather curb them, so that they will not wear each other out but will instead be harmonized into a whole called happiness" (6:58, p. 78). But this does not solve the problem I mention in the text.

9. Plato, *Republic* 588d, p. 1196; I discuss the question whether these thinkers are committed to the view that we should identify with reason in *Self-Constitution,* §7.2.10, pp. 140–141; and §7.5.3, pp. 154–158.

10. Perhaps this is overstated. But there is a general problem about some of the phenomena characteristically studied by psychoanalysts, Freudian slips, for example, which is relevant here. Such phenomena have the kind of intelligibility that chosen actions do—we can say what the person's "reasons" for acting as she does are; but they seem to be caused rather than chosen. In this respect, the kinds of "reasons" Ms. A. has for doing boyish things are rather like the "reasons" for loving someone. Those also seem to operate causally rather than as grounds of choice, yet (in some cases) seem to make the love intelligible. I discuss the problem in "The General Point of View: Love and Moral Approval in Hume's Ethics," in Christine M. Korsgaard, *The Constitution of Agency* (Oxford: Oxford University Press, 2009), pp. 263–301; see especially §1.3, pp. 267–270.

11. Lear claims that Ms. A. was not unreflective about her conscious practical identity as feminine, since she had read the feminist literature and "took her feminine dress

to be an expression of her version." He thinks that this shows that reflection was used in the service of staying with those received social images. I think it shows that not every form of babbling to oneself counts as reflection.

12. This isn't explicit, but see *Self-Constitution*, p. xiii, and also §9.1.5, p. 180.

13. Although it isn't exactly the same, see my account of some closely related worries about the efficacy of human action and how they give rise to the need for faith in *Self-Constitution*, §5.2, pp. 84–90.

4. Irony, Reflection, and Psychic Unity

1. This translation is from Plato, *Symposium of Plato*, Thomas Griffith trans.(Berkeley: University of California, 1989). In general, I rely on Plato, *Symposium* in *Platonis Opera* v. 2, Ioannes Burnet ed. (Oxford: Clarendon Press, 1976).

2. Actually, I doubt that Zen Masters are Zen Masters in that sense either.

3. Plato, *Plato: Phaedrus*, C. J. Rowe trans. (Warminster, England: Aris & Phillips, 2000).

4. Compare this to the apocryphal story told of the Oxford classicist Maurice Bowra. His biographer writes: "Another tale concerned Parsons' Pleasure, a bathing establishment in which dons swam and sunbathed naked. On one occasion a boatload of ladies came by, and men hurriedly tied towels around their waists. One man, however, put the towel over his head, arguing that it was by his face that he was known in Oxford. These anecdotes were told about Bowra as they had been told about others before him. Quite simply, they were oral myths intended to define what a great academic might have done." Leslie Mitchell: *Maurice Bowra: A Life* (Oxford: Oxford University Press, 2009), p. 178. If we consider these two images—Socrates with his cloak over his head, "Bowra" with his towel over his head—we can see two very different ideals of integrity at play. "Bowra's" act is marked by *savoir-faire:* there is no conflict there; he effortlessly knows what to do; and he could care less that his genitals are, so to speak, blowin' in the wind. For Socrates, by contrast, the cloak over his head is the outer mark of the conflict he experiences between desire and shame. The integrity of his act flows not from lack of conflict, but rather from its open expression, its acknowledgment, and the active response to it.

5. Plato, *Phaedrus* 229e–230a, in the translation by C. J. Rowe (Eng.: Aris & Phillips, 2000).

6. For an account of this, see Sigmund Freud, *The Interpretation of Dreams,* chap. 6, "The Dream-Work," and chap. 7, "The Psychology of the Dream Process," *SE* 5: 488–621.

7. Freud, "The Unconscious," in *SE* 14: 187.

8. Freud, *The Interpretation of Dreams, SE* 5: 506–507.

9. See also my "Technique and Final Cause in Psychoanalysis," *International Journal of Psychoanalysis* 90 (2009): 1299–1317. See also "An Interpretation of Transference,"

in *Open Minded: Working Out the Logic of the Soul* (Cambridge, Mass.: Harvard University Press, 1998), pp. 56–79; "Transference," in *Freud* (New York: Routledge, 2005), pp. 117–142; "Transference as Worldliness," in *Therapeutic Action: An Earnest Plea for Irony* (New York: Other Press, 2003) pp. 179–211.

10. See my *Freud*, pp. 23–54; "Jumping from the Couch," *International Journal of Psychoanalysis* 83 (2002): 583–593; "Restlessness, Phantasy and the Concept of Mind," in *Open Minded*, pp. 80–122; "Give Dora a Break!: A Tale of Eros and Emotional Disruption," in *Erotikon: Essays on Eros Ancient and Modern*, ed. Shadi Bartsch and Thomas Bartscherer (Chicago: University of Chicago Press, 2005), pp. 196–212.

11. Christine M. Korsgaard, *Self-Constitution: Agency, Identity, and Integrity* (Oxford: Oxford University Press, 2009), p. 25.

12. Here is one of her classic characterizations: "our capacity to turn our attention on to our own mental activities is also a capacity to *distance ourselves* from them, and to call them into question. I perceive, and I find myself with a powerful impulse to believe. But I *back up* and bring that impulse into view and then *I have a certain distance*. Now the impulse doesn't dominate me and now I have a problem. Shall I believe? Is this perception really a reason to believe? I desire and I find myself with a powerful impulse to act. But I *back up* and bring that impulse into view and then I have *a certain distance*. Now the impulse doesn't dominate me and now I have a problem. Shall I act? Is this desire really a reason to act?" Korsgaard, *The Sources of Normativity* (Cambridge: Cambridge University Press, 1996), pp. 92–93 (my emphases).

    In a similar vein, John McDowell invites us to consider a wolf that suddenly acquires rationality: "Suppose now that a rational wolf finds himself in a situation in which some behavior would come naturally to him: say playing his part in the cooperative activity of hunting with the pack. Having acquired reason, he can contemplate alternatives; he can *step back* from the natural impulse and direct critical scrutiny at it. We cannot allow ourselves to suppose that God, say, might confer reason on wolves, but stop short of his giving them the materials to *step back* and frame the question 'Why should I do this?'" John McDowell, "Two Sources of Naturalism," in *Mind, Value, and Reality* (Cambridge, Mass.: Harvard University Press, 1998), p. 171 (my emphasis).

13. Martin Heidegger, *Being and Time*, trans. John Macquarrie and Edward Robinson (New York: Harper and Row, 1962), p. 229. See in general Division I.6, ¶40, pp. 228–235.

14. Indeed, in a series of footnotes, Heidegger is critical of Kierkegaard for not thinking through the distinction between existential and existentiell, between ontic and ontological; *Being and Time*, p. 492 n. iv; p. 494 n. vi; p. 497 n. iii. Kierkegaard's response, I suspect, would be that the very most important matter—becoming a Christian—required a response in which these categories were inextricably mixed.

15. Heidegger, *Being and Time*, pp. 233–234. It is uncanniness, he says, that "pursues Dasein constantly, and is a threat to its everyday lostness in [Das Man]" (p. 234).

16. Korsgaard, *Sources of Normativity*, pp. 101–102 (my emphases).

17. Freud, *Civilization and Its Discontents*, SE 21: 59–145; Jacques Lacan, *The Ethics of Psychoanalysis: 1959–1960. The Seminar of Jacques Lacan, Book VII*, ed. Jacques-Alain Miller, trans. D. Dennis Porter (London: Tavistock/Routledge, 1992).

18. Stephen Engstrom, *The Form of Practical Knowledge: A Study of the Categorical Imperative* (Cambridge, Mass.: Harvard University Press, 2009), pp. 29–30; see also pp. 50–52.

19. Sebastian Rödl, *Self-Consciousness* (Cambridge, Mass.: Harvard University Press, 2007), p. 46.

20. Engstrom, *The Form of Practical Knowledge*, pp. 104–108.

5. Psychoanalysis and the Limits of Reflection

1. Sigmund Freud, letter of January 1, 1896, in *The Origins of Psycho-Analysis*, ed. Marie Bonaparte, Anna Freud, and Ernst Kris (New York: Basic Books, 1954), p. 141.

2. Richard Moran, *Authority and Estrangement: An Essay on Self-Knowledge* (Princeton: Princeton University Press, 2001).

3. Richard Moran, "Self-Knowledge: Discovery, Resolution, and Undoing," *European Journal of Philosophy* 5 (1997), pp. 141-161.

4. Most memorably explored in the work of Stanley Cavell, beginning with *Must We Mean What We Say?* (Cambridge: Cambridge University Press, 1976) and in *The Claim of Reason* (Oxford: Clarendon Press, 1979).

5. Ludwig Wittgenstein, The *Blue and Brown Books*, (Oxford: Blackwell, 1969) p. 39.

6. Ludwig Wittgenstein, *Philosophical Investigations*, G.E.M. Anscombe trans. (Oxford: Blackwell, 1968) p. 189.

7. In his second lecture Lear says that "expression" in the special sense means "a truth-claim . . . that is a manifestation of the very anger about which the truth-claim makes its claim." But this will be true of simple statements of belief, as well as of many other first-person statements, for example, verbal declarations of hope or conviction or regret or even conditional belief. Their statements, too, are manifestations of the very condition I claim for myself, but this is not for reasons that have to do with the replacement of some preverbal natural reaction that is then replaced by some verbal form.

6. The Immanence of Irony and the Efficacy of Fantasy

1. I began discussing Liberaldom in the response to Korsgaard above.

2. A relatively minor point: in the narrative that Moran ascribes to me, he says that I carve up the world in this way: "So, on the one hand, there are the figures of irony

like Socrates and Kierkegaard who see the infinite questionability of our lives and our identities. And on the other hand, there are the figures, like Alcibiades, who 'don't get it' or who are complacently inhabiting their practical identities as though they were matters of simple membership in a group." This is not what I meant. It is true that I think Alcibiades "just doesn't get it" about Socrates' standing still. That is because his description of the scene is indifferent between a case in which Socrates is deliberating about a serious practical problem—one that might conceivably threaten his virtue—and a case in which he is simply absorbed in thought, perhaps thinking about Euclid's parallel postulate. This indifference is, I think, meant to shed light on Alcibiades' character. (I discuss this in the response to Korsgaard.) Plato does want to put on display the peculiar pathology that Alcibiades manifests; but Alcibiades is an extraordinary figure, one who is susceptible to the force of Socratic irony, one who finds it impossible to complacently inhabit any practical identity, one who regularly suffers erotic, uncanny, anxiety. One problem Plato is raising for his readers is: Why is a person so ready for Socratic irony not helped by it?

3. Richard Moran, *Authority and Estrangement: An Essay on Self-Knowledge* (Princeton: Princeton University Press, 2001), p. 85; my emphasis.

4. I will say in passing that I find the very idea of analysts' making constructions a terrible idea. Freud did it, and he wrote about why it was appropriate. (Sigmund Freud, "Constructions in Analysis," in *SE* 23: 257–269.) This is a part of his technique that we would do well to leave behind. Insofar as the above-quoted passage leaves a reader with a sense that it is constructions that analysts have to offer, it also leaves the reader with a distorted sense of what a good analysis consists in.

5. There is a story of a friend telling Picasso that his portrait of Gertrude Stein does not look like her. "It will," he famously replies. This story is probably apocryphal—though based on Stein's own understanding of the artist's role, and her specific appreciation of Picasso.

6. See my "The Heterogeneity of the Mental," *Mind* 104 (1995): 863–879.

7. For an introduction, see, e.g., Hanna Segal, "Notes on Symbol Formation," *International Journal of Psychoanalysis* 38 (1957): 391—397; also in E. B. Spillius, ed., *Melanie Klein Today*, vol. 1: *Mainly Theory* (London: Routledge, 1988), pp. 160–177. Wilfrid Bion, "Attacks on Linking," *International Journal of Psychoanalysis* 40 (1959): 308–315; also in Spillius, *Melanie Klein Today*, pp. 87–101; Wilfred Bion, "A Theory of Thinking," *International Journal of Psychoanalysis* 43 (1962): 306–310; also in Spillius, *Melanie Klein Today*, pp. 178–186; Wilfred Bion, "Differentiation of the Psychotic from the Non-Psychotic Personality," *International Journal of Psychoanalysis* 38 (1957): 266–275; in Spillius, *Melanie Klein Today*, pp. 61–78. Betty Joseph, "Projective Identification: Some Clinical Aspects," in *Psychic Equilibrium and Psychic Change: Selected Papers of Betty Joseph*, M. Feldman and E. B. Spillius eds. (London: Routledge, 1989),

pp. 168–180. Melanie Klein, "Notes on Some Schizoid Mechanisms," in *Envy and Gratitude and Other Works, 1946–1963* (London: Hogarth Press, 1975), pp. 1–24. Richard Wollheim, "On the Mind and the Mind's Image of Itself," in *On Art and the Mind* (Cambridge, Mass.: Harvard University Press, 1974), pp. 31–53; Wollheim, "Imagination and Identification," ibid., pp. 54–83.

8. I discuss this in the Introduction to *The Fifty-Minute Hour*, by Robert Lindner (New York: Other Press, 2002). I hasten to say that this was *not* a psychoanalytic case. I treated this patient on the in-patient psychiatric ward of the West Haven Veterans Adminstration Hospital. We worked together for two years in a nonpsychoanalytic psychotherapy.

9. See my "Jumping from the Couch," *International Journal of Psychoanalysis* 83 (2008): 583–595; "Give Dora a Break!: A Tale of Eros and Emotional Disruption," in *Erotikon: Essays on Eros, Ancient and Modern*, ed. Shadi Bartsch and Thomas Bartscherer (Chicago: University of Chicago Press, 2005), pp. 196–212; "Restlessness, Phantasy and the Concept of Mind," in *Open Minded: Working Out the Logic of the Soul* (Cambridge, Mass.: Harvard University Press, 1998), pp. 80–122; *Freud* (London: Routledge, 2005), pp. 23–53, 117–144.

10. I have tried at least to begin addressing such questions. See "Technique and Final Cause in Psychoanalysis," *International Journal of Psychoanalysis* 90 (2009): 1299–1317.

11. In a note, Moran says that expression in the special sense means "a truth-claim . . . that is a manifestation of the very anger about which the truth-claim makes its claim"—and goes on to say that that will be true of simple statements of belief as well as many other first-person statements. But I was not there trying to give a sufficient characterization of expression in this special sense. I was pointing out one hallmark of an exemplary case.

12. Ludwig Wittgenstein, *Philosophical Investigations*, G. E. M. Anscombe trans. (Oxford: Blackwell, 1978), p. 189.

13. Freud himself told us that every dream has a navel that goes so deep into the unconscious that we cannot plumb it; *The Interpretation of Dreams*, SE 5: 525. I discuss this in *Freud*, p. 104.

7. Thoughts about Irony and Identity

1. Leo Tolstoy, *Youth*, in *Childhood, Boyhood and Youth*, trans. Louise and Aylmer Maude (London: Oxford University Press, 1930), chap. 31, pp. 338–341. While *Youth* is a novel, much of it is autobiographical; See. Henri Troyat's use of the material in his *Tolstoï* (Paris: Hachette, 1965). I treat the material about becoming *comme il faut* as drawn directly from Tolstoy's own experience. In my discussion of *comme il faut* and similar identities, I focus entirely on masculine identity; my use of "he" or "him" is meant to refer to these identities.

2. Christine Korsgaard, to whom I am indebted for discussion about this matter, raised the issue in connection with *cool*.

3. See Anthony Powell, *A Question of Upbringing,* in *A Dance to the Music of Time* I, *Spring* (London: Random House, 2000), p. 30. The whole of *A Question of Upbringing* is illuminating on the enacting of identities of the sort with which I am concerned, and in particular on the significance of clothes, of how they are worn, and of attitudes to smartness of clothes. Templer indeed is capable of wearing utterly wrong clothes as a kind of play on the whole business: "I've bought a wonderfully Widmerpool tie to go home in"; but his too smart clothes in other contexts make his social ambitions too obvious. On one's clothes' being too correct, see also Pierre Bourdieu, *La distinction: Critique sociale du jugement* (Paris: Éditions de Minuit, 1979), p. 278.

4. Jonathan Lear, *Freud* (New York: Routledge, 2005).

5. My description of Tolstoy may be framed in a way that is incompatible with Lear's account in *Freud*. He argued there that, if the elusive question how to live has not genuinely been asked by someone, we cannot take that person's thought about the way he or she is living (or trying to live) to provide an answer to that question, even if the person does take herself or himself to be living (or trying to live) in a way in which it is good to live. I have described Tolstoy as having had a view of what the only good way to live is, at a period in his life that may antedate the time at which what Lear refers to as the "elusive" question arose for him, or was genuinely asked by him. My account of him as having had a view about how one should live depends on his own later description of his views at the time.

6. The idea of a corresponding move in relation to the Socratic view of cookery is mooted by J. E. Tiles, "*Technē* and Moral Expertise," *Philosophy* 59 (1984): 49–66, at p. 59.

7. See also Alain Montaudon, "Le nouveau savoir-vivre: En guise d'introduction," *Romantisme* 27, no. 96 (1997): 7–15. Speaking of the *désinvolture élégant* that characterizes the man of social distinction, he says that it can be achieved only by practice and observation, by imitation and immersion in the social milieu; it's not something you can get out of books (p. 8).

8. Leo Tolstoy, *Ivan Ilych* in *Ivan Ilych and Hadji Murad,* trans. Louise and Aylmer Maude, London: Oxford University Press, 1935, chap. 3, pp. 25–26.

9. Harry Berger Jr., *The Absence of Grace: Sprezzatura and Suspicion in Two Renaissance Courtesy Books* (Palo Alto: Stanford University Press, 2000), p. 12. The only change that I have made is the replacement of Berger's reference to the culture of *sprezzatura* by a reference to the culture of *comme il faut*. The identity of the courtier as presented by Castigliano has significant resemblances to the modern identities of social appearance that I have mainly in view; see, for example, the discussion by Berger, p. 11, of the "effortless if not lazy elegance of sprezzatura," the effortlessness itself being a matter of performance against the background of anxiety.

10. See, for example, John C. Prevost, *Le dandysme en France, 1817–1839* (Geneva: Slatkine, 1982), p. 67. Prevost quotes Eugène Ronteix, *Manuel du fashionable, ou Guide de l'élégant,* written the year after Tolstoy's birth. I have used the expression "*l'art de vivre*" because of its currency in the discussions with which I am concerned, but (as understood in society) it is no "art" at all from the point of view of Socrates in the *Gorgias* and elsewhere.

11. The quotation is from Bourdieu, *Distinction,* p. 280; see also pp. vii and 573 on the role that may be given to art and the appreciation of art in defining what it is to be truly human. Cf. Bourdieu, *Distinction: A Social Critique of the Judgement of Taste,* trans. Richard Nice (London: Routledge, 1984), p. 251. Nice's translation, which I have altered, has "truly humane humans," which would make a connection with Jonathan Lear's reference to becoming humane, at the beginning of his first lecture. Bourdieu has "les hommes proprement humains."

12. Henry James, *The Portrait of a Lady,* description by Countess Gemini in chap. 25; see also the description in chap. 23 by Ralph Touchett, and Isabel's "He has a genius for upholstery," chap. 38.

13. I mentioned in section 1 that what may seem to be cases of people inhabiting the same practical identity may actually differ substantially from each other. This point clearly applies to the dandy and to the Victorian aesthete. So criticisms of such figures may take for granted a particular way of inhabiting that identity, not shared by all who inhabit it; the criticisms may thus be unjust in application to at least some cases.

14. Confidence in the way in which one inhabits a practical identity is part of the social pretense of many identities, including for example that of the doctor. But the performance of easy confidence in one's identity is, as one might say, not what being a doctor is *about.* The importance or usefulness of such a performance can be conceived in various ways; a doctor who has an ironic relation to the practical identity might perfectly well take the enacting of confidence to be as useful to medical practice as a stethoscope. Irony, so far as it is a form of insecurity about being human, is not a challenge to the practical identity of being a doctor in the way in which it is a challenge to practical identities of social appearance, if I am right in taking the performance of ease-in-being-truly-human to be at the heart of the social pretense of such identities.

15. James, *The Portrait of a Lady,* chap. 42. Ralph Touchett gives a similar diagnosis of Osmond in chap. 39, emphasizing that Osmond, who pretends to be master of the social world, is really its "very humble servant," living with his eye constantly on the world's responses to himself.

16. There is a further apparent parallel between Socrates' raising the issue at 515a–b whether anyone has become better through association with Callicles and Isabel's bringing up the issue whether Osmond's supposed great enlightenment and re-

finement have enabled him to make anyone more enlightened and refined. James's presentation of Osmond as admiring and envying absolute political power is another apparent connection with the themes of the *Gorgias*.

17. In correspondence.

18. In my exposition of Doyle's objection, I stay close to his words when I can do so; but I have shortened his argument. His argument as he formulated it applies also to my discussion of Callicles and the "manly man," in the second half of section 5. I have not been able to discuss here all the issues that Doyle raises.

19. See, for example, Angela Hobbs, *Plato and the Hero: Courage, Manliness and the Impersonal Good* (Cambridge: Cambridge University Press, 2000), p. 140; and E. R. Dodds, *Plato, Gorgias: A Revised Text with Introduction and Commentary* (Oxford: Clarendon Press, 1959), p. 294.

20. See Dodds, *Plato, Gorgias*, p. 278 on 486c. Dodds suggests that *elēnchôn* was substituted by Plato for some other participle in the quoted line.

21. See *Gorgias* 487e; but see also 500c and the appendix to this chapter. There are highly contentious questions about Plato's views about gender, which I cannot get into.

22. James Doyle, "The Fundamental Conflict in Plato's *Gorgias*," *Oxford Studies in Ancient Philosophy* 30 (2006): 87–100, at pp. 95–96.

23. Ibid., p. 99.

24. On the breakdown of communication between Callicles and Socrates, see ibid., passim. On the questions discussed in section 5, see also James Doyle, "The Socratic Elenchus: No Problem," in *The Force of Argument: Essays in Honor of Timothy Smiley*, ed. Jonathan Lear and Alex Oliver (London: Routledge, 2009), pp. 68–81.

25. I am grateful to James Doyle and Alice Crary for their very helpful comments.

26. See, for example, 487e and 512e. The question how to live, when it is discussed at 500c, is not explicitly the question how a man should live, and the word *andros* is used only in specifying the first of the alternative sorts of life mentioned by Socrates—the life of a Calliclean man and the philosophical life. But the question itself has gender built into it in any case, even if it is translated as the question how one should live; for who is "one"? The only "ones" about whom one could ask whether or not they should live the life of a Calliclean man would be men.

8. Flight from Irony

1. Melanie Klein, "Envy and Gratitude," in *Envy and Gratitude and Other Works, 1946–1963* (London: Hogarth Press, 1984), pp. 176–246; Wilfrid Bion, *Second Thoughts: Selected Papers on Psycho-Analysis* (London: Karnac, 1984).

2. Leo Tolstoy, *Childhood, Boyhood, and Youth*, Michael Scammel, trans. (New York: Modern Library, 1994).

3. Ibid., pp. 73–74. See also Henri Troyat, *Tolstoy* (Garden City, N.Y.: Doubleday, 1967).

4. This is a refined version of the Groucho demand: Who are you going to believe, me or your lying eyes?!

5. Tolstoy, *Childhood, Boyhood, and Youth*, p. 351.

6. Diamond quotes the philosopher James Doyle as saying that the concept *comme il faut* "has its home in a world of pure social pretense." A phrase like this can, I think, mislead one into thinking that a case has been made when it has not. It is, of course, true that a concern for being *comme il faut* often requires a heightened concern for social appearances. But, in the case of Tolstoy at least, we have seen that it can be deployed in a (perhaps flawed) attempt to transcend the realm of social pretense. It can be a manifestation of anxiety about the entire social realm. And the words "home" and "pure" are doing rhetorical work where there is no argument. What does it mean to say that a concept has its home somewhere? Aren't homes the kinds of place that one leaves in the morning to go to work? out to dinner? go on a trip? Aren't homes constitutively places where one does not always remain? I agree with Diamond when she says that, if there is a home for the concept, "it is a more unsettled home . . . than may appear." And the word "pure" in a philosophical context conjures up its own associations, and I do not think they are appropriate in this context. I am not sure what it means to say of anything that it is *pure* social pretense. Social pretenses, however self-conscious and mannered, tend to point beyond themselves. In the discussion of Tolstoy I have tried to show how that might be.

7. See, for example, Sigmund Freud, "The Dynamics of Transference," in *The Standard Edition of the Complete Psychological Works of Sigmund Freud,* ed. and trans. James E. Strachey (London: Hogarth Press, 1981), 12: 99–108; "Remembering, Repeating and Working Through," ibid., 147–156; "Observations on Transference-Love," ibid., 159–171; Postscript to *Fragment of an Analysis of a Case of Hysteria,* in *Standard Edition,* 7: 112–122.

8. Freud, Postscript to *Fragment of an Analysis of a Case of Hysteria,* 117.

9. On the Observing Ego and the Experiencing Ego

1. Sigmund Freud, *New Introductory Lectures on Psycho-Analysis,* in *The Standard Edition of the Complete Psychological Works of Sigmund Freud,* James Strachey ed. and trans. (London: Hogarth Press, 1981), 22: 58.

2. Richard Sterba, "The Fate of the Ego in Analytic Therapy," *International Journal of Psychoanalysis* 15 (1934), pp. 117-126.

3. Freud, *New Introductory Lectures,* SE 22: 89.

10. Observing Ego and Social Voice

1. Aristotle, *Rhetoric* II.2–4; many editions; but see *The Complete Works of Aristotle,* ed. Jonathan Barnes, vol. 2 (Princeton: Princeton University Press, 1984), pp. 2195–2202.

Commentators

CORA DIAMOND is University Professor and William R. Kenan Jr. Professor of Philosophy emerita at the University of Virginia.

CHRISTINE M. KORSGAARD is Arthur Kingsley Porter Professor of Philosophy at Harvard University.

RICHARD MORAN is Brian D. Young Professor of Philosophy at Harvard University.

ROBERT A. PAUL is Charles Howard Candler Professor of Anthropology and Interdisciplinary Studies at Emory University.

Index

Finkelstein, David, 110; *Expression and the Inner,* 52, 53
First-person authority, 109–111, 112, 126–127
Fliess, Wilhelm, 103
"Flight from Irony" (Lear), response to Cora Diamond, 154–163
Freedom, Kantian, 105
Freud (Lear), 133
Freud, Sigmund: on functioning of repression, 54; *Interpretation of Dreams,* 90; *New Introductory Lectures in Psychoanalysis,* 164–165; on philosophy and psychoanalysis, 103; on pretense-transcending aspiring, 45; *Project for a Scientific Psychology,* 168; remembering and compulsion to repeat, 61; on superego, 101; on transference, 68–69, 162–163; "Unconscious, The," 90; on unconscious as alternative form of mental activity, 90
Freudian unconscious, 89–90
Fundamental ironic question, of Kierkegaard, 134

Gender identity, 81–82, 93–94
Gorgias (Plato), 22–23, 134–137, 140–141, 148–153
Groundwork of the Metaphysics of Morals (Kant), 78–79

Happiness, Death, and the Remainder of Life (Lear), 104
Harmony, 91
Heidegger, Martin, *Being and Time,* 98
Historical transmission, Christianity and, 7
Homme comme il faut. See Comme il faut
Human, becoming, 3, 37, 142, 153
Human agency, 79–80
Human dignity, principle of, 101
Human qualities, 3–4; irony and, ix

Humans: animal life compared with, 10; teacher's role in developing well-being, 11
Humorous self-recognition, 118

"I," use of word, 166, 167
Id, Freud on, 45
Identity: consciousness of, 53; in ironic moment, 18–19; irony and forging of, 103; as subject of ironic experience, 81. See also *Comme il faut;* Practical identity
Ignorance, Socratic, 35–36
Illusion, Christendom as, 8–9
Imaginative life, verbal description of, 124–125
"Immanence of Irony and the Efficacy of Fantasy, The" (Lear response to Moran), 115–127
Immediacy, in self-knowledge, 109
Infinite negativity, Kierkegaard on irony as, 32–33
Inner, the, Wittengenstein on, 111
Inner speech, for observing ego, 168
Inside and outside image of, 116
Integrity, 66; moral and metaphysical, 76
Internal reality, 70
Interpretation of Dreams (Freud), 90
Ironic anxiety, 116–118
Ironic disruption, 21; being *comme il faut* and, 131–132; Diamond on, 129; of identity of *comme il faut,* 148; Lear's response to Diamond on, 155, 159; of practical identity, 22, 31; in psychoanalysis, 60. See also Disruption
Ironic existence, 9, 30–36, 152; capacity for, 42–43; vs. practical identity, 161–163; of Socrates, 32
Ironic experience: disruption of life's possibilities and, 31; identity as subject of, 81
Ironic moment, teaching in, 18–19
Ironic question, 62–63; fundamental, 134
Ironic uptake, as uncanniness, 16–17

Unconscious motivations, 50
Unconscious practical identity, making
conscious, 57–63
Unconscious source of self, making
conscious, 51–57
Unity: for agency, 76; irony and, 100;
practical identity and, 79; psychic,
63–67, 89

Verbal expression of emotion, as therapeutic option, 54–57
Verbalization, as replacement of unconscious manifestations, 55
Verbal symbols, 168

Virtue(s): ironic questioning of, 62–63;
Socrates on, 33, 35, 36
Vlastos, Gregory, 32–33, 36
Vygotsky, Lev, 167

"We," 166
Williams, Bernard, on Plato and pretense-
transcendent aspiring, 44
Winnicott, D. W., 167, 170, 176
Wittgenstein, Ludwig, 53, 55; on first
person, 109, 110, 112, 126; on replacing
sensation with verbal utterance, 110–111
Words, self-expression in, 113–114, 123
Worldview, unconscious, 46